DATE DUE

OE 23 '94			
OE 16 98			
MY 11 99			
MR 2 '00			
AG 5 '04			
JY 27 '05			

DEMCO 38-296

MAINSTREAMING AND THE AMERICAN DREAM

SOCIOLOGICAL PERSPECTIVES ON PARENTAL COPING WITH BLIND AND VISUALLY IMPAIRED CHILDREN

Howard L. Nixon II

Preface by
Irving Kenneth Zola

American Foundation for the Blind, New York

Mainstreaming and the American Dream: Sociological Perspectives on Parental Coping with Blind and Visually Impaired Children
is © 1991 by
American Foundation for the Blind
15 West 16th Street, New York, NY 10011

The American Foundation for the Blind (AFB) is a national nonprofit organization that advocates, develops, and provides programs and services to help blind and visually impaired people achieve independence with dignity in all sectors of society.

95 94 93 92 91   5 4 3 2 1

Printed in the United States of America

Library of Congress Cataloging-in-Publication Data

Nixon, Howard, L., 1944-
    Mainstreaming and the American dream: sociological perspectives
on parental coping with blind and visually impaired children /
Howard Nixon II
        p.   cm.
    Includes index.
    ISBN 0-89128-191-6 (alk. paper)
    1. Parents of handicapped children—United States. 2. Children,
Blind—United States—Family relationships. 3. Visually handicapped
children—United States—Family relationships. 4. Mainstreaming in
education—United States.   I. Title.
HQ759.913.N59   1991
649'.1511—dc20   91-6866
                                                            CIP

It is the policy of the American Foundation for the Blind to use in the first printing of its books acid-free paper that meets the ANSI Z39.48 Standard. The infinity symbol that appears above indicates that the paper in this printing meets that standard.

To Matthew, who taught me more than he will ever know

CONTENTS

FOREWORD

In 1975, the U.S. Congress passed P.L. 94-142, the Education for All Handicapped Children Act (now the Individuals with Disabilities Education Act), guaranteeing a free and appropriate public education with special education, related services, and individualized education programs (IEPs) for each child with a handicap. Today it is clear that the "mainstreaming law," as it was commonly called, was not just landmark educational legislation but civil rights legislation as well.

It may have been especially difficult for educators of the visually handicapped to anticipate major changes as a result of the new law because, unlike children with other disabilities, blind and low vision children had been in regular classes in public schools since the 1940s. Indeed, in a sense, educators of blind children invented mainstreaming and developed many of its programming concepts, such as resource rooms, self-contained classrooms, and the use of itinerant teachers.

Nevertheless, because P.L. 94-142 was as much civil rights as educational legislation, the blindness field was not immune to the growing pains the implementation of the law generated and continues to generate. These dislocations have many roots. Laws do not change attitudes or provide people with new knowledge and skills overnight. The resources needed to produce educational change are always underestimated, and competition for the same dollar increases. This last factor especially affected public school education of the visually impaired because expansion of services for persons with other disabilities was all too often done at the expense of visually impaired students. For example, many of the children highlighted in this book are receiving what are supposed to be specialized services, but they receive them from special education teachers trained in other disabilities.

Thus, expectations often outpace reality to such an extent and on so many fronts that frequently we are quick to brand bold new initiatives as failures. But we *cannot* afford to brand mainstreaming a failure. If we believe that persons with disabilities have a right to assume useful roles of their own choosing in the larger community, we must first believe in the basis for that participation--a sound, high-quality, integrated educational system. We therefore have to take all steps necessary to make sure mainstreaming succeeds. This may mean a willingness to confront realities we would prefer to avoid and to look at the situation in new ways. I am pleased that the education of the visually handicapped field is already demonstrating the willingness and ability to do this on several research fronts. For example, a wide range of projects centering around literacy, social skills, and definitional development and implementation of appropriate placement models are healthy indications that professionals are open to changing roles for themselves in order to help their students succeed.

The awareness of the central role parents of disabled children play in the education process is another indicator of the desire to make integrated education succeed. Indeed, if the expectations of parents of disabled children were raised too high too early in the implementation of the mainstreaming law, perhaps the expectations of educators about the roles parents could play have been unrealistic as well. In *Mainstreaming and the American Dream: Sociological Perspectives on Parental Coping with Blind and Visually Impaired Children,* Howard Nixon makes a major contribution to more successful integrated education on several fronts. Nixon's sociological framework is in itself innovative for a field that has been more rooted in psychological thinking than in sociological analysis as the solution to problems. Encouraging us to look at being a parent of a child with a visual impairment as only one of many roles parents play every day is an important contribution. Nixon's use of a qualitative, in-depth interview methodology provides rich data on the complexity of parents' lives, the many roles they juggle, and their relationship with the educational system. Similarly, the interviews with educators shed new light on the dynamics of their relationships with parents as well as with the educational system. Finally, the development of a sociological approach to where parents are in terms of "adjustment" to a child's disability provides educators with unique guidance that can only enhance the relationship between professionals and parents.

Mainstreaming and the American Dream is a research monograph that should stimulate much new and needed research. At the same time, it is a book that provides practicing educators with ideas and strategies they can use today—a rarity among research monographs.

Susan J. Spungin
Associate Executive Director, Program Services
American Foundation for the Blind

PREFACE

In the title of this book, Howard Nixon aptly links mainstreaming and the American Dream. It is a linkage steeped in our history. Although the U.S. Constitution and the Bill of Rights ensured certain fundamental opportunities for all people in this country, the Supreme Court stated quite clearly in *Plessey* v. *Ferguson* (1876) that a "separate but equal" education was good enough for some. Not until 1954 in the decision of *Brown* v. *the Board of Education* did the law of the land officially change. But while court decisions and legislation can define rights and occasionally guarantee resources, they do not automatically change attitudes and behavior. What is true in regard to race is also true in regard to disability.

The 1960s marked the early legislative push for equality of opportunity in education for children in the United States. It too has involved a protracted struggle and evolved from the thrust to move funds and materials from needy children to children with special needs. This movement has been fought through the courts, through legislatures, and through school districts. It has resulted in the creation of boards and of councils and bureaus on federal, state, and local levels, as well as a direct translation of efforts into principled statements and detailed regulations. But when push comes to shove, equality of educational opportunity is, as Nixon lays out, still primarily part of the parent's responsibility and job. No one seems to be able to attend to it better. Maybe no one can.

As a study focused exclusively on the parents of blind and visually impaired children, this book bears eloquent witness to how far as a society we have come and how far we have yet to go. People with visual impairments have had a longer history of societal mainstreaming than perhaps people with any other disabilities. Yet from the experiences of the parents in this study, we can see that this long history has progressed further in the development and availability of assistive technology than in the development of general attitudes toward children with disabilities and the children's attitudes toward themselves. Although each of the parents in Nixon's study did not have to reinvent the wheel in learning to cope with their children's disabilities, they initially all had to find their own way. And though all of them seem to be coping with varying degrees of success, it was not without considerable difficulty.

Nixon goes to great pains to show that there is a wide range and variability among visual impairments and that children with low vision may have very different experiences from and in some cases a more difficult time than children who are blind. Yet as a person with a mobility impairment and with a long professional familiarity with disability in general, I was struck with the similarity of issues and coping strategies among all who try to resolve the promise and difficulties of mainstreaming.

In trying to capture these issues Nixon brings to this study more than an ordinary commitment to truth and social justice. Early on the following explanation appears:

> I am a sociologist, and I have studied and written about a variety of social issues and problems. Like a number of the other works I have written, this book is based on my research, but, in an important sense, the book and the research are unlike other things I have done as a sociologist. They are personal. I am not just an observer of parents of impaired children or merely an objective scholar writing about their experiences. I have shared the experiences of the parents I studied because I am one of them. I am a father of a visually impaired child.

Nixon recognizes that others might be concerned about this "personal perspective," and he states straightforwardly that

> ...my main goal was not to produce a detached "objective" analysis of parents of impaired children. Instead, it was to help people understand what it is like for parents to deal with their children's impairments, both within their families and in society. It was impossible for me to stop being a parent as I carried out my research and prepared this book. But rather than "biasing" what I saw and wrote about, my parental experience gave me a vantage point from which I could see and understand much more than could a "detached" or "objective" observer.

These are more than just context-setting comments. Again and again Nixon reflects on his research findings in relation to the experiences of himself and his wife. Although this makes *Mainstreaming and the American Dream* a document told doubly, from a parental perspective, it is not a professional-bashing treatise. In separate chapters Nixon sympathetically describes the professional's dilemmas and at the end of his analysis details how parents and professionals can work toward improving their communication and, ultimately, the well-being of the child.

With the end of the Cold War and consequent fiscal windfalls in doubt, many parts of the world in turmoil, and economic uncertainty prevailing, human services and related promises, such as those concerning the mainstreaming of all Americans with disabilities, are being cut, bent, and broken. It has thus never been more appropriate to understand better the services we do have and how we can secure and improve them in a cooperative vein. And it is a time to appreciate, understand, and support those who ultimately make mainstreaming and the American Dream possible—the parents of children with disabilities.

Irving Kenneth Zola, Ph.D.
Department of Sociology
Brandeis University

ACKNOWLEDGMENTS

This book could not have been written without the help of many people. Most particularly, I want to express my sincere gratitude to the parents and professionals who generously gave their time and shared their experiences with me as participants in my research. I was able to carry out my research efforts with the support of a sabbatical leave from the University of Vermont and a grant and fellowship from the university. My Vermont colleagues in sociology, Jan Folta and Frank Sampson, and in special education, Susan Brody Hasazi, provided important encouragement and advice. Bob Bogdan, a sociologist and special educator at Syracuse University, taught me about qualitative research and reinforced the principle of respect for the people who are the focus of such research. I also would like to acknowledge institutional support from the University of Washington and Appalachian State University. Janet Truman, at the University of Vermont, and Joyce Rhymer, at Appalachian State University, provided valuable secretarial support. I am especially indebted to two people at the American Foundation for the Blind, Mary Ellen Mulholland, director of publications and information services, and Natalie Hilzen, managing editor, for their professional competence and enthusiastic support of me and my work. Wendy Almeleh, the copyeditor, did a superb job, turning my awkward or unclear language into readable text. Finally, I would like to say it is an honor to have had Irving Kenneth Zola contribute the preface to this book. I deeply appreciate his willingness to have done so.

These acknowledgments would be incomplete without mention of my family. My wife, Sara; my children, Matthew, Luke, and Daniel; and my mother and father have been great boosters. My wife and children remained patient, understanding, and encouraging during the years of work on this project. Sara and I have worked together to try to become better parents of all our children, and we have made a special effort to understand the distinctive needs of children with impairments. Matthew, who is visually impaired, has directly and indirectly taught us many things, and I hope the insights gained from and through our life together will be evident in the ensuing pages.

—H.L.N.

INTRODUCTION

I am a sociologist, and I have studied and written about a variety of social issues and problems. Like a number of the other works I have written, this book is based on my research, but, in an important sense, the book and the research are unlike other things I have done as a sociologist. They are personal. I am not just an observer of parents of impaired children or merely an objective scholar writing about their experiences. I have shared the experiences of the parents I studied because I am one of them. I am a father of a visually impaired child.

Some professional colleagues questioned whether I could be sufficiently objective in preparing this book, because I have been both a parent and an advocate for other parents and their impaired children. Although I have tried to draw from the rich perspectives and knowledge of other scholars who have studied impairments, disabilities, and handicaps in society, my main goal was not to produce a detached "objective" analysis of parents of impaired children. Instead, it was to help people understand what it is like for parents to deal with their children's impairments, both within their families and in society. It was impossible for me to stop being a parent as I carried out my research and prepared this book. But rather than "biasing" what I saw and wrote about, my parental experience gave me a vantage point from which I could see and understand much more than could a "detached" or "objective" observer.

Being a parent of an impaired child also enabled me to gain the cooperation and trust of the other parents with whom I spoke, and it encouraged the parents to be open and expansive in talking about their experiences. I also spoke to many educators and other professionals who work with impaired children and their families. Because I am a professional sociologist, as well as a parent, I was able not only to gain access to them but to obtain a great deal of cooperation from many of them. For parents, though, I believe that my being a parent was much more important than were my professional credentials as a sociologist and an academician.

I must emphasize, however, that this book is based on systematic research, which included intensive interviews of parents and professionals and careful observations of parental interaction with blind and visually impaired children, educators, other professionals, and members of the community. (The questions asked of parents and professionals during the interviews are presented in Appendix 1 and Appendix 2, respectively.) What distinguishes my approach is the *blending* of personal and scholarly perspectives. This blending enabled me to understand aspects of parental experiences that I might have missed or seen more superficially if I had assumed the detached pose of a researcher or relied only on a parental perspective.

PURPOSE OF THIS BOOK

A major purpose of this book is to pass on to others at least a portion of the increased understanding and empathy I developed in the course of my research and writing. This book is not merely *about* parents; it also is *for* them, as well as for the people on whom they depend for education and other services and for others who have only a vague idea about what dealing with impairments is like for impaired people and their families. The major concerns of the parents in my study revolved around the desire to have their impaired children and their entire families treated as "normal" and part of the mainstream of American life and their hope that their children would have the same chance for a normal, happy, and productive life and for conventional success as does everyone else in society. These are important themes of this book, and they are reflected in the title *Mainstreaming and the American Dream.*

Key Parental Concerns

It was easy to become complacent after the passage of P.L. 94-142, the Education for All Handicapped Children Act of 1975, and subsequent related laws, including P.L. 99-457, the 1986 early childhood amendments to P.L. 94-142. Many parents thought that these changes in the law meant that their children's needs would be met in the classroom and perhaps even in the larger society. Many parents and dedicated professionals have since realized, however, that there is no reason for complacency. Despite the mandated free and appropriate education and the hope it engendered that mainstreaming would be a panacea, children with impairments have not been fully integrated into their schools, have not received the full range of educational resources, programs, and services they need, and have not been fully accepted as "normal" children in their schools or communities.

Parents have carried the burden of these disappointments, but despite disappointments, frustrations, and fears about the future, they generally have learned to cope fairly well and, as a result, have helped their children deal fairly well with impairment and its implications. With more understanding of the challenges that parents face, other members of society, including the professionals who work with disabled children and their families, can make these challenges easier. I believe that understanding and empathy from others are potentially powerful means of making the lives of these children and their families easier and more rewarding.

Among the battery of professionals who may be involved in the lives of families with impaired children, general and special educators often play a leading role. Because they spend so much time with the children, educators can have a profound impact on these children's lives and the experiences of the children's parents. You will read about parents who seem to deify educators, and you will read about parents who vilify them. Educators—and other professionals—may be loved or despised for the right or wrong reasons, but it is clear that parents' lives are more difficult when they believe they cannot depend on the competence and caring of the people who are supposed to serve their children. I hope educators and other professionals will find in these pages a picture of parents of impaired children that will generate the kind of understanding and empathy that is needed to develop a cooperative relationship with parents and a productive and satisfying relationship with their impaired children.

Diversity of Parents and of Coping Styles

The picture of parents that is presented here necessarily is a complex mosaic, rather than a print of a single color and design, because there are significant differences, as well as important similarities, among parents, and their experiences are complex. This diversity and complexity must be recognized if professionals are to understand and respond effectively to the particular circumstances of individual parents.

I tried to respect the individuality of parents, even as I searched for patterns of commonality that connected their experiences to other parents. What was especially interesting was that such factors as social class, age, gender, the presence of multiple impairments, and even the impairments of parents themselves were not always the predictors of differences in parental coping that I initially expected. It is noteworthy that even in my relatively small sample of parents in 23 families, there was a great deal of diversity in factors such as age, gender, impairment, social class, and other social circumstances.In this sample were parents who experienced poverty, life on the street, and serious substance abuse and others who enjoyed the comforts of middle-class affluence; parents with little formal education and parents with a great deal of formal education; parents with unstable employment and those with major corporate or professional jobs. There were parents who first became parents as teenagers and those who entered parenthood later in life, parents with a blind child and those with a child with low vision whom people refused to treat as visually impaired, and parents who were visually impaired themselves and others who never even met an impaired child before they had one of their own. There were also single parents, noncustodial parents, devoutly religious couples, a faith healer, couples who had no faith in God, alcoholic parents, stepparents, couples with the mother at home and the father with a job outside the home, dual-career couples, couples struggling to keep their marriages together, and others with stable marriages.

I had difficulty getting formal interviews with nonwhite parents, but my observations and interviews with professionals provided some insights about black and Asian families. I therefore cannot say much with confidence about racial and ethnic minority parents, except that their formal contacts with the schools and service providers were at best strained and typically limited. Perhaps in saying this, I have said a lot.

It must be added, though, that given the growing number of nonwhite and other minority children in the population of impaired children, the strained and limited relationships between minority families and the schools and service providers deserve serious attention from those in the fields of education and the human services. Furthermore, there is a need for research that is specifically focused on disabled minority children and their families. My experience suggests that meaningful minority-oriented research in this area may have to be done by, or with the assistance of, minority researchers, just as successful educational programs and services for minority children and their families may require the involvement of respected minority educators, professionals, or members of the community who can bridge the gaps caused by interracial tension, resentment, suspicion, or distrust.

Especially because my primary focus was parents of visually impaired children, I will not claim that my sample was representative of all parents of impaired children. I will argue, however, that there are many things about the experiences of the varied sample of parents I studied that can be informative for all parents of impaired children—and for those with whom they and their children come in contact. Furthermore, the diverse backgrounds I just described indicate that professionals who deal with impaired children must be prepared to deal with the wide spectrum of family circumstances that characterize contemporary America. Simple or convenient stereotypes simply will not work. The diversity of the backgrounds and circumstances of the parents in my sample, as well as major features of each family situation, can be better appreciated by reading the "Profiles of Families" in Appendix 3.

As I suggested, parental coping may be complex, and I hope to make that complexity clear and understandable in distinguishing significant differences in a number of its aspects. Most of the past research and writing about parental coping have been psychological in nature, and these works provide important insights about parental experiences with impairment. As a sociologist, however, my primary focus is on the social and cultural aspects of parental coping. That is, I am primarily interested in how impairment relates to parental values, aspirations, and roles and to the interaction of family members with each other and other people and institutions in their communities and society. I will try to show that there are connections among the kind of meaning parents attribute to impairment, their sense of power and responsibility regarding their children's impairments, the type of orientation they have toward life in their families, and the ways they interact about impairment with other people in society, including teachers and other professionals.

More needs to be said here about the sociological perspective for those who are not familiar with it. In American society, with our strong individualistic values, it often is easier for us, including many human service professionals and educators, as well as other members of society, to think and talk in psychological rather than in sociological terms. Thus, there may be a tendency to look at problems of parental coping as matters of individual personalities, beliefs, feelings, or behavior. The sociological perspective I present is meant to shift attention to the social and cultural contexts of parental coping and to the ways that parents interact with others as they cope with their children's impairments. I do not question the value of psychological and other perspectives, but I want to show how the understanding of parental coping can be enhanced by focusing on the influence of societal institutions and cultural values and norms; on patterns of social interaction and social relationships; and on the enduring social networks, such as families, friendships, and communities, that tie people to each other and to larger institutions in society. Although individuals' attitudes, feelings, or actions are not ignored, they are understood in terms of the social and cultural contexts from which they have emerged and the social relationships in which they are expressed and given meaning.

Because we live in a society that often demeans people with impairments and creates obstacles to their full social participation, parents' experiences with impairment can be viewed in terms of their explicit or implicit responses to the forces of prejudice and discrimination in society. In fact, the shock or disappointment of learning that one has an impaired child may be explained as much in terms of the negative societal meaning of impairment as of the incapacity that impairment will cause for the child.

I assume that parents' awareness of the negative meaning—or *stigma*—of impairment is a product of their everyday experiences. I also assume that the ways parents cope with the everyday realities and possible stigma of their children's impairments will be significantly influenced by what they have learned from other family members and significant others outside their families. Thus, in this book, I focus on ways in which parents attribute meaning to their experiences, construct roles that reflect their understanding of impairment, and rely on networks of real or ostensible social support that play a critical role in creating, sustaining, or modifying their understanding and treatment of their children.

STRUCTURE OF THIS BOOK

Chapter 1 of this book therefore presents important general concepts and perspectives for understanding the social process of parental coping with impairment. Chapter 2, which discusses family dynamics, social networks, and social support in relation to parental coping, ends with a brief description of the nature of my research concerning parents of visually impaired children. The ensuing chapters present the results of my research, specifically on general patterns of parental coping, the needs and support networks of parents, relationships of parents with professionals, the integration of parents and their visually impaired children in the mainstream of the school and society, and parental perspectives on the future. At a number of points, my personal perspective is incorporated into my discussion of the experiences of the parents I studied. In fact, in Chapter 1, I begin to convey what it means to be a parent of an impaired child by sharing a portion of my own experience.

Chapter 1
COPING WITH THE STIGMA OF IMPAIRMENT

When my wife and I were being interviewed as prospective adoptive parents, we were asked if we would take a child who was "different." The term *different* was meant to imply racially different or impaired in some way—for example, physically, mentally, or emotionally or in sight or hearing. We really had not given much thought to this question. Upon reflection, we decided that our only clear desire was to have a "normal, healthy baby," and we figured that because it was to be our first child, we probably would be best equipped to handle one who was not "too different." We gave no further consideration to this question until almost three years later, when we discovered that our "normal, healthy child" was visually impaired. That it took nearly two years of our child's life to discover a serious visual loss may seem strange, but with "invisible" impairments, delayed detection is not unusual. However, the important point here is the irony—and shock—of discovering that our child was, indeed, "different."

For me, the discovery of visual impairment and the role of a parent of a visually impaired child did not come easily. I did not expect them, and at first I did not willingly accept them. I went through many of the stages of coping described in the literature: shock, anger, frustration, acceptance, and action. My child went from being ignored by "the system" to underserved to appropriately educated, first in a largely segregated special education preschool center, then in the mainstream of our local school. One year, during my sabbatical leave thousands of miles from our home, my son had to be in a segregated resource room part of the school day to get essential services. He was in a segregated school, and he had few social contacts outside school and almost none with peers who were not impaired. We were relieved to return home after that year. Our move to another state a couple of years ago necessitated new efforts to achieve appropriate accommodations in the school and to establish friendships with people who understood and adapted appropriately to our son's impairment.

My wife and I have learned that success for our child and for us as parents is never unqualified and that the road to it has many bumps, curves, detours, and dead ends. As parents of two other children who are not impaired, we realize that these are general lessons of parenthood. Having an impaired child, however, means that there is not the same clear road map of conventional expectations for parenting—contained in the advice columns and best-selling parenting manuals—to prepare us in advance for the major transition points and life changes that are uniquely associated with impairment. Part of the reason for writing this book is to help parents know what to expect.

Jerry Adler, a *Newsweek* writer and parent of a child with a birth defect, wrote that having an impaired child is "every parent's nightmare."[1] For a while it surely was ours. After the initial shock, we experienced much of the emotional pain and anxiety that writers, scholars, and other parents have described as reactions to having an impaired child. However, it also is true that, like other parents, our experience with our impaired child and his impairment has been much richer and more complex than our early feelings suggested.

To begin to understand parental coping, I start by going back to the beginning—to when parents learn "the news." After discussing the initial discovery of impairment by parents, the chapter turns to key concepts that are needed to understand basic aspects of the coping experiences of parents of visually impaired children in the research I report here.

INITIAL DISCOVERY OF IMPAIRMENT

Even in the case of congenital impairments, the initial discovery may take much longer than the first few minutes, hours, days, or weeks after birth. In the early years, doctors usually are the first to give the impairment a technical name. After school begins, educators may be the first to suggest a label for a child's condition. Regardless of whoever first offers an official diagnosis, parents frequently suspect that something is wrong before anyone else does.[2] In fact, Barsch found that all the parents of children who were blind or deaf or had cerebral palsy or Down's syndrome he interviewed in his research had concerns about their children in the first six months after birth. Yet, only a minority of their impairments were diagnosed that early.[3]

Because all professionals who are likely to have contact with impaired children or their families have at least a distant awareness of the nightmare that news of an impairment can create for parents, none is likely to find it easy to be the messenger of this news. However, it seems that among those faced with this task, doctors often have the greatest difficulty handling it. In most cases, it is the doctor who ultimately makes the diagnosis that carries the greatest weight in certifying a child's impairment, and research has indicated that the attitudes of health professionals can profoundly affect the reactions of parents to the birth of their impaired child.[4]

Yet doctors may find that the child's impairment presents a confusing clinical picture. They may share the parents' concerns and desire for clarification, but the ambiguity of the child's condition may require that they "wait and see."[5] In some of these cases, though, doctors may postpone telling parents the news even after the picture has become clear. Thomas observed that under these circumstances, doctors and their medical associates may engage in "planned parental ignorance," leaving to parents the discovery and initial expression of their child's impairment.[6] In this way, the burden of relabeling the child from "normal" to "impaired" or "handicapped" is shouldered by parents, and some of the tension of giving an official diagnosis is diffused for the doctor.

Whether confrontation with the doctor is immediate, as in the case of an obvious abnormality, or delayed, as in the case of more ambiguous conditions, parents typically find their contact unsatisfying and often unsettling. My research showed that the parents' responses to getting the "official news" from a doctor tended to be confusion, anxiety, and anger or frustration. Parents often were unhappy with doctors because of the way they delivered the news. Doctors appear to perceive their role under such circumstances as being akin to the grim reaper, and their often limited understanding of the implications of impairments for the adjustment of children and their families, coupled with their busy schedules and stereotyped views of "the handicapped," can make it difficult for them to be anything other than perfunctory, technical, and confusing—even when they want to be helpful.

At times, it seems that doctors rely on medical jargon because it is easier and more efficient and obfuscates or dulls the sting of the truth for parents. When doctors speak plainly, honestly, and accurately about impairment with parents, they may feel the parents' frustration about the inability of medicine to provide a remedy and have to face more directly and intensely the parents' anger, pain, and disappointment. Even when doctors can offer some hope for improvement of the impairment through medical intervention, they may have difficulty conveying that hope in terms that reassure and make sense to parents because their medical training little prepared them to communicate their expertise in a way that parents can understand and that shows their own concern and caring. Thus, the crisis that parents experience when they learn the news about their children's condition frequently is exacerbated by the awkward, impersonal, misleading, or otherwise confusing way doctors convey it.[7]

Even when physicians or other messengers of the initial news are sensitive, honest, and plain speaking, parents may not at first hear or understand what they are being told. The shock of hearing a diagnosis—even when the parents recognized there was a problem and pushed for the diagnosis—can temporarily prevent parents from thinking clearly, listening, and asking relevant questions.[8] The initial shock has been characterized as a period of pure emotion in coping with the lost dream of a "perfect child."[9]

Shock and a sense of loss may seem inevitable reactions to learning the news of impairment. However, parents' reactions and the intensity and duration of their reactions are shaped both by expectations, hopes, and dreams predicated on "normalcy" and by cultural conceptions of impairments and their implications in our society. That is, parental reactions bear the imprint of a societal lens that conveys to the parents what it means to be impaired. The nature of the "eyeglasses" that American society provides parents to interpret and react to their children's impairment is discussed next.

IMPAIRMENT, DISABILITY, AND HANDICAP

Making conceptual distinctions among *impairment, disability,* and *handicap* is important in clarifying how cultural beliefs and social practices shape how we interpret and deal with impairment and impaired people in everyday life.[10] An *impairment* essentially is a biomedical condition; it is an organic or functional disorder that is the basis for disabilities and handicaps. People may be impaired as a result of disease, an accident, or a defective gene. To say that someone is *impaired* implies that something is missing anatomically, structurally, or physiologically. There are different ways of categorizing impairments, and one general and comprehensive way is in terms of physical, organic, emotional, sensory (such as affecting sight or hearing), and speech impairments.

When an impairment persists for several months and interferes with a person's capacity to use certain skills, perform certain tasks, or participate in certain activities or roles, that person is disabled. Although impairments underlie disabilities, the presence of an impairment does not tell how disabled a person will be. Disability varies across situations, roles, tasks, and activities. A person is disabled to the extent that impairment prevents him or her from exhibiting the skills needed to meet normal expectations for roles, tasks, or activities in a particular situation. Thus, disability is *situational* incapacitation and varies to the extent that situations require skills a person does not have or will not use.

To illustrate the variable and situational nature of disability, consider the case of a blind child who must try to keep up with classmates without the benefit of special devices, such as tape recordings, readers, and braille. This child's sight impairment is likely to result in a serious learning disability *under these circumstances*. However, the same child in the same classroom could have a much-less-serious learning disability if there were devices that provided access to the same learning materials and information used by classmates. Similarly, a deaf child will have a serious learning disability in a classroom without an interpreter and with hearing classmates and a hearing teacher who cannot use sign language. The inability to hear will pose a barrier to communication with classmates that will make the deaf child socially disabled as well. The presence of an interpreter or, even better, of a teacher and classmates who can sign could significantly lessen the communication, learning, and social disabilities created by the combination of hearing impairment and the absence of adaptations to it.

An impaired person becomes *handicapped* when that person is cast into a socially inferior status merely because he or she is impaired or disabled. The interaction of impairment and disability with a person's psychological makeup, the resources available, and social attitudes in a situation adversely affect the performance of ordinary roles. Like disability, handicap is situational, and it is an incapacitation that is the result of, in part, the failure to adapt the environment or social relationships to limitations created by the impairment. However, more than disability, a handicap incorporates a negative value judgment of the impaired person's social or moral worth.

To illustrate, a person born without eyes (called "bilateral anophthalmia") is visually impaired as a result of a genetic defect. The inability of this person to travel independently without a cane or a dog guide means that this person will have a disability in trying to get around without these aids in unfamiliar circumstances. The disability may largely or entirely disappear when the devices are available. However, when the regulations of an airline do not permit dog guides on an aircraft and the blind person depends on a dog for independent travel, blindness becomes a handicap and the blind person is a victim of prejudicial and discriminatory treatment that can be called handicapism.[11] That is, because of blindness, the person is socially disadvantaged or singled out for inferior treatment. When the discrimination is built into the rules, regulations, or laws of an organization, community, or society, it can be called *institutional handicapism.* Institutional handicapism may be difficult to uproot because it is part of the social order or routine way of doing things and for this reason seems to be so rational or justifiable.

Impaired people may be handicapped by the unwillingness of others, including parents, other loved ones, and professional service providers in potentially important networks of social support, to allow them to use their abilities. For example, many people probably could not imagine a blind person sky diving, playing golf, or water skiing, and they would be unlikely to encourage or allow their blind children to do these things. However, Tom Sullivan is blind, and in his autobiography, *If You Could See What I Hear,* he describes his participation in these and a number of other activities that other people often tried to prevent or discourage him from doing.[12] That is, Sullivan uses his admittedly exceptional talents, courage, and persistence to take advantage of available opportunities to overcome potential handicaps and disabilities.

Not everyone handles an impairment as effectively or receives as much support as does Tom Sullivan, and some even handicap themselves by undervaluing their abilities or importance as people and not trying to do things they are capable of doing. The handicapping process in society has effects on the self-conceptions and behavior of people with impairments and disabilities. It is self-reinforcing to the extent that handicapist values, attitudes, and social practices cause these people to accept the disadvantaged status imposed on them by the nondisabled majority and perform roles that reflect stereotypical conceptions of their incompetence and inferiority. This process, by which impaired people contribute to their own handicapping, is both self-demeaning and self-inhibiting, and it ultimately contributes to the reinforcement of handicapism and its outcomes.[13]

Stigma and Handicap

For many impaired people, their impairment is an attribute that can become a *stigma*. Goffman defined stigma in terms of a deeply discrediting attribute, but he recognized that an understanding of the dynamics concerning stigma requires a focus on relationships, not attributes alone.[14] What might have been an ordinary relationship or social contact is transformed by the awareness of a stigma, which becomes the focus of attention and turns the other person away from the one who is stigmatized. The stigma is, according to Goffman, "an undesired differentness from what [was]...anticipated," and it sets the stigmatized apart from those not seen as departing negatively from conventional expectations, whom Goffman calls "normals."[15]

As a result of the discrediting caused by their stigma, impaired people may feel shame and confusion trying to manage their "spoiled identity" and deal with their devalued status.[16] Once impaired people are stigmatized by being labeled sick, deviant, or handicapped, they may become victims of a self-fulfilling prophecy that reinforces their tarnished identity and disadvantaged or minority status.[17]

Understanding how people with impairments are handicapped as a minority group depends on the identification of important contextual factors that activate a deviant labeling of the impairment and transform the perception of that differentness into a stigma.[18] Among the types of contextual or situational factors that could affect labeling and stigmatization are the resources and power of people with impairments that could insulate or protect them, to various degrees, from being discredited; the social distance between impaired people and normal people who may label and stigmatize them; community tolerance for differentness, deviance, and impairment or disability; and stimulus properties of the impairment itself, such as its severity, visibility, or type, that could turn it into a stigma.[19]

Parents and the Courtesy Stigma

Parental awareness of the stigma of impairment can be seen as an important part of the process that helps produce parents' shock, disappointment, sadness, and shame following the news that their children are impaired. Parents who recognize the stigma of impairment also may have a dim or clear awareness of the possibility that their intimate connection to their impaired children could lead others to think of *them* in terms of the impairment stigma. Parents of impaired children may be granted a measure of courtesy membership in the company of those sharing their children's stigma. That is, through their close connection to their children, membership in the stigmatized group may be extended to them by the group. However, the acceptance of such membership could bring with it a "courtesy stigma" for parents when they are in the company of members of society who do not share their children's stigma. This courtesy stigma, which identifies parents with a stigmatized group, may subject them to the same avoidance, rejection, or ridicule experienced by their stigmatized, impaired children.[20] Because parents of impaired children may not find themselves completely accepted by groups of impaired people who have extended courtesy membership to them but who have reservations about doing so, they may turn to other parents like themselves or to professionals to find acceptance. Or, to escape the sting of stigma, they may try, to the extent possible, to ignore, deny, or otherwise minimize their children's impairments and disabilities.

The severity and visibility of certain types of children's impairments and disabilities can affect the ability of parents to minimize their impaired children's conditions. Despite the real consequences of stigmatization and the courtesy stigma, there also are real disabling consequences of impairments that can be difficult to ignore or disguise. Without exaggerating the salience of stigma, one may still argue that parents' efforts to deal with the stigma of their children's impairments and their associated courtesy stigma often are an important aspect of parental coping with impairment in their families.[21] In fact, the handicapping effects of stigma or concern about them can make it substantially more difficult for parents to cope with their impaired children's disabilities.

Parental Coping with Impairment

How parents think about their situation with regard to impairment and how they view impaired children provide the foundation for their coping with impairment and their children. An especially significant aspect of how they interpret their children's impairments is likely to be their thoughts about the applicability of labels or names for impairments to their children. In turn, their acceptance or rejection of these labels tends to be related to whether or how they think about stigma in relation to them.

The ideas parents learned about impairments and impaired people before their experience with their impaired children do not suddenly become transformed by the discovery of impairment in their own families. Indeed, as was already suggested, negative stereotypes of the stigma of impairment help create the nightmare that follows the news that a child is impaired. Experience with their impaired children can profoundly affect these initial stereotypes of impaired people as sick, helpless, ugly, strange, incompetent, deviant, or otherwise inferior.[22] The education that experience provides for parents can substantially change how they think about their impaired children, and the stories of parents I interviewed will show that some parents went from ignorance and fear of visual impairment to highly sensitive understanding and acceptance of it. However, stereotypes do not change to the same extent or in the same ways for different parents. Deeply rooted misconceptions and prejudices steeped in stigma can be difficult to uproot in a society that continues to foster stigmatized conceptions of impairments. Stigma is not overcome by experience alone.

A variety of persistent negative stereotypes perpetuate the stigma of blindness for many in American society.[23] The parents of visually impaired children I interviewed either ignored this stigma because they did not openly or fully acknowledge the visually impaired status of their children; recognized the stigma but denied its relevance to their children by understating the visual impairment; recognized the stigma and its possible relevance to their admittedly visually impaired children; or denied the relevance of stigma because neither their children nor the visual impairment was seen as deviant in social or moral terms. As one might expect, the severity and visibility of their children's visual impairments were related to the parents' interpretations of their children's conditions and the implications for them as parents. The impact of these factors on parental coping will be discussed in detail later in the book when the results of the research are presented. However, it is important to recognize here that parents' understanding of their children's impairments formed distinct patterns that were differentiated by a combination of the salience of the stigma of blindness and the acknowledgment of the applicability to their children of the label of blindness and the things symbolically associated with it (such as braille, the white cane, and a dog guide).

The amount of parental experience with their children's impairments and the severity and visibility of the impairment did not have simple, direct, or uniform effects on how parents coped. Instead, the effects of the parents' experience and the characteristics of the impairment were

mediated by the meanings of blindness held by parents, which were filtered by the degree to which the parents had learned to relate stigma to
blind (and other impaired) people. A major influence on this learning
process is assumed here to be the networks of social support in which
parental experiences are embedded. That is, parents learn to deal with
stigma when they receive support from others who understand and
empathize with their situation. Stigma diminishes to the extent that
others' attitudes about impairment lose their pejorative and demeaning
sting.

APPROPRIATE INTERACTION AND INTEGRATION

I suggested earlier that the mainstreaming of disabled children into regular schools that occurred after the passage of P.L. 94-142 was seen by
many as a panacea that would rectify all the perceived past ills from the
segregation of children with impairments. However, as a parent of a
child in a community preschool of three and four year olds with no
other impaired children, I learned early that our visually impaired
child's presence in a classroom with "normal" children had as many
hazards as benefits. The teacher had no training to deal with visually
impaired children and had no idea what to do when other children
became angry with our son when he unintentionally stepped on their
artwork, took someone else's hat or boots by mistake, or isolated himself because other children either fended off his efforts to socialize or
made fun of him. The aide tried to protect him, but the lead teacher felt
something more dramatic needed to be done to make the other children
understand our child's impairment and disabilities.

Without consulting with my wife or me, the lead teacher decided to
turn the class into an encounter group one day. Our son's classmates
were encouraged to tell him all the things he did that bothered them,
and he was supposed to respond. It is not surprising that he was devas-
tated by this experience. There was nothing he was able to say in
response, and as result of this "encounter" with his classmates, he
tucked himself deeper into his shell. His ordeal ended a week or so later,
with the end of the school year. As a resilient three year old, he eventually resumed being the cheerful child he was before things started dete-
riorating at school.

I learned about this incident from another parent and was infuriated.
Despite, or perhaps because of, my anger, I decided to wait one week to
express my feelings, until the end-of-the-year conference with the
teacher. My wife and I thought our son would be "safe" in school during

the final week because we learned that his aide had become even more protective and he was allowed to play by himself. School ended, parental conferences were held, and none was scheduled for us. When we tried to reach the teacher, we discovered that she had left for vacation.

We finally sat down with the teacher six weeks after school ended. It was evident that she was regretful about her experiment in group psychology but felt uncomfortable talking about it. With nearly two months of reflection, my wife and I continued to feel indignant, but we were more capable of seeing that our son's teacher wanted to do the right thing but did not know what the right thing was and did not think to ask for our help. She may have been driven to try her experiment because, in his one visit that year, the state visual consultant in special education had observed the class briefly and informed the teacher that "everything looked fine." The teacher apparently concluded that she would therefore not receive any help from the state consultant despite the fact that she knew everything was not "fine," and she then decided on her experiment. She discovered quickly that her experiment was a failure and probably encouraged the added protectiveness of the aide. Fearing our reaction, she tried to avoid us.

This example illustrates a number of points, but the one I want to emphasize here is that the attempt to achieve integration simply by putting an impaired child together with other children without impairments is naive and may lead to negative results. A teacher once said to me that understanding visual impairment is "common sense." My son's sad experience definitively refutes that contention. He had to endure an unpleasant preschool experience because the conditions at his school did not foster the kind of understanding, empathy, or acceptance needed to integrate my son into the regular flow of interaction with his schoolmates. Appropriate integration, in which disabilities are taken into account but do not inhibit opportunities for interacting and developing relationships, does not occur by chance.

The Process of Understanding

Impaired children have relationships with children without impairments that approximate those that these other children have with each other when there is understanding and empathy and the disabilities of impaired children are appropriately taken into account. Mean-spirited prejudice, stigmatization, and discrimination may be hurtful and degrading to impaired children and to their families. Similarly, reticence and protectiveness may be stifling and frustrating.

Parents, themselves, sometimes may be the source of difficulty for their children. My research and my own experiences have clearly shown that competent, caring, and sensitive teachers and other professionals with expertise in working with people who have impairments can play an important role in teaching parents, other educators and service providers, children, and members of the community about appropriate interaction and integration. Whether they learn from teachers of visually impaired children, other professionals, visually impaired adults, or their experience with their children, it is essential that parents understand and accept a valid definition of their children's impairments and disabilities. Such understanding and acceptance are essential because the conception of their children's condition that parents convey to other people through their daily conversations and other actions may significantly influence whether these other people interact appropriately with the children.[24]

This process of understanding is akin to what Davis calls "breaking through" and "deviance disavowal."[25] It should not be assumed that the determination of valid definitions of impairment and disability are simple, straightforward, precise, or objective matters. Even if an impairment can be diagnosed in fairly precise medical terms, its implications for disability in different situations can be ambiguous. Nevertheless, at least when a real disability is acknowledged along with real abilities, it is possible to achieve the more open, honest, and appropriate interaction that "breaking through" implies.

Because the parents I interviewed typically had children with moderate impairments that could be made relatively invisible, there often was tension between their denial of deviance and deviance disavowal (hereafter termed the *disavowal of deviance*).[26] The special problem of interaction in cases of moderate and invisible impairments is the temptation to engage in denial of deviance. Whatever their children's impairment, parents may fear the threat to sociability that impairment could pose for them or their children. For example, as Davis observes, sociability could be threatened by a tendency to focus interaction on the stigma of impairment, by the awkwardness that people may feel about expressing their true feelings about a "handicapped" person, by possible confusion created by the inconsistencies between ideas about stigma and the apparent positive attributes of the impaired person, and by ambiguity about the actual capabilities of the impaired person in joint activities.[27] Although all parents of impaired children could perceive such threats, parents of moderately and less visibly impaired children may be most tempted to deal with these threats by disguising their child's impairment or denying it.

The effort to "pass" as normal has been discussed in relation to hearing impaired and visually impaired people.[28] Higgins proposes that for these people, passing may involve trying to maintain the fiction that "nothing unusual is happening" (in interaction).[29] For some parents, the fiction may be largely or solely their own construction. To the extent that their children try to play along, the collusion effort represents "fictionalized normalcy," in Thomas's terms.[30]

Efforts to disguise moderate and less visible impairments can be seen as a reaction to social marginality as well as to stigma.[31] Caught between the worlds of the severely and obviously impaired and "normals," parents of moderately and less visibly impaired children may be uncertain about their children's or their own status. The denial of deviance and fictionalized normalcy are the ways they try to escape from the strains of such an uncertain status and the perceived certainty of being labeled deviant for having a stigma in their families.

Although disguising an impairment and denying deviance may seem to resolve certain tensions and problems, such efforts create strains of their own in situations where an impaired child is expected to act in ways that overtax his or her capabilities.[32] Excessive striving under these circumstances can lead to severe role strain. In the end, the role demands may result in the impaired child being "found out," which not only defeats the purpose of the original charade but may lead others to cast even more aspersions on the parents and their child than if they had initially acknowledged the impairment. Nevertheless, stigma remains a significant obstacle to that voluntary acknowledgment.

Fewell and Gelb propose that the severity of visual loss is an important factor in coping with visual impairment and that the presence of some sight makes a difference in parents' responses to their impaired children.[33] Partial sight allows or encourages parents to delay their acknowledgment of impairment and disability longer than does near or total blindness. In addition, parents may "valorize" residual sight with mild or moderate visual impairment and pretend their children see better than they actually can.[34]

When parents of mildly or moderately visually impaired children minimize or deny the impairment, they and their children are likely to feel strains from the fiction they are acting out. Yet when the marginality of their children's impairments makes the impairment seem relatively invisible (though not necessarily absent) in many situations, parents can become confused and anxious from the ambiguity. Thus, it is not surprising that a study found that blind adolescents coped better than did partially sighted adolescents with perceptions of pity and acceptance and that parents have found blindness less difficult to accept than partial sight.[35] In the latter regard, Fewell and Gelb note that a mother of a blind child in one of their parent discussion groups expressed relief that she was free of the uncertainty about the future of her child's visual condition; she preferred the certainty of irreversible blindness to the ambiguity and uncertainty of partial sight.[36] Such uncertainty or anxiety can be a major dimension of parental emotional coping with impairment. Caught in the marginality of partial sight, parents may find it easier—for a while—to treat their children as fully sighted or sightless.

Disavowal of Deviance and Normalization

Parents who engage in the disavowal of deviance reject society's verdict that their children's impairments are a stigma. They break through in their relationships with other people to establish social identities for themselves and their children that are "normal" in their moral dimension but do not preclude attention to disability, *when appropriate*.[37] The disavowal of deviance and normalization imply that a blind person or a person in a wheelchair can be accorded the respect of a "normal" person without denying that there are things the person cannot do or needs help with in certain situations. When parents disavow—rather than deny—the deviance of their impaired children, they are asserting both their children's and their own normalcy. By doing so, they have defused the threat of stigma and have become comfortable with the idea that their children and families may be different but are not socially or morally inferior.

In my research, I found that the placement of blind children in residential institutions had declined substantially in recent years owing to the deinstitutionalization movement and much social and cultural pressure on parents to raise even severely impaired children at home. The bulk of the reduced population in these institutions consists of children and youths with impairments causing profound developmental delays or serious problems of social integration, such as blindness with deafness. Thus, for most parents of impaired children, institutionalization is not an option.

A family with fewer coping resources, skills, and accommodative routines could be expected to have more trouble with impairment in spite of their intention to do the best they can.[38] A family with a limited capacity or desire to cope well may believe that they cannot afford a disabled child and, as a result, may deny the disability, create a fiction of normalcy, and impose excessive or inappropriate demands on the child. A family that is rich in coping resources and skills may overcompensate for the disability and end up creating a "fictionalized handicap" by overprotecting their impaired child.

PARENTAL SELF-DEFINITIONS AND INTERACTIONAL STYLES

Parents in families with a greater coping capacity may believe they have more power to do something about their children's impairments. A greater sense of control may make it easier for them to handle the stigma of impairment and to disavow deviance. Furthermore, Voysey proposes that the combination of parents' perceptions of their power and their responsibility for their children's impairments explains the interactional styles that parents adopt in response to their impaired children.[39]

By "responsibility," Voysey means the degree to which parents or others perceive parents as the source of the impairment, either genetically or through negligence of their parental duties. She assumes that the perceived power of parents to affect their children's impairments or disabilities depends on the nature of the impairments or disabilities, the parents' knowledge of it, and their resources. According to Voysey, these perceptions are not static; they are always open to negotiation or change. However, Voysey argues that the definitions of responsibility and power that parents accept at a given time are important influences on how parents handle their impaired children and the moral interpretation of their own actions as parents. These moral interpretations help shape the ways parents interact with others in relation to impairment.

Styles of Interacting

Treating responsibility and power as dichotomies produces four logical combinations. Voysey proposes that for situations related to three of these combinations, parents or others could adopt a typical line or style as an appropriate way to deal with impairment outside their families or in public and to establish or maintain the "good character" of the parents. In the fourth situation, the absence of such a line or style could make parents cautious in public interactions involving their impaired children because they fear that their reputation will be doubted. The four dichotomies are as follows:

Not responsible/have power. In Voysey's conception of this situation, an impairment is known to be physical and not hereditary, and some improvement (though not a cure) is possible. With regard to the relevance of perceived responsibility and power concerning disability, one could add that parents would not think they were holding back their children but would believe that they were able to lessen the amount of the children's disabilities in one or more settings or roles. In Voysey's words, the interpersonal style adopted or proffered under such circumstances is "coping splendidly."

Responsible/have power. In this situation, such as when a birth defect could not have been predicted, parents feel guilty even though others, such as doctors and family members, try to discourage them from blaming themselves. Self-blame may be a significant source of motivation to do things for their children; the parents may be driven to be assertive and demanding in their quest for services and may "shop around" for services. However, their sense of personal responsibility may be a source of some ambivalence. Thus, even while they search for services, they may not want to draw much attention to their children in routine, everyday interactions except when impairment is made an issue. When it is, they may dramatize their efforts to help and talk about their sacrifices for their impaired children as a means of minimizing threats to their good character as parents.

Because these parents have a sense of power and want people, including themselves, to believe they have done all they can, their pursuit of services may become paradoxical at times. Although they say they want help from others, they may not really trust that others can do as much for their children as they can. Voysey calls this style "making amends."

Not responsible/no power. Voysey suggests that this situation is similar to bereavement and includes cases of "tragic" impairment, such as severe and irreversible congenital brain damage. Because the parents believe they cannot help their children with the impairments or disabilities, they are unlikely to think others can offer real consolation. Because they are not held responsible, others may offer sympathy. To keep their good name, these parents have to learn to take sympathy graciously and "well-intentioned but ignorant" advice with patience. Their style, in Voysey's terms, is "stoic acceptance." However, this acceptance surely is not as deep as that of parents who are coping splendidly. These parents may be stoic, but their acceptance and the understanding on which it is based may be shallow and transparent. In short, their style is stoic and is based on transparent acceptance.

Responsible/no power. Parents of autistic or mentally ill children often may have found themselves in this situation in the past. In the absence of obvious physical causes for the children's condition, professionals, in explaining the origins of the children's problems, frequently made parents the scapegoat.[40] Because they feel powerless and cannot make amends in such a situation, parents can be expected to try to hide their "guilty secret" and limit their interaction regarding their children to those who share responsibility for the children or whose potential disapproval is tempered by knowledge of the parents' good character in other areas. Voysey proposes that parents' circumspect reticence in interaction was derived from the lack of culturally acceptable ways of handling the interaction in their situation. Even if they personally "accept" their children's condition, they may find public interaction to be problematic and avoidance the easiest solution to their dilemma.

Perception and Style

It is important to emphasize Voysey's point that the interactional styles that parents adopt to manage their parenthood and others' impressions of them are not tied to the particular personalities of parents or to the particular impairments of their children. Instead, from Voysey's perspective, these social coping styles are shaped by how parents define their situations in terms of responsibility and power. Because these perceptions can change, so can the parents' interactional styles. The definitions of their situations are "to some extent negotiable issues."[41] As Voysey further argues, although the first three situations provide parents with a legitimate or socially acceptable means of handling interaction regarding their impaired children, it should be apparent that parents in these situations will not be exempt from stigmatization, embarrassment, or other threats to their respectability or sense of normalcy. Nevertheless, especially in the situation in which parents cope splendidly, they are likely to perceive fewer threats to their parenthood and to handle those that arise more easily than in more tenuous or suspect situations.

DYNAMICS OF PARENTAL COPING AND ACCEPTANCE

Life in any family can change dramatically from one day to the next, and impairment can force families to deal with important and unanticipated stresses, problems, or crises on a number of occasions. In general, though, life is a series of smaller and less dramatic adjustments that parents may not even notice.

Cogswell cites studies by her and by Davis in which the researchers had observed families' accommodations to disability that the families themselves had not noticed.[42] Davis saw the tendency for families to say nothing has changed as a result of the disability as a clue to the subtle nature of the coping process. That is, family coping with disability is a steadily unfolding cumulative process in which there is an ongoing succession of shifts in roles and identities around a core of predisability roles and identities. Because the changes from day to day may be minor and continuous, they may be difficult to notice. However, because the results are cumulative, the overall impact on the family over an extended period can be major, despite the family's failure to recognize how much they changed or accommodated in response to the impairment or disability. Thus, the appearance of equilibrium or sameness at various times in the life of a family with an impaired child may belie a dynamic and ongoing process of coping. At times, there may be crises caused by dramatic changes in the child's impairment or disability, but most of the time the changes may be so subtly embedded in the routine patterns of everyday life that life may not seem to change at all.[43]

Although parents may go through a variety of experiences with their impaired children, it is not inevitable that they will have to endure or suffer through a succession of traumatic episodes, deeply troubling thoughts, or highly problematic social encounters. The precise course and content of their experiences with impairment and their children often seem much less clear and predictable than do many stage models and other conceptions of parental coping would have us believe.[44]

Much of the literature on parental coping seems to dwell on various forms of "pathology" or difficulty. Although pathology or difficulty may be common aspects of parental coping, at least for a while, it is insufficient or inappropriate to rely solely on preconceived notions of pathology, abnormality, or maladjustment to understand the varied and complex coping responses of different parents and parents over time. These pathological views may reflect a medical, clinical, or intervention perspective aimed at curing or fixing something. When conveyed to parents by professionals or other agents of socialization to impairment, these conceptions can become part of a stigmatizing process that may, indeed, make the parents' coping problematic. The results of my research will show, first, that even after many years of coping, some parents were not doing "splendidly" or did not fully "accept" the nature, severity, or implications of their child's impairment and, second, that the amount of pain or suffering that parents revealed varied considerably more and in more complex ways than many pathological views imply.

My research suggested that there may be considerable variation in how much parents suspend their beliefs about what they have taken for granted, in how much they feel a need to redefine good and evil, in how much they must discover what is "really important" in the face of impairments, in how much they see themselves suffering, or in how much differentness they acknowledge about their lives. Parents' efforts to minimize impairments or their implications may create an appearance of acceptance and normalcy that masks real problems with impairments or disabilities in their families that they do not seem to recognize.

Voysey found that most of the parents she studied were able to "accept" impairment in some socially acceptable way.[45] This finding suggests that most parents learned gradually or quickly to define their situation and to act, in various degrees, in apparently unexceptional or "normal" ways. In Voysey's terms, those who coped splendidly achieved the ideal form of action.[46] That is, they felt they had power without a sense of personal blame. They pursued "a day-to-day 'pragmatic' approach to piecemeal problems."[47] In seeing their lives and their impaired children in these terms, they were realistic and able to treat their everyday frustrations and disappointment as ordinary or normal. Thus, their situation was different only in degree from the experiences of all parents, because all parents face some frustration and disappointment in their everyday lives.

It seems apparent from past research that to cope effectively, parents must be able to acknowledge impairments and disabilities and to accommodate to them without accepting notions of the moral inferiority or deviance of these social differences. They must learn to handle interaction regarding impairment in ways that are free from the hold of others' stigmatizing definitions and expectations. They must learn to take the initiative, break through, and negotiate terms for thinking about impairment and accommodating to it that are both nonstigmatized and realistic.

The circumstances of the lives of parents, their impaired children, and other family members change. Thus, parents who have learned to disavow deviance and to cope splendidly are never completely assured that they will not feel the sting of misinformed and hurtful opinions or attitudes or the need to accommodate to them. Life may seem to continue as it has been, but as Cogswell suggests, we change whether we notice it or not. Parental coping and acceptance are dynamic and ongoing processes. In the midst of their everyday coping with impairment, parents may feel, think, and act in slightly different ways than in the past. In some cases, the cumulative impact of these minor deviations may be a major change in their style of coping or acceptance of impairment. Educators and other professionals need to know about changes in a child's family situation to be able to recognize and respond effectively to the changing behavior and needs of the child. When professionals develop stereotypes of the children and families whom they serve, they may have difficulty seeing important changes, and the failure to recognize, accept, and be responsive to change can undermine professionals' effectiveness.

LOOKING AHEAD

The parents of visually impaired children I interviewed displayed patterned differences in their ways of coping with their children. These differences generally reflected important differences in how parents viewed the stigma of blindness, how much they accepted the realities of their children's impairments, and how they saw their responsibility and control in relation to their children's impairments. The model of parental coping presented here incorporates these elements, which have been major themes of this chapter, along with general ideas about how individuals are socialized by personality and by situational, cultural, and social structural factors. An important aspect of parental coping that has not yet been discussed in detail is the social networks that provide parents with social support and mediate the effects of the major cultural and institutional forces of the society on parents. Two major kinds of social networks for parents of impaired children are the family and networks of supportive relationships outside the family. In the next chapter, family dynamics, social networks, and social support are discussed in relation to parents' coping with their child's impairment.

NOTES

1   J. Adler, "Every Parent's Nightmare," *Newsweek*, 16 March 1987, 56-66.

2   H. Featherstone, *A Difference in the Family: Living with a Disabled Child* (New York: Penguin Books, 1981), 178.

3   R. H. Barsch, *The Parents of the Handicapped Child: Study of Child Rearing Practices* (Springfield, IL: Charles C Thomas, 1968), 80, 83.

4 M. S. Collins-Moore, "Birth and Diagnosis: A Family Crisis," in *Chronic Illness and Disability through the Life Span: Effects on Self and Family*, ed. M. G. Eisenberg, L. C. Sutkin, and M. A. Jansen (New York: Springer Publishing Co., 1984), 49.

5 Featherstone, *A Difference in the Family*, 178.

6 D. Thomas, *The Experience of Handicap* (London: Methuen, 1982), 96.

7 Collins-Moore, "Birth and Diagnosis," 39.

8 Featherstone, *A Difference in the Family*, 180.

9 E. P. Scott, J. E. Jan, and R. D. Freeman, *Can't Your Child See?* (Baltimore: University Park Press, 1977).

10 These distinctions can be found in a variety of sources, including F. Bowe, *Handicapping America: Barriers for Disabled People* (New York: Harper & Row, 1978), 16; and Thomas, *The Experience of Handicap*. Roth has written that although disabled and able-bodied people are biologically different, it is not the decisive difference between groups. "Handicap is a social construction. There is a biological substratum, but what it means to be handicapped to others and oneself is overwhelmingly social and decisively political" (56). See W. Roth, "Handicap as a Social Construct," *Society/Transaction* 23 (March-April 1983): 56-61. This is the key sociological insight of this section.

11 See R. Bogdan and D. Biklen, "Handicapism," *Social Policy* 7 (1977): 14-19.

12 T. Sullivan, with D. Gill, *If You Could See What I Hear* (New York: Signet/ New American Library, 1975).

13 This discussion of the self-handicapping and the self-reinforcing nature of handicapism is based on H. L. Nixon II, "Handicapism and Sport: New Directions for Sport Sociology Research," in *Sport and the Sociological Imagination*, ed. N. Theberge and P. Donnelly (Fort Worth, TX: Texas Christian University Press, 1984), 162-176.

14 E. Goffman, *Stigma: Notes on the Management of Spoiled Identity* (Englewood Cliffs, NJ: Prentice-Hall, 1963), 1-2.

15 Ibid., 5.

16 G. L. Albrecht, "Socialization and the Disability Process, in *The Sociology of Physical Disability and Rehabilitation*, ed. G. L. Albrecht (Pittsburgh: University of Pittsburgh Press, 1976), 3-38.

17 See H. Becker, *Outsiders: Studies in the Sociology of Deviance* (New York: Free Press, 1983); K. Erikson, "Notes on the Sociology of Deviance," in *The Other Side*, ed. H. Becker (New York: Free Press, 1964), 9-21; and Nixon, "Handicapism and Sport."

18 I have noted elsewhere (Nixon, "Handicapism and Sport," 167) that even those (such as Gove) who have pointed out the limitations of societal reaction theory in the analysis of disability and rehabilitation have acknowledged that labeling and stigmatization processes tend to be important in handicapping impaired people. See W. R. Gove, "Societal Reaction Theory and Disability," in *The Sociology of Physical Disability and Rehabilitation*, ed. G.L. Albrecht (Pittsburgh: University of Pittsburgh Press, 1976), 57-71.

19 See W. R. Gove, *The Labeling of Deviance* (New York: John Wiley & Sons, 1975); and I. Katz, *Stigma: A Social Psychological Analysis* (Hillside, NJ: Lawrence Erlbaum Associates, 1981), 121.

20 Goffman, *Stigma*, 31. See also R. B. Darling and J. Darling, *Children Who Are Different* (St. Louis: C. V. Mosby, 1982), 36; and Thomas, *The Experience of Handicap*, 138.

21 P. C. Higgins argued that deafness is not only a stigma but an impairment that has serious disabling effects on communication with hearing people. Furthermore, he suggested that the primary concern about an impairment—especially deafness—is often to accomplish the tasks of everyday life. In this context, the management of a spoiled identity may become a secondary or even negligible concern. See P. C. Higgins, *Outsiders in a Hearing World: A Sociology of Deafness* (Beverly Hills, CA: Sage Publications, 1980). As Nash and Nash observed, Higgins's view corrects an "overstigmatized" conception of deaf people. However, neither Higgins nor Nash and Nash would suggest the *lack* of salience of stigma in the lives of deaf or otherwise impaired people. See J. E. Nash and A. Nash, *Deafness in Society* (Lexington, MA: Lexington Books, 1981), esp. 78-79.

22 The roots of negative attitudes toward and stereotypes of impaired people are discussed by H. Livneh, "On the Origins of Negative Attitudes Toward People with Disabilities," *Rehabilitation Literature* 43 (1982): 338-347. The nonacceptance, stigma, stereotypes, and prejudice associated with the minority group status of impaired people are discussed by E. C. Wertlieb, "Minority Group Status of the Disabled," *Human Relations* 38 (1985): 1047-1063.

23 See R. A. Scott, *The Making of Blind Men: A Study of Adult Socialization* (New York: Russell Sage Foundation, 1969), esp. chap. 2.

24 E. Thomas, "Problems of Disability from the Perspective of Role Theory," *Journal of Health and Human Behavior* 7 (1966): 2-13.

25 F. Davis, "Deviance Disavowal: The Management of Strained Interaction by the Visibly Handicapped," *Social Problems* 9 (1961): 120-132. See also F. Davis, *Passage through Crisis*, (Indianapolis: Bobbs-Merrill, 1963).

26 See H. L. Nixon II, "Invisible Impairments, Deviance Reactions, and Appropriate Integration: A Case Study of Adjustment to Visual Impairment in Mainstream Sports" (unpublished manuscript, 1988).

27 Davis elaborated on the nature of each of these types of threat to sociability raised by an impairment. See Davis, "Deviance Disavowal: The Management of Strained Interaction by the Visually Handicapped."

28 Drawing from Goffman (*Stigma*), Higgins (*Outsiders in a Hearing World*) and Nash and Nash (*Deafness in Society*) discussed hearing impaired people's efforts to pass. Efforts by moderately visually impaired people to pass as normally sighted were discussed by R. R. Fewell and S. A. Gelb, "Parenting Moderately Handicapped Persons," in *The Family with a Handicapped Child: Understanding and Treatment*, ed. M. Seligman (Orlando, FL: Grune & Stratton, 1983), 175-202.

29 See Higgins, *Outsiders in a Hearing World*, esp. pp. 155-162.

30 Thomas, "Problems of Disability."

31 See, for example, E. V. Stonequist, *The Marginal Man: A Study in Personality and Culture Conflict* (New York: Charles Scribner's Sons, 1937).

32 I describe problems of pursuing "fictionalized normalcy" in the often demanding and competitive realms of mainstream sports in Nixon, "Invisible Impairment."

33 See Fewell and Gelb, "Parenting Moderately Handicapped Persons," esp. 185-186.

34 See G. C. Lairy and A. Harrison-Covello, "The Blind Child and His Parents: Congenital Visual Defect and the Repercussion of Family Attitudes on the Early Development of the Child," *AFB Research Bulletin*, no. 25 (1979).

35 E. L. Cowen and P. H. Bobrove, "Marginality of Disability and Adjustment," *Perceptual and Motor Skills* 23 (1966): 869-870.

36 Fewell and Gelb, "Parenting Moderately Handicapped Persons," 182-183.

37 See Davis, "Deviance Disavowal"; Elizabeth Boggs, a parent advocate for mentally retarded people, observed that some parents like the idea of normalization because it is useful in "glossing over the realities of difference." She also stated that some professionals liked it for the same reason. The concept of normalization associated with the disavowal of deviance does not "gloss over the realities of difference." Rather, the realities of the difference of impairment and disability are accepted without attendant notions of moral inferiority or social deviance. See E. Boggs, "Who's Putting Whose Head in the Sand?" in *Parents Speak Out: Then and Now*, ed. H. R. Turnbull III and A. P. Turnbull (Columbus, OH: Charles E. Merrill, 1985), 39-54.

38 Shapiro made a useful distinction between *coping responses* as actions, thoughts, words, or feelings elicited by stressors from an impairment or disability and *coping resources* as things that could be used to mediate responses to a stressor. Coping resources include personality attributes; prior experience in stressful situations; aspects of an impairment or disability that make it harder or easier to handle; socioeconomic factors, such as social class, marital status, educational attainment, financial status, and religious affiliation; and access to formal and informal support systems. Coping responses are a buffer between life stress and impairment for parents of impaired children and are a means of achieving some sort of regular or routine adjustment to impairment and their impaired children. See J. Shapiro, "Family Reactions and Coping Strategies in Response to the Physically Ill or Handicapped Child: A Review," *Social Science and Medicine* 17 (1983): 913-931.

39 M. Voysey, "Impression Management by Parents with Disabled Children," *Journal of Health and Social Behavior* 13 (1972): 80-89; and M. Voysey, *A Constant Burden* (London: Routledge & Kegan Paul, 1975), 146-153.

40 Frank Warren, a former journalist, a consumer activist for people with autism, and the father of an autistic child, presented a scathing attack on professionals who have explained autism in terms of parental pathology. On the basis of his reading of relevant evidence, he asserted: "No known factors in the psychological environment of a child have been shown to cause autism." See F.

Warren, "A Society That Is Going to Kill Your Children," in *Parents Speak Out: Then and Now*, ed. H. R. Turnbull III and A. P. Turnbull (Columbus, OH: Charles E. Merrill), 217. Of course, what is relevant in the present context is what parents believe or are made to believe by others.

41   Voysey, *A Constant Burden*, 152.

42   See the discussion "Nothing Has Changed" (165) in B. E. Cogswell, "Conceptual Model of Family as a Group: Family Response to Disability," in *The Sociology of Physical Disability and Rehabilitation*, ed. G.L. Albrecht (Pittsburgh: University of Pittsburgh Press, 1976), 139-168. Cogswell cited Davis's study of children with polio and their families (*Passage Through Crisis*) and her study of paraplegics (see B. E. Cogswell, "Socialization into a Role: A Study of the Rehabilitation of Paraplegics" [Ph.D. diss., University of North Carolina, 1965] and B. E. Cogswell, "Self-Socialization: Readjustment of Paraplegics in the Community," *Journal of Rehabilitation* 34 [1968]: 11-13).

43   In this context, one may see a fine distinction between "structure" and "process." Social structure can be seen as a snapshot at a specific point in time of continually evolving or challenged rules, roles, and relationships. The continued change of or challenge to routinized and expected patterns of social rules, roles, and relationships reflects the influence of social process. See H. L. Nixon II, *The Small Group* (Englewood Cliffs, NJ: Prentice-Hall, 1979), 49-50, for a discussion of social structure and social process from a similar dynamic perspective.

44   See, for example, E. Kubler-Ross, *On Death and Dying* (New York: Macmillan Co., 1969); and P. W. Power and A. E. Dell Orto, eds., *Role of the Family in the Rehabilitation of the Physically Disabled* (Baltimore: University Park Press, 1980).

45   The parents interviewed by Voysey ("Impression Management" and *A Constant Burden*) were predominantly working-class mothers, and their impaired children ranged in age up to nine years and had "relatively severe" and "probably permanent" impairments. Her research was conducted in Britain.

46   Voysey, *A Constant Burden*, 221.

47   Ibid.

Chapter 2
FAMILY DYNAMICS, NETWORKS OF SOCIAL SUPPORT, AND PARENTAL COPING

In Chapter 1, it was proposed that dealing with the fact of a child's impairment can be a lifelong experience for parents and that the impairment may be a source of recurrent or chronic stress extending long beyond the initial stressful event of discovering impairment. After the shock of initial discovery, the stresses from impairment may reflect the practical difficulties of "objective" disability or the more subjective but just as real difficulties of esteem, identity, and status posed by stigma, deviance, or handicap. Nevertheless, an important fact about parental coping is that parents do not cope alone.

PARENTAL COPING IN A SOCIAL CONTEXT

Even if parents are single and feel alone or isolated, at the very least they cope along with their impaired children as part of a family. When their family unit consists only of a parent and an impaired son or daughter, the family is represented by the parent-child relationship. Obviously, the dyad of a parent and a child is the simplest family structure, and most families have more members and more complex webs or networks of social affiliation. However, whatever their composition or complexity, the structure and dynamics of these family relationships tend to be central elements of parental coping with a child's impairment.

In their families, parents directly confront the stresses of their children's impairments as a parental responsibility and seek support to cope with impairment. Single parents may have difficulty satisfying their needs for support through family relationships. Even in dual-parent families, family relationships may be unable to satisfy the range of parents' needs for support. In such cases, parents may turn outward for support. Thus, parental coping may be embedded primarily or centrally in the family, but it also occurs in a larger context of relationships with kin, neighbors, friends, educators, service providers, and organizations in the community or larger society. The impact on parental coping of impairment-related social relationships inside and outside the family, the amount and kinds of support these relationships provide, and the major patterns of social integration of parents of impaired children are the focus of this chapter. However, it is first necessary to present a brief definition of *social support* and some basic distinctions among types of support.

If support is broadly defined as help with socioemotional well-being, understanding, or role performance, then certain relations can be identified as being essentially supportive and others as being less supportive or not supportive.[1] In broad terms, one can distinguish among *expressive* support relations (including affection, recognition, and esteem-enhancing communication); *informational* support (including information, advice, guidance, referral, and empathic understanding); and *instrumental* support (including concrete goods and services or financial assistance).[2] Different strands of supportive ties may vary in intensity, as well as in reciprocity.

Parental Coping in Families

Families, like individual parents, cope with impairment in different ways. A general conceptual distinction between the ways family systems cope with stress is between morphostasis and morphogenesis.[3] Morphostasis refers to a tendency for families as social systems to try to maintain the same structure or pattern of relationships as in the past, whereas morphogenesis refers to a tendency to adapt the family structure to stresses and pressures for change. Morphostatic families tend to have relatively rigid rules, roles, and relationships, whereas morphogenic families tend to be more flexible. Morphostatic families tend to turn inward during times of crisis, stress, or pressure for change, whereas morphogenic families may form ties outside the family at such times. Thus, the boundaries of morphostatic families tend to be relatively impermeable or closed, whereas the boundaries of morphogenic families are more permeable or open.

I assume that impairment has some degree and type of distinct impact on parents and their families, as well as on the impaired children, but this impact may not be faced as immediately or directly as in the families with older adventitiously disabled members that Cogswell studied. In Cogswell's research, impairment usually occurred in late adolescence or adulthood.

My research focused on families with children who typically were congenitally impaired or became impaired in the first few years of life. I found that parents can take months or years to get a clear diagnosis of their children's impairments and even longer to acknowledge and try to come to terms with it. They may take this long because of a kind of inertia in family relations (like that found in one morphostatic case by Cogswell) or because the family network already is overtaxed or over-stressed and has little capacity to handle another major stressor. In some cases, the discovery of impairment may not become a crisis because the impairment is mild or moderate and "invisible" or because the family was organized before impairment to provide strong support.[4] Of course, if parents' failure to treat the discovery of impairment as a crisis or significant stress reflects an unwillingness to confront the disabling implications of the impairment, parental and family relations may become strained and problematic.

Parents will have an easier time delaying the recognition of impairment and ignoring the implications of the disability when the impairment is their children's rather than their own. A family also may function with fewer stresses and strained relationships when they ignore the impairment of a child, rather than of a member with adult responsibilities. Nevertheless, a child's impairment can profoundly change family members and relationships, especially when the impairment is severe. It also is true that the roles, relationships, and patterns of support that existed in the family before the discovery of impairment are likely to affect how parents and the family cope with the discovery and implications of impairment.

Marital ties offer the greatest potential for physical closeness, accessibility, commitment, interdependence, and opportunities for intimacy within the family, and they offer the widest range of possible forms of support. However, precisely because so much support may be expected from the marital tie, demand may exceed capacity, producing stress. The support or stress that parents experience in their marriages is likely to affect and reflect the ties they form with their impaired children, the ties they seek outside their families, the ways they think and feel about impairment and their impaired children, and the patterns of coping throughout the family network.

Husbands and wives are likely to rely especially on each other for support in coping with their impaired children. However, dealing with impairment may be stressful, and turning to a spouse for help could place a strain on the marriage. Thus, the reliance on one's spouse for support to cope with an impaired child suggests the possibility of a paradoxical interdependence of support and stress in coping.[5] That is, relationships on which parents rely for support may themselves become a source of stress when the demands for or expectations of support in these relationships exceed the capacity of the relationship to be supportive.

The problem in seeking understanding from one's marital partner after discovering that your child is impaired is that the situation typically is just as novel and ambiguous for the partner. As a result, a husband and wife may reinforce their uninformed stereotypes and create shared attitudes that fail to account for the realities of their child's impairment. When marital comparison and communication processes produce more uncertainty, anxiety, and stress regarding impairment than they alleviate, marital relations may be threatened.

For both mothers and fathers, fulfilling the full range of obligations of both marital and parental ties while dealing with responsibilities outside the family can be a difficult balancing act. This balancing act is likely to be even more difficult with an impaired child in the family, and the payoff from dealing with this increased stress or role strain may not be readily apparent to family members. Although most families are likely to develop coping patterns that enable them to hold together despite even severe impairments, stresses and strains in roles and relationships from the objective or perceived demands of impairment still may be a regular part of family life. Families who were cohesive and adaptable and who communicated well before the discovery of impairment seem likely to cope most effectively with disruptions of family patterns caused by impairments.[6] Similarly, marriages that were cohesive, adaptable, and had good communication before impairment seem likely to be the most successful at enduring the stresses and strains that impairment can produce.

Single Parents

Few parents seem capable of handling their children's impairments entirely within their families. For single parents, support from outsiders would seem especially valuable.[7] However, research by Mednick suggests that the support on which these mothers or fathers rely to cope with their children's impairments has a dual character.[8] Social-support relationships breed dependence for those being helped, and increased dependence allows others to increase their power as they give more support. Thus, single parents of impaired children seem vulnerable to the dilemma of the dual character of social support precisely because they perceive this help to be so valuable to them.

Single parents, particularly single mothers who are unemployed and have limited economic resources to take care of their impaired children and their other children, will have needs for support that go beyond impairment. Their range of needs may make it difficult or uncomfortable for them to ask for all the help they need. The more they feel they must ask, the more keenly they may feel the sharp edge of lost control from the support they receive and the more ambivalent they are likely to feel about asking for help in the future.

When support comes from relatives and friends with whom single parents have had enduring close ties and cannot be fully reciprocated, the discomfort from their ambivalence may become acute and cause resentment. This resentment may make single parents reluctant to ask for help from these sources in the future. The parents' reluctance can become a dilemma from which there is no escape, however, because if support is not requested, it may not be forthcoming, and in such cases the single parent is left to fend alone with the obligations and stresses of parenting an impaired child and his or her siblings.

Thus, although a single parent escapes the pressures of having to juggle parental and marital obligations with outside responsibilities and the special demands posed by impairment, there may be no escape from the dilemma of trying to balance the needs for support and the desire to maintain primary control over her or his family and personal life. Voysey's analysis implies that no parent—married or single—can cope splendidly without some sense of power or control regarding his or her child's impairment or disability.[9] However, single parents, even more than parents with partners, will need various kinds of support over time. Like married parents, they have to learn the appropriateness of different kinds of potential support ties in different situations. In this vein, I would argue that the set of support ties that ultimately enable single and married parents to cope splendidly will empower them with understanding and resources and address their emotional needs so they can disavow deviance and help their impaired children and families do the same. Parents are most likely to find and benefit from these ties when their families are linked by good communication; are cohesive enough to make their collective welfare important; flexible and adaptable enough to accommodate the changing conditions of impairment and demands of disability; and open enough to be able to accept outside help when the family network is stressed by the demands on it.

SUPPORT FROM PERSONAL COMMUNITIES AND DISABILITY NETWORKS

Parents in morphogenic families that allow or encourage relations with outsiders may find help for coping with their children's impairments both from informal networks that Wellman, Carrington, and Hall call "personal communities" and from more formal ties in disability networks.[10] Personal communities offer support through the "significant ties" that they actively think about and maintain (though not necessarily on a regular basis). Significant ties in such networks can include "intimate" or socially close ones with relatives and friends, as well as "routine" ties that are not as close or frequent, such as relations with neighbors, more distant relatives, and co-workers and contacts maintained by telephone or mail.[11]

Parents of impaired children may form ties in both personal communities and formally organized disability networks either as individuals (whether single or married) or as couples. Wellman, Carrington, and Hall found that in many cases, people viewed their ties to married persons as joint ties to the husband and wife as a couple, and they suggested that much of the support given to married persons may be intended for the couple.[12] However, for married couples, the crisis, stresses, and strains in roles and relationships produced by their child's impairment could divide parents or result in different responses that divide them. In such cases, parents often will seek or receive support as individuals, even though their purpose may be to find ways to bolster their marriage as they try to deal with the impairment.

Parents who seek or receive support from intimate or routine ties outside their families may be reassured or bolstered by the caring that is expressed. Yet they still may have no better understanding of their children's impairments or how to deal with them, and they still may lack important material resources (such as money, equipment, and programs) to help their children. In some cases, as with grandparents and other intimate family members, parents may find they have to give support to others who are having difficulty coping with the children's impairments. Some research has indicated that when parents turn to their parents, they find no support.[13] This suggestion helps explain the finding that families with impaired children have smaller social networks than do families without impaired children.[14] The willingness of people in usually intimate or routine ties to help with parental coping may be limited by such factors as the severity or stigma of impairment. Of course, they are precisely the kinds of things with which parents may need the most help.

Although they may appreciate and benefit from expressive and instrumental support from relatives and friends, parents still may feel a need for additional support to help them understand their children's impairments. Informational support from professional experts can help parents understand, but such support may not provide parents with the deeper level of meaning or empathy they feel they need. A parent of a child with Down's syndrome was quoted as saying in this regard, "You need somebody who can say, 'I know exactly how you're feeling'.... No one can do that except another parent."[15] The fact that there are differences in types of social integration implies that relations with other parents of impaired children will not appeal to all parents with impaired children. However, those who are coming to terms with the reality of their children's impairments and disabilities may have a strong need for such parent-to-parent ties on an individual or group basis to fill in a gap in their understanding and to reassure them about their children's future.

Educators and other professionals I have known have tended to assume that parents need help from individual parents or from parent groups only in their children's early years. Some parents make this assumption, too. My research shows that the need for social support from other parents, as well as from others, fluctuates over time and often intensifies at crucial transitional points in a child's or family's development.

I found it useful to get information and advice from parents and experts in the field of visual impairment when our son was a preschooler, when he entered public kindergarten (and a mainstream situation), when our family moved to another community and another state, when our son was in a resource room part of the school day, when we were looking for a camp and other recreational opportunities for him, and when he became a teenager.

I anticipate some anxiety or uncertainty for us all about the upcoming transition to high school and the related issues of dating, a part-time job, and planning for college or a job and life on his own after high school. I know he could benefit from the chance to talk to peers who have successfully handled these challenges and changes, and my wife and I could learn much from parents who have already navigated these waters, from successful visually impaired adults, and from professionals in the areas of the education and rehabilitation of blind and visually impaired persons. My wife and I have found, though, that despite our efforts to remain informed about our son's needs and available services, we often cannot find appropriate help at the time we need it. We have learned to become resourceful and to trust our own judgment, but we also know that we cannot fully meet our son's impairment-related needs. The varied and changing needs for social support of the parents in my study, which often were closely linked to their children's needs, is a major focus of later chapters. The notion of appropriate (and timely) support and the influence of support groups and professionals on parental coping receives special attention in those chapters.

Parent-to-Parent Support Ties

When parents of impaired children find other parents they perceive to be like them and have regular opportunities for face-to-face interaction, their relationships may develop an intensity and significance that are usually associated with those of families and close friends. Although parent-to-parent ties may be beneficial, they are not necessarily a panacea. In fact, parental coping could be damaged if other parents are not inclined or able to offer helpful support. Parent groups could attract angry, bitter, frustrated, or misinformed parents who offer only negative peer models or counterproductive coping strategies. Furthermore, some parents may be confiders, willing to engage in self-disclosure and mutually expressive support, whereas others may not want to talk about their feelings or want to help others understand and deal with theirs. Traditional gender-role socialization tends to discourage men from confiding or disclosing. However, women also may feel uncomfortable about openly expressing troubling or painful thoughts and feelings. Powell suggests that in times of crisis, people tend to turn to their primary social networks of family members and friends for support.[16] However, I have already noted the possible limitations of such networks when the crisis involves an impaired child and it is a novel or ambiguous experience for the people to whom parents usually turn for help.

Even though parents may be in social contexts that are conducive to forming new ties with disability networks and may want to enhance their own or their children's coping, organized parent groups or programs may not appeal to them. There are parents who feel best served by ongoing informal contacts with one or two other parents. There are parents who prefer ongoing involvement in a more organized group matched to their personalities and personal needs and aims. There are parents whose needs are adequately met by membership in a national or regional parent association. There also are parents who are able to get the help they feel they need through involvement in a time-limited parent group or program and others who receive valuable expressive, informational, or instrumental support from one-time individual contacts with other parents. Of course, at any given time and for various reasons, there are likely to be a number of parents who are uninterested in or unaware of any form of impairment-related parent-to-parent support.

A mother in my study who had not finished high school said she would be embarrassed to be in a support group because she was not good at talking. I suspect that a number of parents with a similar educational or social-class background also feel intimidated or out of place among the better educated and more articulate middle-class parents who often dominate the membership of support groups, especially more organized groups. In fact, I frequently was struck by the sharp and penetrating observations and insights expressed by the less formally educated parents I interviewed. It is difficult, though, to motivate such parents to join formal parent groups or to help them feel comfortable in the company of people whose lives seem different from theirs. If it is possible to get parents to focus more on their similarities in relation to their impaired children than on their differences, parents of different social backgrounds may find that they can interact comfortably and effectively with each other.

Differences of social class, race, ethnicity, age, and gender should not be underestimated, however, as obstacles to parent-to-parent ties. They are the basis for differences in many types of social interest and involvement in society in general. When impairment is important or urgent enough, these differences may be overcome, at least until the sense of urgency or crisis subsides, as parents seek whatever help they can find from whoever can provide it. The portion of my research concerning parent groups and other forms of parent-to-parent support is a major focus of Chapter 5.

Formal Support Networks

Whether parents want to develop new ties to help them cope will be affected by how they are coping at the time. How they are coping at a particular time and the amount and kind of support they are receiving will reflect and be influenced by their involvement in formal disability networks, as well as in personal communities of impairment-related ties. Formal disability networks provide direct support to parents or impaired children, such as medical and rehabilitative services, education, parent training, counseling, and financial help. They also influence how parents interpret and come to terms with impairment when parents treat them as authoritative or helpful.

The importance of formal services to parents or their impaired children may seem obvious, although some parents of impaired children may reject them. (The important function of weak formal ties in the spread of information about available support was discussed earlier.) In many cases, professionals may be most valuable to parents when they serve as indirect links or bridges to sources of direct support for parents themselves or their families, rather than just for the impaired children. For example, a teacher who develops a strong tie to an impaired child but rarely sees the parents may be helpful to the parents in suggesting (directly or through the child) a contact in a parent- support group or the name of an agency that can provide parents with financial assistance or respite care. Because networks of disability organizations, professionals, and services in a community rarely are fully linked as systems, parents easily can get lost in the community service "maze." Referrals from weak ties in such networks often are essential in helping parents identify their needs, define them with labels (such as "preschool screening," "parent training," and "respite care") that people in disability networks understand, and contact appropriate organizations or individuals for help.[17]

Relations with professionals are not without risks or problems for parents (or professionals), as the earlier discussion of doctor-parent relations should have indicated.[18] Parents may resent the authority or respect the expertise of professionals or perhaps feel some mixture of resentment and respect. Whatever the case in specific relationships between parents and professionals, parents will be more influenced by the professional than the professional will be by them, and they will need the professional more than the professional will need them. Parents will be able to reduce the imbalance in the power-dependence ratio in their ties to professionals when they have a broad array of support ties in their families, personal communities, and formal disability networks and when they believe they have access to alternative support ties that are equivalent to the current relationship with the professionals.[19]

One of the important ways that professionals can wield power over parents is in their role as gatekeepers.[20] In this role, professionals' decisions can determine the access of the impaired children, the parents, or whole families to specific supports, such as programs, financial assistance, and other resources. It is easy to see in these ties the dependence and vulnerability of parents and their families as well as the power of professionals.

Parents may find that their perceived need for support for themselves, their impaired children, or their families clashes with feelings of frustration, intimidation, debasement, or anger that comes from formal ties to professionals or agencies. They also may find that they do not understand the jargon that professionals use to talk to them. Furthermore, they may discover that professionals privately hold unflattering or demeaning opinions of them and apply pejorative labels to their parenting. Perhaps what is most threatening to parents is the possibility that reliance on specialized help from formal disability networks will reinforce the stigma on the children and families and increase their social distance from "normal" society.[21]

STABILITY, CHANGE, AND PARENTAL COPING IN NETWORKS

The discussion at the end of Chapter 1 underscores the dynamic nature of the coping process for parents. Just as parents change their orientations to their children's impairments, the social networks, contexts, and situations in which they cope also change. In fact, one can conclude from the discussion in this chapter that changes in parents' personal networks and the situations in which they confront impairment will reflect and affect how they cope.

The concept of morphogenesis implies flexibility and adaptability, and moderate amounts of flexibility and adaptability in families are associated with effective family coping. However, parents who face a variety of past and potential disruptions in their lives and stressful demands from their children's impairments and disabilities are likely to want some security and stability in their lives. Indeed, if they are to have a sense of order and control in their lives, there must be some predictability.[22] Parents can be expected to derive most of their security from the stability at the core of their personal networks, which are made up of intimate and routine ties to family, friends, neighbors, and, in many instances, co-workers.

Formal ties may be essential to parents or their children in particular contexts or at particular times of their lives. However, to the extent that they exist because of the children's attachment to them, they can be expected to change as the children change. For example, when a child changes schools, parents usually stop seeing teachers at the old school. Changes in other ties may alter parents' approach to coping or their capacity to maintain certain weak ties, which can lead to changes in relationships for them, their impaired children, and the other family members. This change may be illustrated by a mother who gets a part-time job and no longer has time to observe her impaired child in rehabilitation or in the classroom.

When parents respond to impairment in different social situations, they are tied to social networks that provide them with various kinds and amounts of support for their coping. The family is the primary social network of parents, and the orientation of parents to their family and the actual support the family provides have a major impact on how parents, their impaired child, and the entire family cope with impairment. Parental coping also is shaped by ties with outsiders in personal communities and more formal networks. Parental ties to outsiders will be influenced by ties within the family and the way the family as a whole functions. The integration of parents in society can take different forms that reflect, among other factors, their impairment orientation toward their impaired child, their interactional style, and their family orientation. The different ways in which these orientations and styles are related to societal integration and to each other will be revealed in the presentation of results from my study of parents of visually impaired children in future chapters. The nature of this research is summarized in the next section, which concludes this chapter.

THE RESEARCH: AN OVERVIEW

My research focused on interviews with 33 parents in 23 families with a blind or partially sighted child. Its use of an open-ended in-depth interview approach for parents supplemented by interviews of professionals and observations provided a detailed understanding of various dimensions of parental coping. The interviews were conducted over a six-month period in a major metropolitan area on the West Coast.[23] Most of the interviews with parents were conducted in the parents' homes, but 4 of the parents were interviewed in the project office, and 2 were interviewed by telephone. The average length of these interviews was three hours. Interviews with professionals were conducted at the professionals' offices or by telephone and varied in length more than did those with parents; they ranged from an abbreviated 30-minute phone session to a detailed 4 ½ hour in-person interview. Most of the interviews with professionals were full scale and were conducted in person.

Parental Sample

The aim of the first phase of the study was to interview all the parents of visually impaired children without other severe impairments who officially received resource-room or itinerant visual impairment services from special educators in "Central City" in the metropolitan area where the research took place.[24] In effect, the operational definition of visual impairment in these cases was official eligibility for special education. The 23 parents from Central City who actually were interviewed were from 15 (79 percent) of the 19 families in that city who had children in the visual impairment program of the public schools and whose first language was English. The 17 visually impaired children of the interviewed parents in Central City were less than 1 percent of all the children receiving special education in the city, which provided special services to approximately 8 percent of the students in its public schools.[25]

Following interviews with parents in Central City was a second phase of purposive parent sampling, intended primarily to increase the geographic diversity of the sample of parents and to add parents of preschoolers and multiply impaired children.[26] This sampling procedure added 10 parents from 8 families in 5 cities and towns within 50 miles of Central City.

There was a total of 42 parents in the 23 families represented in the study. Of the 33 parents interviewed, 21 were mothers and 12 were fathers. Eighteen of the families were dual-parent families. In 10 of these families, both partners in the couples were interviewed. A summary of major descriptive characteristics of the entire parent sample appears in Table 1.

Gaps in this sample (in relation to the population of the metropolitan area of Central City) included black families (only one partial phone interview) and Asian families who were not fully fluent in English (only indirect or informal contacts in school settings and phone contacts to solicit participation). In addition, the sampling procedure excluded parents whose visually impaired children attended private schools or residential schools for blind children. However, according to school officials in Central City, there were relatively few impaired school-age children in their city whose main impairment was visual and who did not attend the public schools.

Whatever the actual percentage of families with a visually impaired child in or out of the public schools, only one family with a school-age child in this study had their child outside the public school system of their city or town during the time I conducted my research. This child's family lived outside Central City, and the child was a fourth grader who had transferred from a public school to a parochial school at the beginning of fourth grade. One other family with two visually impaired children had their children in a number of different private schools over the years, but both were in public school at the time of the research. Thus,

Table 1. SUMMARY OF DESCRIPTIVE CHARACTERISTICS OF THE SAMPLE PARENTS

Characteristic	Number
Parents interviewed	33
Gender of parents interviewed	
Mothers	21
Fathers	12
Total families	23
In Central City	15
In five other communities	8
Total parents in families	42
Visually impaired children in families	25
Blind	4
Severe low vision	4
Moderate low vision	15
Mild low vision	2
Multiply impaired children	10
Current family situations of parents interviewed	
Dual parent	18
Single parent	5
Age range of parents interviewed	20 to mid-50s
Age range of children	6 months to 19 years
Race of parents interviewed	
Caucasian	32
Black	1
Parents, families, and the school-age distribution of their visually impaired children	
Preschool	4 mothers and 2 fathers in 4 different families
Elementary	9 mothers and 4 fathers in 10 different families
Middle–high school	8 mothers and 6 fathers in 9 different families

Note: Parents' socioeconomic status was not measured by objective means and is therefore not included in this table. However, the economic status of families in the sample ranged from "needy" (receiving public assistance) to "having plenty" (upper middle class).

essentially this was a study of parents of visually impaired children who lived at home and attended public schools if they were of school age. The relatively small number of interviewed parents reflected the in-depth interview approach and the low incidence of visual impairment in children and youths. However, because the population of parents with visually impaired children in the sampled communities was relatively small, the small number of parents interviewed in this research was fairly representative of that population on many major socio-demographic dimensions—with the notable exceptions already mentioned. Thus, despite the limited representation of nonwhite minority parents, which may have partially reflected an underidentification of their children for special education, the patterns of parental coping revealed in this study offer insights across a wide range of parents and parental experiences. Even when parental coping differs from the patterns I found, recognition and understanding of these differences should contribute to sensitivity toward and insight into important aspects of the meaning of parental coping with impairment.

Professional Sample

Professionals were interviewed to expand and deepen my understanding of parental coping and to learn more about the professionals themselves and their values, attitudes, and roles regarding visual impairment and visually impaired children and their families. Interviews with professionals were conducted concurrently with the interviews with parents. The sampling of professionals began by contacting all administrators and special educators associated with the visual impairment program of Central City, as well as service providers in agencies serving the visually impaired community in and around the city. Sampling was extended by a snowball procedure, whereby those professionals who were contacted in the first phase of sampling were asked to suggest other service providers with experience relevant to this study. Formal interviews were conducted with 35 "professionals," of whom 3 were volunteers with extensive enough experience to qualify as "experts" in recreational programs for visually impaired youths and adults. The range of fields represented by these professionals included, in addition to recreation, services for visually impaired people, special education, vocational education, educational administration, parent counseling and advocacy, social work, medicine, and university-based research and consulting.

Issues Explored

The major areas of questioning for parents (which were also reflected in the interviews with professionals) concerned (1) family-context factors (family size, composition, background, resources, life and routines, and culture), (2) impairment-context factors (severity, background and onset, diagnosis, and prognosis), (3) parental-coping factors (awareness and understanding of impairment, perceived responsibility and power, self-conception and commitments, child care and control, problems and pressures, the future, and parental role differentiation), (4) societal integration (school, child's social and recreational activities, and parents' integration), and (5) social support (needs, formal support, and general and informal support).

My understanding of parental experiences and responses was deepened and broadened by the professional interviews and by informal contacts with both parents and professionals. My informal and repeated contacts with certain parents and professionals resulted from my dual role as a researcher and a parent of a visually impaired child. This dual role increased the range and number of my informal contacts with parents at general school functions and other functions explicitly for visually impaired children or their families. It also brought me into more frequent contact with a number of professionals in the school my child attended.

Despite the limited size of the sample of parents, mine is one of the few studies of impairment in the family to include families with impaired children at virtually all the key stages of a child's life cycle. The 25 children in the 23 families in this study (2 families had 2 visually impaired children) included an infant (of 6 months), preschoolers, children in elementary school, and adolescents in middle school and high school (up to age 19). The ages of parents ranged from 20 to the mid-50s. Although this design allowed only tentative conclusions to be drawn about how individual parents change over time, it enables one to see that different parents cope differently but that they do so not necessarily because of the age of their children or even their own age. Variations in general patterns of coping among the parents I interviewed are presented in the next two chapters.

NOTES

1   See H. L. Nixon II, "Reassessing Support Groups for Parents of Visually Impaired Children," *Journal of Visual Impairment & Blindness*, 82 (September 1988): 271-278; T. L. Albrecht and M. B. Adelman, eds., *Communicating*

Social Support (Newbury Park, CA: Sage Publications, 1987); and R. M. Milardo, ed., *Families and Social Networks* (Newbury Park, CA: Sage Publications, 1988).

2   L. L. Eggert, "Support in Family Ties: Stress, Coping, and Adaptation," in Albrecht and Adelman, *Communicating Social Support*, esp. 89-91.

3   A general social-systems treatment of these ideas is in W. Buckley, *Sociology and Modern Systems Theory* (Englewood Cliffs, NJ: Prentice-Hall, 1967). These ideas were used to analyze family responses to disability in B. E. Cogswell, "Conceptual Model of Family as a Group: Family Response to Disability," in *The Sociology of Physical Disability and Rehabilitation*, ed. G. L. Albrecht (Pittsburgh: University of Pittsburgh Press, 1976), 139-168.

4   See R. S. Weiss, "The Provisions of Social Relationships," in *Doing Unto Others*, ed. Z. Rubin (Englewood Cliffs, NJ: Prentice-Hall, 1974), 17-26; M. Argyle, and A. Furnham, "Sources of Satisfaction and Conflict in Long-Term Relationships," *Journal of Marriage and the Family* 45 (1983): 481-193; B. H. Gottlieb, "Social Support and the Study of Personal Relationships," *Journal of Social and Personal Relationships* 2 (1985): 351-375; and N. Lin, "Modeling the Effect of Social Support," in *Social Support, Life Events, and Depression*, eds. N. Lin, A. Dean, and W. M. Ensel (Orlando, FL: Academic Press, 1986), 173-209.

5   J. Eckenrode and S. Gore, "Stressful Events and Social Supports: The Significance of Context," in *Social Networks and Social Support*, ed. B. H. Gottlieb (Beverly Hills, CA: Sage Publications, 1981), esp. 52-53, 56.

6   Cohesion, adaptability, and communication have been shown to be major dimensions of successful coping with stresses by "normal" intact families at all stages of the family life span. Olson, McCubbin, and their associates derived these three basic dimensions of family behavior from a conceptual clustering of over 50 concepts used to analyze marital and family dynamics. These three factors were the conceptual cornerstones of the model they used to explain family coping in the 1,140 dual-parent families (in 31 states) in their research. In their study, the families that coped best generally had *moderate*—not extreme— levels of cohesion and adaptability that were facilitated by good communication, and they were called "balanced" families. This model applied to marriages as well as to large family networks. See D. H. Olson, H. I. McCubbin, and associates, *Families: What Makes Them Work* (Beverly Hills, CA: Sage Publications, 1983).

7   See, for example, P. F. Vadasy, "Single Mothers: A Social Phenomenon and Population in Need," in *Families of Handicapped Children: Needs and Supports Across the Life Span*, ed. R. R. Fewell and P. F. Vadasy (Austin, TX: Pro-ed, 1986), 221-249; and L. Wikler, "Single Parents of Mentally Retarded Children: A Neglected Population" (paper presented at the American Association of Mental Deficiency Meeting, Miami, FL, 1979).

8   M. T. Mednick, "Single Mothers: A Review and Critique of Current Research," in *Family Processes and Problems: Social Psychological Aspects*, ed. S. Oskamp (Newbury Park, CA: Sage Publications, 1987), 184-201.

9   M. Voysey, *A Constant Burden* (London: Routledge & Kegan Paul, 1975).

10 B. Wellman, P. J. Carrington, and A. Hall, "Networks as 'Personal Communities,'" in *Social Structures: A Network Approach*, eds. B. Wellman and S. D. Berkowitz (Cambridge, England: Cambridge University Press, 1988), 130-184.

11 Ibid., esp. 137-153.

12 Ibid., 140.

13 A. Birenbaum, "On Managing a Courtesy Stigma," *Journal of Health and Social Behavior* 11 (1970): 196-206; and J. McDowell and H. Gabel, "Social Support Among Mothers of Mentally Retarded Infants" (unpublished manuscript, George Peabody College, Vanderbilt University, Nashville, TN, 1981).

14 McDowell and Gabel, "Social Support Among Mothers of Mentally Retarded Infants." See also I. M. Sonnek, "Grandparents and the Extended Family of Handicapped Children," in *Families of Handicapped Children: Needs and Supports Across the Life Span*, eds. R. R. Fewell and P. F. Vadasy (Austin, TX: Pro-ed, 1986), 99-120.

15 C. Lavin, "When Being a Family Is Special," *Burlington Free Press*, 31 January 1985.

16 D. R. Powell, "Individual Differences in Participation in a Parent-Child Support Program," in *Changing Families*, eds. I. E. Sigel and L. M. Laosa (New York: Plenum Publishing Corp., 1983), 203-224.

17 S. Rubin and N. Quinn-Curran, "Lost, Then Found: Parents' Journey through the Community Service Maze," in *The Family with a Handicapped Child: Understanding and Treatment*, ed. M. Seligman (Orlando, FL: Grune & Stratton, 1983), 63-94.

18 See H. Featherstone, *A Difference in the Family: Living with a Disabled Child* (New York: Penguin Books, 1981), esp. chap. 7; and R. B. Darling, "Parent-Professional Interaction: The Roots of Misunderstanding," in *The Family with a Handicapped Child: Understanding and Treatment*, ed. M. Seligman (Orlando, FL: Grune & Stratton, 1983) 95-121.

19 For sophisticated general theory to explain power relations in social networks, see B. Markovsky, D. Willer, and T. Patton, "Power Relations in Exchange Networks," *American Sociological Review* 53 (1988): 220-236.

20 See H. W. Smith, *Introduction to Social Psychology* (Englewood Cliffs, NJ: Prentice-Hall, 1987), 403-404.

21 See the discussion of similar problematic implications of the "professionalization of handicap," or increasing specialization among disability professionals, in D. Thomas, *The Experience of Handicap* (London: Methuen, 1982), 182. Problems and strategies of linking formal and informal support networks are considered in C. Froland, D. L. Pancoast, N. J. Chapman, and P. J. Kimboko, "Linking Formal and Informal Support Systems," in *Social Networks and Social Support*, ed. B. H. Gottlieb (Beverly Hills, CA: Sage, Publications, 1981), 259-275.

22 Turner argued that predictability is a fundamental interaction condition. See R. H. Turner, "Personality in Society: Social Psychology's Contribution to Sociology," *Social Psychology Quarterly* 51 (1988): 1-10, esp. 4.

23   The study was conducted in the mid-1980s, but the precise year is not given to protect the identity of the people who were interviewed.

24   Fictitious names are used for places and people in this study to protect the confidentiality of all participants. Because the study focused on personal social networks of parents rather than on the structural characteristics of full-scale networks in their communities, this method of treating the identity of places and people does not create significant problems in the analysis of the results.

25   In fact, one of these 17 visually impaired young people from Central City was a recent high school graduate at the time of the interview. For this reason and because this person was still a teenager, the youth is treated as part of the high school population in the data analysis.

26   See, for example, R. C. Bogdan and S. K. Biklen, *Qualitative Research for Education: An Introduction to Theory and Methods* (Boston: Allyn & Bacon, 1982).

Chapter 3
VISUAL IMPAIRMENT AND PARENTAL DENIAL AND MINIMIZING

The thought of blindness often scares people. In 1976, a public opinion poll indicated that cancer and blindness were the most feared "ailments."[1] The association of blindness with cancer as a dreaded sickness reveals much about people's attitudes toward this impairment and people with this impairment. This type of attitude is different from the view held by many blind people about their blindness. For example, Kenneth Jernigan, the outspoken leader of the National Federation of the Blind, a major advocacy organization of and for blind people, has said that "with training and opportunity, we can reduce blindness to the level of a mere inconvenience." However, he added that "we also know that custodialism, discrimination, denial of opportunity, and putdowns can make our blindness a veritable hell—as terrible as it has been... thought to be."[2] The clear implication to be drawn from Jernigan's observations is that it is not the inability to see that is frightening or terrible; it is stigmatization or handicapism that makes life especially difficult for people who cannot see.

VISUAL IMPAIRMENT IN SOCIETY
Many degrading misconceptions and stereotypes of blindness and blind people can be found in literary works and the Bible, the contemporary

mass media, and public attitudes in American and other societies.[3] These misconceptions and stereotypes fuel a stigma of blindness and handicapism for blind people. There are occasional examples of sensitive and nonstereotypical portrayals of blind people in the mass media, and this kind of treatment of blindness and blind people has seemed to increase somewhat in recent years in literature, films, and television.[4] Nevertheless, there is no reason to conclude that the stigma of blindness has disappeared from American culture; that blind people no longer face barriers erected because they are blind; or that the acceptance of a child's blindness no longer is a problem for parents, relatives, and others who are in contact with the child. In fact, my research clearly showed that blindness remains stigmatizing, difficult to accept, and even somewhat frightening for many parents and others in the parents' and children's networks of contacts.

Following the discussion in this chapter of visual impairment and basic elements of parental coping, I consider evidence of two different types of parental coping patterns and show how the differing significance of stigma distinguishes two types of coping in which parents do not accept the full reality or disabling implications of their children's impairments. These types of coping are called *denial* and *minimizing*, and these terms reveal how parents think about the reality of impairment for their children and themselves. In the next chapter, I present evidence of two other parental coping patterns, called *protectiveness* and the *disavowal of deviance*. These latter types of coping involve a great deal more acceptance of the reality of impairment than do denial and minimizing, but they, too, are distinguished by the amount of importance parents place on stigma. The meaning of each of these forms of coping with impairment, as well as its connection to particular types of interactional style, family orientation, and societal integration, will be presented after the discussion in the next section of the nature of visual impairment.

THE NATURE OF VISUAL IMPAIRMENT

As a stigma, a basis for disability and handicapism, and a cause of crises or stresses, visual impairment is like other types of impairments. However, parents with a visually impaired child are likely to see their coping as different in one or more respects from coping with other types of impairments. They may believe that coping with their child's visual impairment is different because they have learned distinctive stereotypes or other cultural images of blindness, because they do not want to

associate their child with other impairments they se
matized, or because they see distinctive characteristics (
ment that they do not see in other types of impairment.
be unwilling to equate their child's condition with the
other visually impaired children.

It has been suggested that the difference between near or total blindness and partial sight is likely to be an important difference that affects how parents see their child and respond to his or her visual impairment and its disabling implications. Thus, a child's visual impairment may be perceived by professionals and parents as being similar to other types of impairment conditions in salient respects, and it may be seen as different, even from the visual impairment of other children. The perceived similarity or dissimilarity of their visually impaired child or the child's impairment in relation to other impaired children and their impairments is likely to be an important factor that shapes the kinds of ties parents seek and sustain to gain support for their coping.

As a sensory impairment and in medical terms, visual impairment has many variations. Furthermore, the term *visual impairment* has been defined differently—to apply only to partial sight or in a more encompassing way to all degrees and types of visual loss. For the purposes of this study, the term, as used here, applies broadly to conditions in which sight cannot be corrected to an acuity of better than $20/70$ (the threshold for reading ordinary newsprint) in the better eye or where the field of vision is less than 20 degrees or both. Operationally, this definition applies to children and youths who are likely to be sufficiently sight impaired to be eligible for special-education services in a special program or resource room or on an itinerant basis. This conception of visual impairment encompasses a range of conditions, from low vision, in which there is partial sight, to total blindness, in which there is no light perception. Total blindness is relatively rare among young people. The prevalence rate of visual impairments in the under-20 population in the United States has been estimated at approximately 5 per 10,000.[5] Only about 2 percent of all visual impairment is congenital or develops in early childhood. The other 98 percent develops "adventitiously" after early childhood. People who are referred to as "legally blind" have a corrected acuity of no better than $20/200$ in the better eye or have a visual field of less than 20 degrees.

Some children have visual impairment along with one or more other types of impairment. For example, specific visual impairment conditions may be combined with cerebral palsy; hearing impairment; mental retardation; epilepsy; attention deficit disorder and other specific learn-g disabilities; spina bifida; and an assortment of other physical, emotional, and health impairments.[6] In most cases, the presence of multiple impairments is likely to complicate and intensify the coping experience of parents. Depending on the nature and relative severity of the multiple impairments, the presence of one or more other impairments could compound the perceived stresses of visual impairment or distract attention from it.

THE NATURE OF PARENTAL COPING

It was my aim in this research to listen to parents and professionals, observe them, and use what they said and did as a basis for identifying general types of parental coping and finding themes, patterns, and experiences common to each general type.[7] I respected the relevance and importance of what people told me and then tried to interpret the meaning of it and discern whether there were patterns that linked or distinguished perspectives and experiences of parents. Thus, in presenting my research, I often will cite, sometimes at length, what parents (or professionals) said or did and then give my interpretation of it.

The basic conceptual frameworks that describe parental coping emerged from what I heard and saw in my research and were developed and refined through my application of relevant sociological ideas and research. It is important, both from a research standpoint and for practical reasons, to accept parents' perceptions of their experiences as real and valid to them, whether or not they seem appropriate and constructive. Even when parents expressed ideas or recounted experiences that appeared to contribute to their coping difficulties, I assumed that what they said reflected their perception of their experiences, and, hence, it formed the basis of my interpretation of what coping with impairment meant to them.

My research uncovered shades of difference—in understanding, feeling, and action—within generally similar contours of parental coping. Indeed, in probing deeply into anyone's perceptions and life, it is impossible not to see their uniqueness. Thus, in the search for common threads, themes, and patterns and broadly general types of distinctions, it is important not to gloss over the individual differences that this research approach is especially suited to uncover.

Parental coping may be viewed as an ongoing and dynamic process that defines and redefines the relationship of parents to their impaired children. I have suggested that two central issues in parental-role relationships with their impaired children concern the salience of the stigma of impairment and the willingness of parents to accept the reality of impairment and its disabling implications. By combining the factor of the salience of the impairment stigma with the factor of the acceptance of the reality of impairment, I distinguished the four types of parental impairment orientation—denial, minimizing, protectiveness, and disavowal of deviance—that were mentioned earlier (see Table 2).

Denial refers to a parental orientation in which the impairment stigma is salient and the reality of the child's impairment is not accepted. *Minimizing* refers to a parental orientation in which the impairment stigma is not salient and the reality of the child's impairment is not accepted. A *protective* parental orientation occurs when the impairment stigma is salient and the reality of the child's impairment is accepted. *Disavowal of deviance* refers to a parental orientation in which the impairment stigma is not salient and the reality of the child's impairment is accepted.

The terms *denial*, *minimizing*, and *protectiveness* occur frequently in the literature on parental coping, but they rarely are defined as they are here.[8] The *disavowal of deviance* (derived from the term *deviance disavowal* in Davis' seminal work on interaction between disabled and nondisabled people) is less commonly found than the other terms in the literature on parental coping or general coping.[9] Parents who disavow deviance reject the verdict of society that their children's impairments are a stigma. They break through in their relationships with other people to establish social identities for themselves and their children that are "normal" in their moral dimension but do not preclude attention to disability, when appropriate.

A second dimension of the relationship of parents to their impaired children that was found to be important in this research was suggested by Voysey's conception of parental interactional styles.[10] As was noted earlier, parents' interactional styles reflect perceptions of their responsibility for their children's impairments or disabilities and their power to do something about the impairments or disabilities. These interactional styles are closely related to parents' sensitivity to stigma and acceptance

Table 2. PARENTS' IMPAIRMENT ORIENTATIONS

Impairment Orientation	Stigma Impairment	Acceptance of Impairment
Denial	Salient	Not Accepted
Minimizing	Not Salient	Not Accepted
Protectiveness	Salient	Accepted
Disavowal of Deviance	Not Salient	Accepted

of the reality of their children's impairments, which are incorporated in parental impairment orientations. The major interactional styles of parents are avoidance, stoic acceptance, making amends, and coping splendidly, and they generally follow Voysey's language. (See Table 3.)

Avoidance occurs when parents feel a sense of responsibility for their children's impairments or disabilities and believe they have no power to affect the impairments or disabilities. Stoic transparent acceptance occurs when parents feel they are not responsible and have no power. In the case of making amends, parents feel responsible but also believe they have power to do something about their children's impairments or disabilities. Coping splendidly occurs when parents feel they are not responsible and believe they have power.

My research suggested a correlation between a parent's impairment orientation and his or her interactional style regarding impairment. The denial orientation tended to be correlated with avoidance, the minimizing orientation with stoic transparent acceptance, the protective orientation with making amends, and the disavowal of deviance with coping splendidly.

Parental Coping and Family Orientations

For the parents in this study, Cogswell's concepts of morphostasis and morphogenesis were useful ways of describing their orientations to their families.[11] Rather than using these terms to describe the actual functioning of family systems, I use them here mainly to describe parental orientations to family interaction and family functioning. A morphostatic orientation is relatively rigid, inward looking, and closed toward outsiders and is referred to here as a rigid family orientation. A morphogenic orientation is relatively flexible, outward looking, and open toward outsiders and is referred to here as a flexible family orientation. This study found that parents who coped by denial and avoidance tended to have a rigid family orientation. Parents who coped by minimizing and stoic transparent acceptance tended to have a marginally flexible family orientation. Parents who coped by being protective and making amends tended to have a relatively flexible family

Table 3. PARENTS' INTERACTIONAL STYLES

Interactional Style	Perceived Responsibility	Perceived Power
Avoidance	Responsible	No Power
Stoic Acceptance	Not Responsible	No Power
Making Amends	Responsible	Power
Coping Splendidly	Not Responsible	Power

orientation. Parents who engaged in the disavowal of deviance and were coping splendidly tended to have the most flexible family orientation.

Types of Parental Integration

Parental coping tends to bear the strong imprint of the nature of a parent's orientation to the dynamics of family life. In addition, it is shaped by the nature of ties with outsiders in "personal communities" of kin, friends, and neighbors and in more formal networks.[12] Whether parents want to develop new ties to help them cope will be affected by how they are coping at the time. How they are coping at a particular time and the amount and kind of support they are receiving will reflect and be influenced by their involvement in formal disability networks as well as in personal communities of impairment-related ties.

The combination of parents' comments about their experiences with "outsiders" and the ideas of Darling and Darling and of Nash and Nash suggested four basic types of parental integration in society.[13] The distinctions are based on differences in the range and intensity of "normal" (not impairment-related) ties of parents and the nature of their pursuit of general and specialized ties to informal and formal disability networks (to professionals and other service providers, advocates, voluntary associations, agencies, parent support groups and other individual parents of impaired children, and impaired children and adults and their families). I assume that normal ties may be customary (similar to the past) or restricted in range and intensity (compared to the past). I also assume that ties to disability networks will be strongly pursued, moderately or weakly pursued, or rejected. The maintenance of customary ties may minimize a parent's sense of distress about impairment, but that sense will be precarious when parents reject ties to disability networks. Combining the two main dimensions of integration produces four types of parental integration—isolation, biased normal integration, biased disability subcultural integration, and dual integration, which are shown in Table 4.

Table 4. TYPES OF PARENTAL INTEGRATION

Parental Integration	Range and Intensity of "Normal" Ties	Pursuit of Ties in Disability Networks
Isolation	Restricted	Rejected
Biased Normal Integration	Customary	Rejected
Biased Subcultural Integration	Restricted	Strong
Dual Integration	Customary	Weak to Moderate

Isolation involves a restricted range and intensity of normal ties because parents are wary of new ties and have difficulty sustaining old ones. It also involves the rejection of ties to disability networks because parents are careful to avoid the potentially stigmatizing influence of associating with people connected to impairment. Biased normal integration involves parents' maintenance of the customary range and intensity of their "normal" ties and the rejection of ties to disability networks because these ties are perceived to be irrelevant. Biased (disability) subcultural integration involves a restricted range and intensity of normal ties because parents also are wary of new ties and have difficulty sustaining old ones. However, in this case, parents strongly pursue ties in disability networks. Dual integration involves the maintenance of the customary range and intensity of normal ties and a weak-to-moderate pursuit of ties to disability networks.

Four Parental Coping Patterns

The four parental coping patterns proposed here integrate elements of the parents' impairment orientation and interactional style with elements of family orientation and societal integration. The correlations among the four main elements in each pattern are summarized in Table 5.

In presenting the parents' comments that defined each coping pattern and that clarify their different shades of meaning, I will indicate the number of mothers, fathers, and couples who displayed the pattern. I also will identify parents in terms of the family numbers in the "Profiles of Families" in Appendix 3. To preserve the confidentiality and anonymity I promised each participant in this study, it is necessary to avoid giving details that could lead to the identification of specific individuals. By referring to the family profiles and the background information provided in the discussion of individual parents and families, readers can gain a sense of the different life circumstances from which parental

Table 5. A COMPOSITE MODEL OF PARENTAL COPING PATTERNS

Pattern	Impairment Orientation	Interactional Style	Family Orientation	Societal Integration
A	Denial	Avoidance	Rigid	Isolation
B	Minimizing	Stoic Transparent Acceptance	Marginally Flexible	Biased Normal
C	Protectiveness	Making Amends	Flexible	Biased Disability Subcultural
D	Disavowal of Deviance	Coping Splendidly	Flexible	Dual

experiences with impairment emerged. By keeping in min'
ferences, along with the variations in experience within (
coping pattern, one should find it difficult to think of par
of simple stereotypes.

Attention initially will focus on the perspectives and experiences of
parents who displayed denial and the types of interactional style, family
orientation, and societal integration that tended to be associated with
it. The final part of this chapter focuses on patterns of parental coping
related to minimizing.

Pattern A: Denial

Pattern A—denial-avoidance-rigid-isolation—which generally will be
called "denial," applied to 3 of the interviewed parents, 2 fathers (families 3 and 20) and a single mother (family 9). The role orientation
reflected an awareness of the stigma of blindness, along with an
unwillingness to acknowledge the full reality of impairment for the
child. The different dimensions of meaning of denial, along with other
elements of this pattern, may be seen in the comments of one of the
fathers in this category. He was the father of a teenage daughter with
low vision:

> I always think about the fact that [my child's] visual impairment is
> [not noticed] by others, like teachers. I don't understand visual
> impairment at all. I take that back. I understand how she can see,
> but psychologically ... I don't understand. She has adjusted through
> the years to see what is normal for her. I try to help her in every
> way, but she wants to drive [a car]. It's hard to tell her she can't.
> Who knows? Maybe they'll be able to cure it. I want her to have as
> normal a life as possible. She doesn't think she is visually impaired. I
> brought her up to think she's as good as anyone else. [I have] a com-
> pletely different view than my wife [who was "protective" in both
> our terminology and this father's]. I tell [my daughter] she is capa-
> ble of doing anything. My wife constantly tells her she's hand-
> icapped and legally blind. I want her to feel she's a whole person,
> not half.... Sight is the most important thing you can have.... My
> daughter is normal, and I am proud of her. I don't think of her as one
> of those people with a cane.

This father's comments reveal a great sensitivity to the stigma of
blindness and an unwillingness to accept the reality of his daughter's
visual impairment, which are characteristic of denial. Avoidance is
based on both a sense of responsibility and a sense of powerlessness
regarding impairments or disabilities. However, powerlessness seemed
to be a much more salient basis for avoidance for all the parents who
displayed this pattern.

Relationships with professionals. The avoidance displayed by parents who engaged in denial incorporated frustration, alienation, or antagonism. These feelings seemed especially evident in the case of the single mother, who showed no inclination to come to grips with her son's low vision. She strongly asserted, "[My son] is not blind!" This mother was poor and seemed to have no sense of connection to her son's school or teachers. She and her son lived with her extended family. She talked about her child "doing fine when he was left alone by stupid people [in the school system]." Special educators and other teachers gave me information that revealed a different picture of the visual functioning of this woman's son. They said he had significant problems seeing and described the resistance they confronted in trying to get the mother to take her child to eye appointments his teachers had scheduled for him. Because he often "misplaced" his glasses when he took them home, they kept a second pair for him at school.

This case shows how difficult it can be for parents and professionals to establish a cooperative relationship when parents deny the reality of their children's impairments. One reason why teachers could not gain the cooperation of this mother may have been the general alienation she felt because she was poor and could not identify with the middle-class values and expectations of educators and schools. In fact, all three of the denying parents seemed to have been pushed toward avoidance by difficult relationships with professionals that spawned their sense of powerlessness about their children's impairments and disabilities.

Because bad or good relationships with educators and the schools were a major theme in parental experiences, they will be considered throughout, in the parents' comments on their experiences, but especially in Chapter 6, where parent-professional relationships are the central focus. In the case of the alienated mother just described, one sees how important it is for professionals to be sensitive to the alienation and powerlessness that parents of less affluent or culturally different backgrounds may feel in their dealings with community institutions and their representatives. It is easy to blame or criticize denying parents for their "irresponsibility" or "ignorance," but the reasons for denial usually are much more complex and may include the way parents *believe* they are treated by people who represent powerful community institutions like the school. What school officials and teachers saw as helpful behavior, such as setting up eye appointments and providing glasses, the single mother thought of as interference in the lives of her son and herself. It was evident in the interviews with all the denying parents that they shared a sense of frustration about their inability to direct their children's lives in the way they intended.

Family relations. All three denying parents described strained family relations. The family orientations, at least of the two fathers, could be described as rigid. The father's comments that were just quoted reflect his basic disagreement with his wife about how to handle their daughter. In fact, at the time of the interview, these parents were having serious disciplinary problems with their visually impaired daughter, whose teenage desire for independence had turned into rebelliousness. The daughter was having problems in school and had run away from home a couple of times. Her father seemed lost, in part because his traditional conception of fatherhood and family did not apply well to the "nontraditional" circumstance his family was confronting, especially visual impairment and extreme rebelliousness.

The second denying father said, "I have not concerned myself much with [visual impairment]." His visually impaired baby was the product of his second marriage. He was under a great deal of stress, from strained relations with his former wife and his current one and from a financial struggle to sustain his fledgling small business. His wife accused him of "lying" about his lack of concern about their baby's vision, saying he was constantly asking the nurses questions about it. He asserted, however, that he was concerned much more about other medical crises the child was experiencing that related to premature delivery and about the medical bills that were piling up.

This father was angry, and he lashed out at the doctors whom he blamed for his baby's visual impairment. He was angry that they delayed telling him and his wife about their baby's loss of vision following their postsurgical treatment of the baby for other problems. Indeed, he and his wife discovered the baby's visual impairment only after they suspected a change in vision, extracted some information from a nurse, and confronted the primary physician directly. However, a reluctant confirmation was all they received. In the ensuing couple of months, this father was unable to obtain answers to any of his questions, which fueled his frustration. Ironically, then, he actively sought information from medical personnel while he tried to avoid contacts with others in disability-support networks. In fact, his attempted avoidance of disability-support ties was not successful. Soon after his daughter's birth, he reluctantly became involved in a support group for parents of premature infants.

This father acknowledged that visual impairment might become a bigger concern after his child was through her other problems. However, he was uncomfortable talking about his daughter's visual condition and his adjustment to it. He said, "I am adjusting on my own.... I am not looking for somebody to talk to." He was like the other father who displayed this pattern, who said, "A man to me is a man. You're not supposed to be a sissy." Both men clearly manifested denial, avoidance (at least regarding the dimension of powerlessness), and a rigid family orientation.

Because the children of all three denying parents were connected to a disability network to some degree, their parents were at least indirectly tied as well. Thus, none was truly "isolated." Yet, subjectively there was some sense among these parents, and a number of others, that their own world or their children's had contracted as a result of visual impairment or that contacts with disability networks should be avoided or were not worth being pursued.

What especially distinguished these parents who exhibited Pattern A was their clear denial of the implications of their children's visual impairments and their failure to come to terms with the reality of it in their own and their children's lives. It is not enough, though, merely to state these observations. It also is necessary to say that the patterns of coping displayed by these parents were not marks of their character or products of their personalities. These patterns should be understood, instead, as products of the parents' immediate and more enduring social, cultural, and economic life circumstances and the nature of their relationships in their families and with significant and powerful others outside it, such as educators and doctors.

Prospect for change. Parental coping is a dynamic process, which means that it can change with changing life circumstances, especially with changes in resources and relationships that affect the parents' and the children's capacity to understand visual impairment and to deal with visual disabilities. In Chapter 4, I discuss other parents who first denied their child's impairment and later learned to disavow, with experience and the support of others.

I must acknowledge that with little prior knowledge or experience regarding impairments or impaired persons, my own initial responses to the news of my child's impairment bordered on denial. Whatever understanding and acceptance I have gained as a parent of an impaired child have come from the education I have received from a variety of highly competent teachers and rehabilitators of visually impaired persons; from visually impaired adults; from advocates for impaired children and adults; and, perhaps most important, from listening to and observing my son.

I recognize that it is easy to jump to moral judgments about people who are "deniers" or who cope in other ways that may seem inadequate, but I hope this personal acknowledgment and a realization that patterns of coping have reasons or causes will short-circuit such judgments. An important purpose of this book is to show that parental coping varies and can change. In trying to understand why coping varies or changes, one must look closely at the differences in life circumstances, resources, and relationships that characterize different parents or the same parents at different times. The next section shows how minimizing parents differed from those who denied.

Pattern B: Minimizing

Pattern B—minimizing-stoic transparent acceptance-marginally flexible-biased normal integration—which generally will be referred to as *minimizing*, applied to five of the interviewed parents. These parents were a married couple (family 10), two other mothers (both visually impaired themselves and one a single parent, in families 19 and 23), and one other father (in family 21). Five other fathers (in families 11, 12, 14, 22, and 23) were not formally interviewed but appeared, from my observations or from comments from spouses or professionals, to be minimizers, too.

Aspects of minimizing. Minimizing parents shared with denying parents a limited acceptance of the real or full implications of visual impairment and a sense of limited power or powerlessness. However, they generally seemed less concerned about the stigma of blindness, less worried about the future, and less inclined to blame someone for problems related to impairment or for the impairment itself. The marginally flexible nature of their family orientation allowed these parents to engage in an ordinary range of "normal" relationships outside the family. However, they were characterized by biased normal integration because their failure to accept their child's impairment led to their rejection of ties to disability networks as irrelevant. These parents accepted sympathy graciously to keep their good name but tended to view special efforts to help them with the impairment as well intentioned but ignorant. Those whose children had moderate or mild and relatively invisible impairments were likely to try to have their children pass as normal, if possible.

The difference between minimizing and denying patterns is illustrated by two mothers of visually impaired teenagers who were visually impaired themselves. Because visual impairment had been part of their own childhood and youth, they had learned to deal with the possible stigma of their impairment and, as stoics, were not worried about their children being stigmatized. Perhaps because they felt they understood firsthand the experience of visual impairment and were not inclined to be worriers, they tended not to address the full impact of impairment and disability on their children's lives.

One of the mothers was much more visually impaired than was the other. A self-described "welfare recipient," she said her job prospects had been hindered by her visual impairment and her failure to finish high school and develop marketable job skills. She was made acutely sensitive to the social difference of being blind when she was an adolescent. As a young teenager, she was transferred from a regular classroom into a special education resource room. She said, "You didn't dare let anyone see you in the resource room." She learned to "go with the flow to avoid embarrassment," which meant trying to pass as normally sighted and fit into the "normal" peer subculture to the extent it was possible. As a mother, she recognized how visual impairment intensified her teenage daughter's difficulties with social adjustment and how her daughter was "trying to be as normal as the other kids." She realized her daughter missed things and "was not one of the cool ones." However, she also felt she was more impatient with her daughter because she herself was visually impaired.

She was upset with her mother for coddling and pitying her grandchild after not behaving that way with her when she was growing up. This mother had no pity for her own child, and she stated that her standard response to her daughter's complaints and excuses was, " 'I can't' never did!" Her daughter may have been trying to deny visual impairment and pass as normal in the same way she did as a teenager because the mother was a *minimizing* parent with a strong mainstream or normalcy orientation.

The mother herself made no effort to deny her adult impairment or her child's and even talked about the jokes they made when their mutual visual impairments led to some embarrassing moments (such as not seeing things, bumping into things, and seeing people incorrectly). Yet, her acceptance was a transparent stoic type because she fatalistically accepted her daughter's genetically transmitted impairment as "the way it was supposed to be." She added, "I wish it didn't happen but there's no blaming. There is no time for that. What good would it do anyway?" As a partially sighted single mother on welfare who was unable to drive, she felt no sense of power over her daughter's impairment or disability.

Her one major effort to have her child's impairment corrected through surgery had failed.

This mother valued "a normal life" for herself and her daughter and made no concerted effort to locate special help for either of them. However, as a minimizer rather than a denier, she appreciated the itinerant teacher's supportive attitude and helpful advice to her daughter even though the mother made no effort to solicit the help herself. It is noteworthy, too, that the daughter's contacts with her special education teacher were mainly by phone. In school, the daughter tended to avoid being seen with this teacher or the adaptive devices, such as large print, that the teacher could supply. Her conversations with this teacher generally focused on her "social problems" and only obliquely on the relevance of visual impairment or adaptive devices.

The other visually impaired parent who was a minimizer was only mildly visually impaired. Although she was married, her husband's alcoholism caused her to assume nearly all the parental responsibility during their marriage. The middle-class lifestyle of this family, with both parents usually employed, had been strained in the past year because the father had been out of work. Before the interview, the mother had considered separating from her husband, but marital relations had improved by the time of the interview because her husband recently had returned to work and was making a serious effort to deal with his alcoholism. The combination of this mother's limited impairment and tendency not to be a worrier contributed to her minimizing the significance of visual impairment in the lives of her two visually impaired children. Friends told her, "You've done a good job [as parents] because your kids don't know they're handicapped." Similarly, she never thought of her kids as handicapped.

The fact that both children had been in a special class for visually impaired students for the first few years of school posed no stigma for this mother nor did the fact her son had been in high-level competition for visually impaired athletes. Both her children had spent most of their school life in the mainstream, and she thought of the special sports competition more in terms of athletic accomplishment than of disability. Furthermore, like the other visually impaired mother who minimized, she did not think about blaming herself for her children's hereditary impairments. Like this other mother, she expressed a stoic, almost fatalistic, kind of "acceptance" of her children's impairments, but she still did not place much emphasis on their impairments or disabilities.

This mother's coping pattern made it difficult for her to understand and deal with a recent crisis in her daughter's life that was brought on by her problems with visual impairment. Her description of the crisis reveals why she was so poorly prepared for her daughter's difficulties:

> I felt no stress from visual impairment until my daughter first had a problem last year [as a junior in high school]. I didn't consider them handicapped. They always did what their [normally sighted] peers did. But [my daughter] put a lot of pressure on herself. The pediatrician said I should be concerned about suicide. [My daughter] said, "If I were totally blind, it might be easier." She said she faked it [being normally sighted]. Her brother did it, too [but he didn't feel as much stress] because he was a happy-go-lucky kid, a "good-time Charlie."
>
> Until last year, I thought both of them accepted [their visual impairment] really well. But the psychologist said my daughter tried to be a perfectionist to make up for being handicapped. Her overachievement in school was to compensate. The pressure she put on herself led to her depression. She needed to ease up. I thought she had it under control. Then it flared up again [recently]. This time she went to the psychiatric ward. Because I had a sight problem, I didn't worry [before the crisis]. I'm an up person, and I don't know how to deal with depression. I didn't worry about visual impairment. I am not a worrier, [but] this is frightening.

This mother's poignant story deepens one's understanding of the different levels of acceptance and problems of empathy that even visually impaired parents can have in coping with their children's impairments and the implications. In addition, as this mother's account shows, a parent's approach to coping can leave a substantial imprint on a child's coping—and complicate it. This mother's story also should indicate the need to avoid quick or simplistic conclusions about how a parent's coping influences a child's approach to coping with impairment, for in this family, the older brother responded differently from his sister to low vision. The specific dynamics of parent-child interaction and other ties need to be explored much more extensively before the precise impact of a parent's coping on a particular child can be understood.

It should be added that this mother was responsive enough to her daughter's depression to accept without question her daughter's need for hospitalization after her second serious experience with this illness. She seemed to want life in her family to be the way she recalled family life during her childhood, but she knew that even if visual impairment could be viewed as not being a problem, having a child who was suicidal, as well as a husband who was alcoholic, made it impossible to sustain an impression that life in her family was normal. She had a marginally flexible family orientation, which accompanied her efforts to engage in minimizing, and stoic transparent acceptance regarding visual impairment.

Impact on family. As has been shown, minimizing may mislead one about the deep impact of impairment on a family. In looking at the other cases of minimizing, one will see even more variety in its forms and reasons. The husband and wife who displayed this pattern seemed to do so mainly because their child's impairment was mild and hence easy to ignore. A major reason that the impairment received little attention from this couple in the past, before their son had received corrective lenses and when his impairment was therefore moderate in nature, was that the parents had difficulties adjusting to their parental and marital responsibilities and made only a limited effort to understand the impairment or their child. They admitted some neglect of their child's needs as they struggled with their personal problems. These problems led to a separation, which was followed by a recent attempt at reconciliation. They stated that they wished to pay more attention to their visually impaired son, who was their only child. However, they intended to make few concessions to his impairment. Although they acknowledged the impairment and knew eyeglasses helped, they still expected their son to act "normally." The boy's father said, "I expect the same from him as a normally sighted child.... [Visual impairment] is just something that happened, and you get him glasses. He'll blame problems on his vision if he can."

The mother's comments suggest a connection between expectations and understanding:

> We were fighting against his taking the Metro bus to school at first. But we figured it would teach him not to use his eyesight as a handicap. He has to learn to rely on himself....
> I don't think I understand that much about his visual impairment. I can only go by looking at his [school] work. He can't explain what he sees [he was of elementary school age]. To him, he sees normally. Doctors do not talk where you can understand. [Our son] doesn't like not having his glasses. There are worse things than wearing glasses.
> Sometimes I think he uses his [low vision] as a crutch. He pulls the trick "I can't see it" or "It's blurry" quite a bit with me. With all these questions [in the interview], I'm wondering if we are as concerned as we should be. (*Laughs*)

For this minimizing couple, visual impairment was a relatively insignificant part of life. For the other parent who was a minimizer, impairment was a major issue. However, this father was concerned much less about visual impairment than about the other effects of the motorcycle accident in which his teenage son had been involved over a year earlier. The accident caused serious brain damage for his son. Moderate low vision, which was visible in its effects, was one result of the brain injury, but the son's persistent behavioral outbursts and general lack of emotional control stemming from his accident were much more troublesome to the father. Somewhat like the denying father of the visually impaired baby, dealing with visual impairment was seen in the context of priorities by the father of the teenager. Problems that he perceived as more serious had to be resolved before he could fully acknowledge and attend to the implications of visual impairment. This father's comments clearly display a number of basic elements of Pattern B, at least in relation to visual impairment:

> [My son] hasn't yet accepted the fact of his injury. He still thinks he can go and do as he pleases—like he always did. He knows his left eye is closed, and he can't see that good out of his right one.... It's not like he's blind, though. We try to build his hopes up, not tear them down. We can't tell him he's going to be blind for the rest of his life.... There is not much hope of improvement.... I wish visual impairment was his only thing. We got a psychiatrist for him. We don't know what else to do. I know what the problem is. My son needs to straighten out.
>
> I have very little control. I am more or less a baby-sitter. I laid a hand on him a couple of times in the hospital to bring him around, and all that got me was a record as an adult abuser. Now I just back off and let him rant and rave.... We have an altogether different life now. I am resigned [to] no freedom. I am not crying. What's done is done. You can regret without crying.

This man's stoicism was one of the most striking aspects of his coping, and it was marked by his justifiable sense of futility and powerlessness related mainly to his son's brain damage and its effects on his son's behavior. The repercussions of his son's accident had substantially altered his life, including the stability of his marriage and his plans for a new business after his recent retirement. Yet he did not complain. There were no histrionics. He did not dwell on the impact of impairment on his life. He did not talk about institutionalizing his son. Furthermore, he refused to "burden" others with his problems. Trapped by his custodial role, this man's fondest wish was that the life of his family would return to normal. Thus, along with his tendency to minimize (the visual impairment, in particular) and display stoic transparent acceptance, his family orientation was only minimally flexible, and his strong desire was for biased normal integration. At the time I interviewed him, he was willing to accept outside help, but he had little confidence that it would do any good.

This type of parent may seem inaccessible or uncooperative to some professionals, and, indeed, one professional who had suggested that I try to talk to the father expressed surprise that he actually was willing to do so. Despite the obvious indications of stoicism I found, this father clearly wanted to tell his story to me and convey his willingness to accept help that would make a difference to his son or his family. The lesson here, I suppose, is that educators and service providers should be careful not to write off parents as "inaccessible" or "uncooperative" without first trying to understand them, their situation, and the reasons for their apparent lack of desire to talk or take advantage of services for their children. It is worth repeating that this man was fatalistic, but he still was willing to accept services that could help his child or him. This attitude was common among minimizers.

A willingness to accept help with impairments and disabilities from at least one type of service provider was a major characteristic of nearly all the parents who displayed the protectiveness pattern. These varied manifestations of protectiveness, and their relationship to making amends, flexible family orientations, and biased disability subcultural integration are considered in the next chapter. The combination of coping patterns associated with the disavowal of deviance are also discussed in Chapter 4.

At this point in the consideration of patterns of coping, some comments about the concepts of patterns and categories are in order. The experience of the father whose teenage son sustained multiple impairments that differed in the nature and severity of their disabling effects and their urgency reveals the difficulty of using general categories to describe coping with complex circumstances. This man's case reinforces the need to be mindful of individual differences and complex reactions within categories of coping, and this point will be reinforced again in considering other parental experiences. For this man and for each of the other parents I studied, one pattern of coping tended to be more descriptive of their responses to their children's impairments than any of the other patterns, and the pattern applied to each parent, despite its limitations, provided useful and important insights about how he or she coped.

Although parents in a specific coping category are not all alike and their impairment orientation is not correlated in exactly the same way with interactional style, family orientation, and societal integration, the coping concepts presented in this chapter should be helpful in understanding how differences in parental coping become patterned and how different aspects of coping are related to each other. I believe that the coping categories and the connections among different aspects of coping that emerged in my research may be generalized beyond the relatively small sample of families I studied. That assumption, however, needs to be tested in other settings with parents who are facing challenges other than visual impairment.

NOTES

1 Cited in D. F. Stroman, *The Awakening Minorities: The Physically Handicapped* (Washington, DC: University Press of America, 1982), 91.

2 K. Jernigan, "To Everything There Is a Season: Discrimination Against the Blind," *Vital Speeches* 43 (August 15, 1977): 667. Quoted in ibid., 91.

3 See M. E. Monbeck, *The Meanings of Blindness: Attitudes Toward Blindness and Blind People* (Bloomington, IN: Indiana University Press, 1975); F. Bowe, *Handicapping America: Barriers to Disabled People* (New York: Harper & Row, 1978), chap. 4; and D. Biklen and L. Bailey, eds., *Rudely Stamp'd: Imaginal Disability and Stereotypes* (Washington, DC: University Press of America, 1981).

4 See, for example, J. Kalter, "Disability Chic," *TV Guide*, 31 May 1986, 40-44; F. Koestler, "A Look at the Way Blind People Are Portrayed in Movies," *AFB News*, Summer 1986, 8, 14; F. H. Jarosh, "AFB Talks to 'Mr. Sunshine,'" *AFB News*, Summer 1986, 14; and J. Bateman and E. Warren, "This Week: 'Can't You Feel Me Dancing?'" *TV Guide*, 11 October 1986, 18-19.

5 Statistics cited here were taken from Stroman, *The Awakening Minorities*, 89-90. For additional facts about blindness and low vision, see, for example, I. Bailey and A. Hall, *Visual Impairment: An Overview* and P. C. Cockerham, *Low Vision Questions and Answers: Definitions, Aids, Services* (New York: American Foundation for the Blind, 1990 and 1987, respectively). Stroman also discussed definitions of visual impairment (which he termed *blindness*), demographic characteristics of the population of visually impaired people in the United States, and causes of visual impairment. A clear and straightforward discussion for parents of "Eyes and What Can Go Wrong" is in E. P. Scott, J. E. Jan, and R. D. Freeman, *Can't Your Child See? A Guide for Parents of Visually Impaired Children*, 2nd ed. (Austin, TX: Pro-ed, 1985).

6 For a general overview of the nature of various types of multiple-impairment conditions experienced by visually impaired children, see Scott, Jan, and Freeman, *Can't Your Child See?*, chap. 7.

7 The conceptual framework presented in this chapter also appears in H. L. Nixon II, "Patterns of Parental Coping with a Child's Impairment: Integrating Impairment Orientation, Interactional Style, Family Orientation, and Societal Integration" (unpublished manuscript, 1990).

8 See, for example, P. W. Power and A. E. Dell Orto, eds., *Role of the Family in the Rehabilitation of the Physically Disabled* (Baltimore: University Park Press, 1980); H. Featherstone, *A Difference in the Family: Living with a Disabled Child* (New York: Penguin Books, 1981); R. B. Darling and J. Darling, *Children Who Are Different* (St. Louis: C. V. Mosby, 1982); M. Seligman, ed., *The Family with a Handicapped Child: Understanding and Treatment* (Orlando, FL: Grune & Stratton, 1983); J. Shapiro, "Family Reactions and Coping Strategies in Response to the Physically Ill or Handicapped Child: A Review," *Social Science and Medicine* 17 (1983): 913-931; M. G. Eisenberg, L. C. Sutkin, and M. A. Jansen, eds., *Chronic Illness and Disability Through the Life Span: Effects on Self and Family* (New York: Springer Publishing Co., 1984); G. Henderson and W. V. Bryan, *The Psychosocial Aspects of Disability* (Springfield, IL: Charles C

Thomas, 1984); R. P. Marinelli and A. E. Dell Orto, eds., *The Psychological and Social Impact of Physical Disability*, 2nd ed. (New York: Springer Publishing Co., 1984); and R. R. Fewell and P. F. Vadasy, eds., *Families of Handicapped Children: Needs and Supports Across the Life Span* (Austin, TX: Pro-ed, 1986).

9 F. Davis, "Deviance Disavowal: The Management of Strained Interaction by the Visibly Handicapped," *Social Problems* 9 (1961): 120-132.

10 M. Voysey, *A Constant Burden* (London: Routledge & Kegan Paul, 1975).

11 B. E. Cogswell, "Conceptual Model of Family as a Group: Family Response to Disability," in *The Sociology of Physical Disability and Rehabilitation*, ed. G. L. Albrecht (Pittsburgh: University of Pittsburgh Press, 1976), 139-168.

12 B. Wellman, P. J. Carrington, and A. Hall, "Networks as 'Personal Communities,'" in *Social Structures: A Network Approach*, eds. B. Wellman and S. D. Berkowitz (Cambridge, England: Cambridge University Press, 1988), 130-184.

13 Darling & Darling, *Children Who Are Different*; and J. E. Nash and A. Nash, *Deafness in Society* (Lexington, MA: Lexington Books, 1981).

Chapter 4
PARENTAL PROTECTIVENESS AND DISAVOWAL OF DEVIANCE

It is sometimes difficult to see the distinctions among actual forms of parental coping that are implied by the abstract concepts of coping presented in Chapter 3. It is especially difficult when we focus exclusively on one dimension of coping or when parental coping is in a volatile period. For example, if we concentrate only on the acceptance of impairment or its implications, we may confuse denial with minimizing (because there is a failure to accept in both cases) or protectiveness with the disavowal of deviance (because both reflect relative acceptance). If we look only at sensitivity to stigma, we could confuse denying and protective parents (both are highly sensitive) or, more likely, minimizing and disavowing parents (for whom stigma is not highly salient). When parents are becoming protective after having been deniers, it is difficult to know whether they are more denying than protective or more protective than denying. These examples point to the importance of seeing different aspects of parental coping, such as orientation to impairment, as being more complex than unidimensional concepts would suggest. They also suggest caution in jumping to quick conclusions about how parents typically cope.

Although the complexity and dynamic character of parental coping can make it difficult to see clear-cut differences in coping patterns, the comments of denying and minimizing parents in Chapter 3 demonstrate that there are real, significant, and patterned differences in parental coping. Knowledge of parents' impairment orientation can provide important clues about other aspects of their coping, including their interactional style, family orientation, and societal integration. The correlations among these different aspects of parental coping, which were summarized in the composite model of parental coping patterns presented in Table 5 in the last chapter, will be seen once again in this chapter in the consideration of protective and disavowing parents.

The remainder of this chapter focuses on the perspectives and experiences of protective and disavowing parents. I will first discuss protectiveness (Pattern C) and the other aspects of parental coping that tended to be associated with it and then go on to the disavowal of deviance pattern (Pattern D).

PATTERN C: PROTECTIVENESS

The protective-making amends-flexible-disability subcultural integration pattern, which generally will be called *protectiveness*, applied to 11 parents—3 couples (families 6, 15, and 16) and 5 other mothers (in families 1, 3, 12, 14, and 20). These parents generally differed from denying and minimizing parents not only in their greater acceptance of visual impairment and its implications but in their greater sense of power to do something about the impairment or disability. They generally felt more responsible than did the disavowing parents for the existence of their children's impairments or disabilities.

Protective parents tended to have relatively flexible family orientations that were open to outsiders in disability networks. Their biased (disability) subcultural integration was marked by a concern that people in *normal* networks would not understand their children's impairments and would be critical of or disparaging toward them or their impaired children because of the stigma of impairment, which would restrict their ties in these networks. However, their acceptance of impairment and sense of power and "responsibility" motivated them to become heavily involved in disability networks.

Protectiveness and Making Amends

One of the most unusual contexts for parental coping that I found concerned a young mother who had lost custody of her son to a foster family when she was a teenager and was charged by legal authorities with nonsupport. The child was a victim of abuse by his father, which had caused the head injury that resulted in the child's severe visual impairment. When I interviewed the mother, she was 20 years old, separated from her husband (who was incarcerated), heavily involved in counseling and support groups to improve her parenting skills, regularly involved with her child in a supervised schedule of visits, and deeply committed to developing her capacity and right to regain full parental custody of her child. Her story gives concrete definition to the notion of "making amends":

> I have done a lot to learn about special needs. I try not to blame. I would have to point a finger at myself. It is hard to look in the mirror at times. But it doesn't do any good to blame [myself or my husband]. There is nothing to do [for my child] but physical therapy [right now].... I am learning to deal with responsibility. No one is born a parent. I have come a long way, but it is only the tip of the iceberg. I must prove myself as a parent. I think about the future a lot [in relation to visual impairment]. I don't know where he's going. I have hope, but people create their own future—and problems.

One is struck by the growing maturity and wisdom of this 20-year-old woman. She absorbed much from the support she had received, but she also recognized that she had much more to learn. Meanwhile, she was happy to entrust her child to the care of a loving foster family. As she was "making amends," she was moving from protectiveness toward the disavowal of deviance. She had developed a flexible family orientation, even as a noncustodial mother, as a result of her extensive and intense participation in special support groups to teach her about motherhood and parenting a disabled child.

Other protective mothers spoke about their consuming commitment to their impaired children, their sensitivity to stigmatizing judgments by others, and their own protectiveness. One mother, of a visually impaired baby, was the wife of a denying father cited in Chapter 3. The different coping patterns of these two parents reflect the tension in their marital relationship, which had worsened with the problems following their baby's birth. This mother had benefited from the support of a group of parents of premature infants into which she had pushed her resistant husband. However, she was only beginning to learn about visual impairment, which had been part of her life for just two months. Her protectiveness reflected the recency of her discovery of her baby's vision loss and her negligible past exposure to impairment of any kind:

> Visual impairment is a hard one. I figure life won't be normal for her or me. I'll have to do a lot for her. I had lots of hopes that may never be [realized]. It's sad. I want her to see.... I think about visual impairment every day. Her visual impairment makes her more special.... I blamed myself, my husband, the doctors, whoever turned up the

oxygen [which apparently caused the loss of vision]. Sure, I hold a big grudge against the doctors. I was sure I was being punished for something I did. I am trying to do the best I can, but my main concern is my child and being a good parent.... Life is not normal. I have learned not to think beyond today.... My husband thinks [parental] support is stupid. He will not ask for help. He puts me down for it. I am afraid of getting hurt by building up hope. I'll probably be overprotective.

It is not surprising that this woman said she did not feel she was in charge of her life, which could be seen as a departure from the sense of power that the protective parents tended to have. However, her determination to do everything she could for her child reflected a kind of intentional power that often characterized protective parents. Although protective parents often felt limited control at the moment, they intended to have a strong influence over their impaired children's lives. Their sadness about impairment, their perceived lack of normalcy, the perceived specialness of being visually impaired, their blaming of themselves and others, and their overarching commitment to their impaired children also were common qualities.

A protective couple, a mother and a stepfather of a girl in elementary school, emphasized how special she was, partially in response to stigmatizing comments. Both these parents had lived difficult lives, dealing with life on the street, economic disadvantages, and drugs. They were trying to stabilize their lives and were committed to being good parents. The mother, who had a mild but potentially serious visual impairment herself, wanted her daughter's life to be much better than her own and than in the past. In her comments, one sees her concerns, her protectiveness, and her desire to make amends:

> [My daughter] is handling [visual impairment] well. She sees what she wants. She pretends not to see when she doesn't want to. I want to improve her will to see.... She's special to everyone because she's so bright. Being visually impaired is not as easy as some people think.... People talk behind her back and tease her. She's taunted by her cousins, who call her "retarded." I handle the taunts by ignoring them and explaining them to [my daughter].... Discipline is no problem with her. She doesn't usually need it. She doesn't do anything wrong. I do things for her because I feel sorry for her.... I have control now, but I didn't feel that way before [when I lived on the street and when my husband and I had drug problems]. [I see] what we put the kids through [with the drugs], but now we've turned it around. I am not really sure about the future. I am not ready for the teens.

The stepfather assumed a father's role and, even more than his wife, saw their impaired child as "special." He had grown up in a family with many impaired foster children and had learned from his mother to treat children with impairments as "God's gifted children." He said, "She's one of the least demanding handicapped kids. Visual impairment makes her more special to me. She is an angel; her [younger] sister is a terrorizer." Like his wife, he made a point of asserting in the face of teasing and taunts that "she is *not* retarded!"

These parents were impressed with the child's resource-room teacher, who was visually impaired herself. They thought that she was an excellent role model and that their daughter needed her. As a result, they were reluctant to break the child's ties to her. When one effort by school officials to place the child in a regular classroom failed, the parents were relieved and pleased to have their daughter back in the resource room, where she felt much more comfortable. They wanted her to be mainstreamed in the future but "only when she feels ready."

However, because their daughter's resource-room teacher was the only person in the school whom these parents seemed to trust, it seemed unlikely that they would push for a mainstream placement if it meant less contact with that teacher. Thus, the practical aspects of their daughter's everyday experiences in the school were far more important to them than was the abstract principle or long-term implications of mainstreaming.

This case presents a valuable lesson to those who are trying to understand why parents may not embrace mainstreaming. Parents may think that mainstreaming is not working on a practical level and that it makes them and their children frustrated and unhappy because they believe that teachers are unresponsive or unsupportive or programs are inappropriate for their children's needs. In such cases, parents may be more satisfied when their children are "sheltered" by a "protective" resource-room teacher who identifies with the children and has a better understanding of their impairment-related needs.

Consuming Commitment

In a few cases, such as the one just described, protective parents were willing to entrust their children's welfare to a person with "special understanding." Other protective parents ultimately trusted only themselves to know what their children needed. One mother treated her child as if he were blind for the first three years and became consumed by her commitment to meet all his special needs. She gave up a promising corporate career to take care of her child, and she and her husband had moved several times to find appropriate services for him. Even after she discovered that he was partially sighted at age three and felt bad that she had not allowed herself to believe he could see, she continued to be protective. However, her protectiveness did not mean she was fearful of physical knocks and bruises. It related more to his education, rehabilitation, and socioemotional development. She said:

> In some ways I push him. I let him take his bumps physically, but I protect him too much in other ways....
>
> I worry about embarrassment more for me than for him. I used to worry that people would think he was mentally retarded, but that doesn't bother me now. I am embarrassed by his unusual mannerisms [because of the combination of his visual and neurological impairments]. I see him as different from his peers and *that* bothers me.
>
> Our life is not really normal because of [our son's impairments]. A lot of problems are because of my reluctance to let him be with a lot of sitters. My husband says I've overprotected him. For so many years, I've wanted to do everything. I am at school a lot. I give it my all. Most of the time, it is not fun. It has affected my husband, and I have begun to change my mind about [trying to do everything].

The other protective mother of an elementary-school-age child also spoke about her consuming commitment to her son, her sensitivity to stigmatizing judgments by others, and her protectiveness. Both mothers had to deal with their children's multiple impairments and felt it would be much easier if there were "only visual impairment." Their husbands loved and generally supported them and their impaired children, but both spouses engaged in minimizing that bordered on denial. These middle-class protective mothers also were alike in their "biased" involvement in disability ties and networks stemming from their commitment to their impaired children and their concern about getting appropriate services and education. However, the second mother's impaired child was her only child, which may have accounted for her deeper levels of anxiety, concern, and frustration.

Another parallel between these two protective mothers was their concern about the appearance of impairment. The first mother's concern was caused by the unattractive appearance of her son's eyes and his unusual mannerisms. The source of the second mother's concern was a physical impairment that affected her son's gait and prompted teasing from peers. In this mother's case, the invisibility of her son's low vision and the ambiguity of his learning impairment contributed to other kinds of worries and frustrations. Thus, she had problems about things seen and unseen. Some of the distinctive aspects of her pattern of coping were described in these terms:

> Every mom who has carried [an impaired] child [in pregnancy] blames herself in some way. I've asked, "How come?" But I put my energy into raising my child. Guilt can be carried into advocacy....

The parents [of visually impaired children I know from the support group I organized] who are having problems have low vision kids. Low vision kids are misunderstood and mistreated.... No one in the public schools knows what to do with a low vision child. His teachers missed the low vision.... [It] bothers me when he gets excited and swoops his head around. Others might not understand and think he's weird. Because the other problems are more demanding, I often put visual impairment on the back burner.... Physical care is not that much, but he is never out of my mind, probably because he is always sick.... I am consumed by what's going on with him. I have no choice. I can't walk away. I couldn't handle another child, with my job and my worrying.

Parents of Teenagers

Although one might expect protectiveness in impairment orientation and the tendency to make amends to diminish as a child gets older, time and experience do not necessarily make these elements of Pattern C disappear. In fact, among the parents of teenagers I interviewed, two couples and another mother generally could be classified as protective, and still displayed some evidence of "making amends."

Family 1. One upper-middle-class couple with two visually impaired teenagers had a strong commitment to education. Over the years, they had tried a variety of private and public schools to obtain an appropriate education for their daughters but had little success. The teachers usually did not seem to understand low vision. Their older daughter, who was more visually impaired and had the added complication of a learning impairment, had much more difficulty coping. She developed a serious emotional impairment, with bouts of deep depression and suicidal feelings. This teenager's psychiatric case history was longer and differed in a number of other key respects from the case of the teenager with psychiatric problems discussed in Chapter 3. However, in both cases, visual impairment was a salient problem. In the earlier case, the mother and father were minimizers, and the mother had difficulty empathizing with her daughter. In the case of the protective parents, the capacity for empathy could help explain their protectiveness, which was much more pronounced in relation to their older daughter than to their younger daughter. The mother said:

[Our older daughter] has had difficulties in social interaction. She's always acted like a blind person, with her mannerisms. It's from not getting visual cues. I feel comfortable [in public] now, but I used to feel embarrassed by social "boo-boos."

[Until the past two years] the number-one priority of [our older daughter] was not to be different. Since last year, she felt it was OK to be different and associate with other visually impaired kids....

> She has threatened suicide. We've tried emphasizing and deem-
> phasizing visual impairment. You're damned if you do, damned if
> you don't.... There have been tremendous trials.
> I think we've done a good job overall in letting them know we
> love and support them. We may have pushed the younger one more
> along a [normal] path to compensate ourselves for her sister. We
> worry about the older one finding her niche outside the home. My
> sense of control [over my life] depends on how the kids are doing.
> There is a big void after high school, a big "What if?" .... We try to
> steer them toward things they can do well or feel good about. We
> change our emphases as they get older. We grow as they grow.

This mother and her husband were not as consumed by their children's visual impairments as were the protective mothers with multiply
impaired children in elementary school. In fact, the responses by the
mother of the two visually impaired teenagers suggest that she and her
husband were moving toward the disavowal of deviance. The
adaptability she mentioned, when she referred to growing with her
children, suggests the kind of flexible family orientation that could be
the foundation for the disavowal of deviance. She and her husband,
however, still seemed to be protective because their older daughter's
continuing coping problems made it difficult to get beyond a sensitivity
to social stigma.

Although this couple did not feel much guilt or personal responsibility for the genetic nature of their daughters' visual impairments because
it was not easily identified in their family history, they felt a great deal of
responsibility for finding help to deal with their daughters' (especially
the older daughter's) special needs. They had been in couples therapy,
and in the father's words:

> It made us more aware and sensitive. It led to a desire to get more
> help for [our daughters'] handicaps. Mental health people have been
> very important [to them]. Teachers don't understand visual impair-
> ment. We bridge the gap between school and outside in mental
> health. We need to know help is available. We need to know we are
> doing a good job.

These parents ultimately settled for public school placements for
their daughters. As the mother said, "We've gotten satisfied with less.
We gave up looking for help for the dyslexia [of our older daughter]."
They were seeing signs that their older daughter was beginning to
achieve more emotional stability, with help from the counselor who
befriended her and from a supportive resource-room teacher. They
were encouraging her to accept her therapist's advice to "say good-bye
to her vision and go through grieving so she could acknowledge ver-
bally her limitations." Although encouraged by hints of their older

daughter's progress in coping, they had some concern about their younger daughter's unwillingness to confront her limitations directly.

The father said that his wife had dealt more directly with their daughters' visual impairments and that he had not given as much as he could. He added that he still had "given a lot to the kids." His lengthy interview, one of the longest, clearly indicated how much he, and his wife, had given. Their willingness to give, or sacrifice, and their recognition that impairment continued to pose special problems were prominent aspects of their coping. Also noteworthy was their need to get feedback from significant others that they were doing a good job as parents. They may have appreciated mental health professionals because the professionals provided this kind of support for their parental esteem.

Family 2. The other protective couple with a teenager lived a comfortable, but not extravagant, working-class lifestyle and had a long and stable marriage with traditional family-oriented values. They had not faced serious psychiatric problems with their daughter, but they had significant concerns about her social isolation as a result of her severe visual impairment. The mother spoke about her daughter's problems with the stigma of being in a resource room and her own worries and sense of guilt:

> She doesn't want to feel different. Kids associate visual impairment with being different. She doesn't have too many friends. She doesn't want to be more conspicuous than she is. A lot of people think she can see. We try to understand and don't treat her different. We want her to do everything for herself. But I am more protective than my husband [because] I was an only child.... I just questioned why it happened—what caused it. I thought, "Lord, why did you do this to my child?" I felt guilty. I kept asking the doctors [after the illness that led to her loss of vision]. I wonder how far she would have gone without visual impairment. But maybe she's pushing more because of it.

The child's father was not as protective as was his wife, but he expressed the same mixture of acceptance of visual impairment and regret about it happening that his wife—and a number of other parents—expressed. He also was sensitive to the fact that his daughter studied longer and harder than her classmates and had more "social problems" because she was visually impaired. Ideally, he preferred mainstreaming at the local neighborhood school, but he thought that visually impaired children were "dumped in regular classrooms with teachers who didn't want them." This complaint was frequently expressed in some form by protective parents, as well as by a number of disavowing parents.

Family 3. The final protective parent I interviewed was an exception to the general patterns just described. This mother's visually impaired daughter was a rebellious teenager. (Her husband, who was a denier, is described in Chapter 3.) She shared her husband's sense of frustration, anger, and alienation regarding the treatment of their daughter by the public schools and special educators. However, as her husband's comments indicated earlier, she openly accepted her child's visual impairment, and she was willing to reveal her deeply rooted worries and concerns about her daughter, her parental role, and visual impairment. Her willingness to do so was the reason her husband felt she dwelled too much on her daughter "being handicapped and legally blind" and was too protective. She was upset that teachers "didn't seem to want to be bothered with mainstream kids [with impairments]" and that they did not even read the files on her child at the beginning of the school year so they would be aware of her low vision.

This mother was unlike most of the protective parents in her distaste for contact with school personnel and others in disability networks, except doctors and vision researchers. She respected those who offered technical knowledge about her daughter's impairment or might be able to provide some improvement in the future. She and her husband were grateful to doctors who had corrected their daughter's crossed eyes and made her impairment relatively invisible. Ironically, the invisibility of the daughter's visual impairment contributed to a new set of coping problems for her as a teenager—problems that she shared with the other teenagers previously discussed.

Despite the mother's hostile feelings toward school personnel, she still did what she felt she could to help her daughter in school. She said:

> The teachers have been told by me every year about visual impairment and that [my daughter] needed accommodations. They don't go far enough to accommodate. They don't deal with the teasing. IEPs [Individualized Education Programs] don't work out like they are supposed to. The teachers are not committed. She needs to be with so-called normal kids, but teachers need to give an extra push. We hired our own tutor to get her up to grade level. She vegetated in the visual impairment program due to a poor teacher. I have respect for one mainstream teacher who took the extra time....
>
> My daughter won't tell anyone she has a visual problem now. To be accepted, she started doing what others did, [and she] got in with a bad crowd. I hope it will be easier for her to admit she has a visual problem when she gets older. Others don't understand low vision unless they've lived with it or experienced it. I hate the word *handicapped*.... I never put kid gloves on. She did everything despite what doctors said....

> I don't know if I've adjusted to [the visual impairment]. I couldn't handle it in her place, but she was born with it. I have been more protective because of her visual impairment, so I can't understand why she [runs away from home].... Parents don't understand that handicaps can be overcome, but the handicaps lead you to expect less.

This mother's comments reveal the sometimes contradictory thoughts, feelings, and actions of parents in response to the problems posed by their children's visual impairments. This mother did not have the biased (disability) subcultural integration of many other protective parents, perhaps because she and her husband valued their independence as a hard-working working-class couple or because, as working-class people, they felt somewhat alienated from the school and disability "systems." Nevertheless, the mother shared with other protective parents a dissatisfaction with the accommodations to her child's visual impairment, an acknowledgment of her own protectiveness, her efforts to get more help for her child, and perhaps a tendency to expect less because of the visual impairment.

PATTERN D: DISAVOWAL

Pattern D—the disavowal of deviance-coping splendidly-flexible-dual integration pattern, which generally will be referred to as *disavowal*— was displayed by 14 parents who were interviewed and seemed to describe 2 other parents who were not interviewed in these families. Disavowal was displayed by both parents in six families (2, 4, 5, 8, 17, and 18), with the mothers in all six and the fathers in four families (4, 8, 17, and 18) interviewed. Also manifesting this pattern among the interviewed parents were a single mother who was visually impaired (in family 7); a divorced noncustodial father (in family 13); and two other mothers, who had been single parents for several years before remarrying (in families 11 and 22). All but one of the parents of totally blind children generally gave evidence of the disavowal. The exception was a stepfather who was not interviewed. The stepfather probably could be classified as a disavower, although his wife said he sometimes restricted and babied his blind stepson. He was significantly older than his wife, who was the primary parent for both her children.

Basic Characteristics

Disavowing parents may have manifested strong evidence of a protective pattern in the past and still may have shown some tendency to be protective at times, even though they generally were disavowers. However, they were different from protective parents because they were not as concerned about an impairment stigma and did not feel the same degree of personal responsibility for their children's impairments or disabilities. That is, they disavowed the deviance or stigma of their children's impairments and coped splendidly with a sense of power without guilt. Of course, not all Pattern D parents displayed the elements of this pattern to the same extent. The disavowal of deviance and coping splendidly may be significantly influenced by a highly flexible family orientation built on the kind of marital support and consensus found in the couples who jointly displayed this pattern. These parents generally were confident and had a sense of balance between the need to accommodate to their children's needs and the children's need to accommodate to the parents' lifestyle and interests. They also tended to be realistic about what they could do for themselves as parents and about what areas of parenting needed social support. When parents who have coped in other ways develop this sense of balance and realism, along with acceptance, openness, power, and confidence, they transform their coping into the disavowal of deviance.

The flexible family orientation of these parents allowed them to continue their customary "normal" ties outside the family and to pursue ties to disability networks to some extent. Their dual integration did not involve the strong pursuit of ties in disability networks because they coped splendidly, which implies a sense of their own power and freedom from guilt about impairments or disabilities, and because they engaged in the disavowal of deviance, which implies balance in their relationships in "normal" and "disability" networks. Disavowing parents were not wary of ties to disability networks, but their understanding of the realities of disability made them inclined to pursue these networks only when they actually needed such ties.

In the two families with preschoolers in this category, the children were blind. In one case, the mother was interviewed. Her family was working class with modest resources, but they had opened their home to a number of foster children. For the past several years, they had provided foster care for a severely developmentally delayed child, for whom they were applying for adoption at the time of the interview. Although chronologically their foster son was of elementary school age, developmentally he was not much older than an infant in many respects and was in effect a preschooler. He had a variety of impairments, and his survival was frequently made precarious by his medical condition. His impairments required constant attention, which drained the energy of his foster mother. Yet, the entire family had come to love him and wanted to make him a permanent member. Although the foster mother worried about keeping the boy alive from day to day, she expressed the kind of acceptance of her severely multiply impaired foster child that is the essence of the disavowal of deviance:

> People make cruel remarks, which especially hurt our 11 year old.... What people see is blindness and a little mental retardation. They don't see all the stuff inside, how much he hurts inside. On the whole, though, people understand.... When they stare or ask, I say, "He's blind and retarded." Kids stare sometimes, but how else are they going to learn? My kids get embarrassed, but I bypass it. I don't care what people think.... I recognize that [our foster child] makes our life different. It's good for my own kids and my day- care kids to be around a handicapped child. Our family is coming around to living in a blind world with [our foster child].

"Coming around to living in a blind world" implies an acceptance that was based on empathy and cut through stigma. However, this case and a number of others clearly show that the disavowal of deviance does not necessarily mean the absence of problems, concerns, anxieties, stresses, or even crises. For example, the other parents of a preschooler, a professional couple whose child was born without eyes and had a neurological delay in growth, continued to struggle with their child's impairments and disabilities. Nevertheless, their struggles did not diminish their capacity to accept and respond to their child. The mother spoke of her coping in the following terms:

> I've never belonged to a normal family or had normal sibling relations. My sister is mentally ill.... I don't believe my son needs to see.... He needs to learn social skills. I worry about how other kids will treat him. My husband thinks our son is not social because we're not. He [our son] won't change our personalities.... I get as much out of talking to parents of kids with other disabilities [as parents of visually impaired kids] as long as the conditions are not real horrendous. I see the day-to-day issues [for parents of impaired children] as 90 percent the same as for any parent.... We are not embarrassed by [our child]. I find more and more that our peers are interested. We talk to anyone about him. We believe there is a lack of public education. We respond by informing people when they say, "How sad!"

The daily demands from her child's special needs tired this mother, who also was employed part time outside the family. She and her husband were concerned, after discovering a neurological impairment when their son was around age two, about whether there would be more to handle. Although the disappointment of discovering that her son was blind at birth was compounded by growing up in a family that was "not normal," this mother accepted her son's impairments, sought the help he needed to cope with them, and took advantage of opportunities to make other people better informed about her son's conditions.

Highly supportive and consensual marital and coparental relationships were the foundation for the disavowal of deviance for her and her husband, as they were for most of the other parents who disavowed. In the comments of her husband, one sees a sense of not being overwhelmed or consumed even by severe impairments. This attitude was nurtured by the involvement of his wife and him in an informative parent training program that was associated with their child's infant-stimulation program. It was an attitude expressed by a number of disavowing parents, and this father articulated it in the following way:

> All in all, I would rate us 9-9.5 as parents. We haven't thrown everything out the window to restructure our priorities [because of our son's impairments]. But it takes energy to do what he needs. Our strengths and weaknesses filter the whole thing. We are doing the best we can. Much of how he is [relates to] how we are as parents and what's important to us.... I try to include him, within his limitations, in the home things I do. [My wife and I] see ourselves as professionals, and we know our scope and limitations as parents. We have realized the need for professionals, that we can't just read a book [to know what to do].

Along with confidence, these comments convey a sense of balance between the need to accommodate to the child's needs and the child's need to accommodate to the parents' lifestyle and interests and a sense of realism about what he and his wife could do for themselves and what areas of parenting needed professional support. When parents who have been protective or have coped in other ways develop this sense of balance and realism, along with acceptance, openness, power, and confidence, they transform their coping into the disavowal of deviance.

Change and Struggle

A number of parents told stories of their growth in coping, but probably the most change was described by the mother of an elementary-school-age girl. This woman's daughter was mildly impaired at the time of the interview, but she was more greatly impaired earlier in her life. However, the change in the mother's coping with her daughter's impairment reflected how much the mother had learned about impairment, her child, and parenting more strongly than it did the change in her daughter's visual condition. The mother's account of her coping reveals how radically parental coping can change over time, with experience and appropriate support. It also reveals the struggle that may be involved in change:

For a long time I didn't accept that there was something wrong with her. It was like it was a reflection on me as a parent, as a mother. I had produced her [and her impairment]. It first hit me when they wanted to put her in special education. I did not see her as handicapped.... [When she was younger] I threw away all her pictures because she looked deformed [with crossed eyes]. I was fighting it. I was used to seeing her, but I didn't like the pictures....

In my first marriage, I had total care. Her father didn't help. He refused to accept or deal with [the visual impairment]. He was unsympathetic and said [when I was first pregnant] that if it was handicapped he'd kill it.... I still do the caring but get much more emotional support [from my new husband].... I saw a psychiatrist about my first marriage. He said I protected my kids too much from realities....

I am proud of overcoming my ignorance, my discomfort in public, and my lack of acceptance. But I had no one to talk to. I never knew anyone who was handicapped before her.... I don't understand visual impairment, but now I have a real good understanding of its effects. I have learned from working with her for seven years....

The transitional kindergarten teacher was the first person who really made me feel comfortable with [my visually impaired daughter]. Before her, I always felt [my child] was different and something was wrong with her. [The transitional kindergarten teacher] gave me a big reassurance and relief.... Experience helping in the classroom [with more severely handicapped children] changed my whole attitude. I am thankful [my child] is not more handicapped. Now I feel, "My kid's handicapped. So what?" I am not as afraid of handicaps now with the knowledge I gained.... It was slow learning. I could have used a lot more understanding in the past. Now I feel, she is my daughter, she has special needs, and she is normal.

The recounting of this mother's experiences reveals the ongoing socialization process that reshaped her impairment orientation, interactional style, family orientation, and type of integration. We see elements of the denial and protective patterns and, eventually, the emergence of a new inclination to disavow deviance and to accept her daughter as she was, see her as normal, and put behind her the sense of stigma she had been taught. She struggled a number of years without the support of the child's father or important ties to professionals or other parents that could propel her beyond denial and avoidance. During those years of struggle, she felt isolated. For most of them she was either separated or divorced and functioning as a single parent. With experience and support from an empathic teacher, she was able to learn to cope more effectively.

Coping differences and spouses. Two other mothers were disavowers but did not have disavowing spouses. One was a single parent, and the other had been one for several years before remarrying. Though both had their struggles in coping with impairment, neither went through an extended period of nonacceptance or perceived stigmatization after the diagnosis of her child's impairment. The single mother's moderate visual impairment and the fact that her son's visual impairment was likely to progress to blindness contributed to her acceptance.

The remarried mother, whose blind son was a teenager at the time she was interviewed, had experienced an initial trauma when her son's life was threatened after his premature birth. After he survived, she received the news that the oxygen that kept him alive had made him blind. The news came from the doctor in a cold, impersonal way. The doctor also seemed to condemn her for getting pregnant before marriage and conveyed the impression that her son was unworthy of the same care given to children born to more "virtuous" mothers. Despite the initial trauma and sense of guilt, this mother took only "one to two days" to accept the blindness. She was relieved her son was alive and said:

> Once I got it in my mind [that he would live], I was thankful he was just visually impaired. I thought, God gives you only what you can handle. Feeling sorry gets you nowhere. So you accept and go on.

It took longer for the single mother than for the remarried mother to come to terms with the prospect of her son's blindness because his blindness was not immediate. The single mother began to see hints of her son's visual impairment when he experienced night blindness at age three. However, it took nearly six more years for him to be diagnosed with retinitis pigmentosa. The diagnosis was complicated by the mother's adoptive status, because she had no family medical history that indicated this condition. She said:

> The first year after discovering RP was hopeless; it was going to be terrible. But I kicked myself. Now we have the attitude it is possible he'll be totally blind and it's OK. He'll learn to work around it. He still has moments of utter terror. [Because] there is no firm prognosis, we go with what we've got. His adjustment changes with his changes [in vision].... Low vision does make a difference, because it is not visible. He's coming to terms with [the idea that] it's OK to be different. My attitude of not caring what others think probably makes it worse for him. [Because he is almost a teenager] he is very sensitive to differentness. We don't even discuss the white cane now, but comparisons with his friend with muscular dystrophy alleviate self-pity. Tom Sullivan is his idol.... My own visual impairment makes me harder on him. I am "tough love." I am not sympathetic to complaints.

This mother's toughness was balanced by love and the responsiveness to her son's special needs that is generally associated with the disavowal of deviance. The facts that she had been a single mother almost since the start of her parenthood (owing to widowhood) and that she was a faith healer and spiritual leader with a peripatetic lifestyle contributed to her sense of independence, adaptability, and faith that she and her son would be able to cope with his increasing loss of vision.

The disavowing noncustodial father waged continuing battles with his protective wife, whom I did not interview, about the special educational rights and needs of their visually impaired child, as well as about the father's self-acknowledged meager financial support of all three of their children. Despite his noncustodial parental status and inadequate child support caused by his pursuit of a precarious new entrepreneurial business, he was highly committed to his children and was a forceful advocate for the rights of his child as a disabled student. His comments reflect an attitude that borders on minimizing the impairment, but they also reveal the underlying acceptance, confidence, sense of power, and responsiveness of the disavowal of deviance:

> The hospital said the only reason my son can see is that he doesn't know he is not supposed to. We treated him as a visual child, and that's why he could see. He doesn't have crossed eyes; he turns his eyes to see. I don't want to correct it because that's how he sees.... He is [most] impaired by the [tense] relationship between his mother and me. He does better than people give him credit for. He tried excuses, but he doesn't get away with it. He needs to learn to cope with other people and teasing. I need to [make myself] aware he has trouble seeing. Otherwise, I forget he's visually impaired—until the IEP [meetings].
>
> So far, visual impairment is not a stumbling block. Ask me in five years. He needs to deal with being a little different. Of course, we're all different, but his difference makes a bigger difference. There is the ambiguity with his low vision that is not true of blindness....
>
> The only stress [for me] from visual impairment is related to the IEP—getting what my son needs. Not so much getting services, but working through a third party and getting agreement between his mother and me. Why should visual impairment be a stress? It just happened. It's no one's fault. You take one day at a time. I don't worry about it. I have no problems with visual impairment. I guess I might feel differently if he were totally blind.

Degree of visual impairment. Thus, blindness does, indeed, create different responses than does low vision for parents and children. However, this difference in the degree of visual impairment does not necessarily imply a difference in the general pattern of parental coping. Parents of blind children are more likely to engage in the disavowal of deviance, but parents of partially sighted children also may disavow deviance, even though they are likely to have different histories of coping.

Strong marital support and a flexible family orientation enhanced the attainment of the disavowal of deviance by couples with blind and partially sighted children. However, the cases of the noncustodial father and of a number of other parents I have presented have shown that unusual or difficult family circumstances also can be associated with the disavowal of deviance by parents of partially sighted or blind children. The ambiguity and social marginality of low vision complicate understanding and acceptance. However, parents of children with low vision seemed able to surmount these complications and disavow deviance if they had helpful ties to disability networks that taught them how to understand, accept, and handle their children's impairments as parents or if they learned to deal with their children's impairments by first disavowing their own.

The noncustodial father and his former wife disagreed about many things, but he said that both of them understood their child's visual impairment and that, in the beginning, their shared orientation toward their son as a "visual child" helped him see. Among the disavowing parents who were married to their original partners, shared attitudes, sentiments, and behavior seemed to combine with substantial mutual affection and respect to help produce and sustain their disavowal of deviance. Mutuality of support was strongly communicated by both parents of the child born without eyes. It also was reported by nearly all the other parents who disavowed deviance and were with their original spouses.

A major element of the disavowal of deviance that distinguishes it from protectiveness is the integration of accommodations to visual impairment into a normal life for the impaired child, the parents, and the entire family. This element was evident in the comments of parents already quoted in this section, and it can be seen in the comments of the other parents who disavowed deviance. For example, the mother of an elementary-school-age boy with moderate low vision said:

> Visual impairment has affected his educational process. Otherwise, he has been able [so far] to do what anybody else does. He just needs certain precautions—more verbal instruction.... I don't feel limited by his visual impairment.... Life is normal. People say, "Wow! How do you do it?" They think you have special qualities. That's a lot of bunk. I'm not different than any other parent.... I take one day at a time. I want him to be accepted as a person—not due to his visual impairment.

Independence and Success

The idea that visual impairment has real effects but does not confer a special *negative or positive* status is part of the process of breaking through to the disavowal of deviance. If parents who disavowed deviance thought their children were "special," it typically was not simply because the children were impaired or disabled. This situation contrasts with comments by a number of protective parents that visual impairment or "handicaps" made their children special. Parents who disavowed deviance talked more often than did protective parents about the independence, success, and normalcy of their children despite obstacles posed by impairment.

The mother of a blind elementary-school-age girl spoke about the independence of her daughter's attitude. She said, "We try to keep her independent and get her to handle problems and situations on her own." Her husband added, "She's independent because we let her be that way." Both said they were more careful about their daughter's safety because she was blind, but overall they placed more emphasis on opportunities than on restrictions. The father said:

> The only thing we can do [for the future] is expose her to possibilities. To her, there are no limitations. She can reach the sky if she wants. *How* she does it will be a problem. She has to understand that society may not let her do what she wants. She has to fight. We also have her interact with blind [adults] to learn how they live.

In these comments, there are elements of optimism, realism, and determination that were found in the comments of many of the parents who disavowed deviance. The parents just quoted would say that their orientation to impairment stemmed from their strong religious faith, but I would add that a highly supportive extended family and the resources and influence of upper-middle-class status also may have contributed to their approach to their daughter's blindness.

The need to be strong advocates and encourage their children to be strong and assertive also were common themes among these and other disavowing parents. Indeed, the previously quoted mother of the blind teenager saw herself as a fighter. She said, "The only way to get things is to fight.... People don't ask, 'Do you want?' You need to take the initiative." Unlike the protective parents, who also saw themselves as "squeaky wheels," advocates, or fighters and felt a need to exert power, the parents who disavowed deviance either felt less frustrated by the results of their efforts or were less consumed by their activism in disability networks. That is, protective parents had biased (disability) subcultural integration, whereas parents who disavowed deviance generally had more balance between their disability and "normal" ties, which is the meaning of dual integration.

The remaining two couples who disavowed deviance were parents of multiply impaired teenagers. On the surface, these couples may seem different. One couple had their visually impaired daughter when they were teenagers without any financial security. Through their hard work, they had achieved the comfortable lifestyle of lower-level industrial management. The other couple was well educated and highly sophisticated, had a comfortable upper-middle-class lifestyle despite the recent financial pinch of investment in a new business venture, and had become parents later in life. In spite of differences in background and lifestyle, there was much that was similar about these couples as disavowers. The combination of important similarities in coping with social and economic differences is another reminder to be careful about generalizing from appearances or stereotypes of social class about how or how well parents handle their children's impairments.

Both couples with multiply impaired teenagers were practical. They believed in "going right to the top" to get what their children needed, and they had little patience for people who offered talk or jargon ("Edspeak" from educators and "Medspeak" from medical people, in the words of one father) instead of action. They shared with other parents who disavowed deviance a mixture of acceptance of their children as they were and a desire to see them achieve a measure of independence and success on their own terms and at their own pace. They also shared a responsive orientation that was not overly sentimental. They were honest but not effusive about their feelings. They believed they received sufficient emotional support from their spouses and had no desire to pour out their frustrations, fears, or other deeply felt emotions to a group of strangers or acquaintances. In fact, one of the fathers of a multiply impaired teenager was stoic, indicating that he had learned as a child that "cowboys don't cry." This man's wife spoke about coping with their child's impairments in the following terms:

> She is so well adjusted to her visual impairment. We haven't sought out things to change her—to make her "normal." What has mattered has been to make things as easy as possible with vision so that she could do what she wanted.... She can take care of herself. She has made it easy on us.

Her husband said they did not like the idea of a cane because their daughter attended a camp for disabled children (which was run by a religious organization) when she was younger, and she returned handicapped by the experience. It took a while to rid her of the inappropriate behaviors she had learned. He seemed to place more emphasis on handicap than on stigma in expressing his feelings about canes, blind people, and her camp experience. Like his wife, he obviously accepted his daughter as she was. Furthermore, he once accompanied his daughter, her resource-room teacher, and her class of visually impaired students on a camping trip, and he spoke about the experience as both educational and enjoyable. He said about his daughter:

> She is normal for her. We don't try to explain her to everyone. She is who she is. I say she's blind in one eye and can't see out of the other. My wife is blind in one eye, too. There is a lot of humor around here.... The visual problem is a small portion of her whole problem. By the time we got to that [after dealing with her nearly dying], we said, "Phew. Is that all that's wrong?" Although she'll always have to deal with it, she'll have no problem with it. I have no big worry about her maturing [at her own pace].

This teenager's invisible low vision caused some misunderstanding, with teachers accusing her of "faking" disability. Her father stated a version of a theme expressed by many parents of children with an invisible impairment: "They should spend one hour in her eyes." However, for him and his wife, as well as for a number of other parents who disavowed deviance and coped splendidly, this call for empathy did not diminish their confidence in their child or their sense of humor about impairment. In the latter regard, it could be argued that the ability to laugh about impairments and disabilities without demeaning those who have them is a significant measure of the depth of acceptance of a person who is impaired. It marked the coping of a number of parents, especially those who disavowed deviance or were visually impaired themselves.

The other couple with a multiply impaired teenager echoed each other throughout most of their interviews. They spoke about their moderately visually impaired and mildly neurologically impaired teenage daughter as being "occasionally inconvenienced" by her impairments. In her father's words:

> It is a fact of life for her. We don't have to live with [her impairments]. She will. It is her life. She understands there are things she can't do, such as drive a car. We are grateful she is partially sighted, but if she were blind, we would have handled that, too. We have accepted her current visual impairment. We are realists.

Although Pattern D may be seen as the most effective form of parental coping, in part as a result of how the pattern is conceptualized, such coping should not be idealized. Even though Pattern D parents generally disavowed deviance and coped splendidly, they were not without worries, problems, or stresses, as may be seen from the following comments which I slightly paraphrased) by the father who was just quoted:

> The future is a big, fat stress. With all the uncertainties of the future, at least [my child] has the closeness of our family as a constant. We protect—but don't overprotect—with our "shelter of love." I know there is an irony about our happy family. It will not prepare our child for the harsh realities of the world, and I worry about when we will not be there for her. We worry about our daughter and worry more as time goes by. Stress is never more than an inch below the surface. She will have to be on her own eventually. But we are concerned about what she will do, how she will handle her finances, how she will handle her life. The future is a question mark, a big blank. She needs more career direction.

This father spoke with the nodding approval of his wife. Many other disavowing parents would have shaken their heads in agreement, even those who professed that they did not worry about the future. Keep in mind that this father was an intelligent, committed, responsible, middle-class parent who was an activist and self-described realist.

PATTERN D AND EFFECTIVE COPING

If effective coping means responding appropriately to the needs of the impaired child, without ignoring the needs of other family members, then Pattern D would seem to represent the most effective pattern of coping among the four described here. Of course, this statement is partly tautological because the basic elements of Pattern D are implicitly defined in normative or idealized terms as indicators of successful coping.

It is especially interesting that a relatively high proportion of the parents in this study tended to conform to Pattern D, and these disavowing parents varied in their socioeconomic backgrounds and status. Increased experience with the child's impairment may help most parents move toward the disavowal of deviance and coping splendidly that mark this pattern, but unless the conditions for a flexible family orientation and dual integration exist, parents seem unlikely to become Pattern D copers. The case of the disavowing mother who was quoted at length demonstrates how coping can be enhanced by a combination of personal experience and adequate and appropriate social support, both inside and outside the family.

Even though the disavowal of deviance, coping splendidly, a flexible family orientation, and dual integration may represent the most effective approach to parental coping with an impaired child, they do not eradicate worries. They also may not purge anger, bitterness, or blame that can surface with the discovery of impairment. Furthermore, parents who learn to disavow deviance and cope splendidly may demonstrate more than occasional evidence of other types of coping. Parents do not instantly learn to cope effectively, and, for some, learning to be "responsible" and effective parents of an impaired child can be a long and stressful journey. In the words of one family counselor, parental coping can be a "roller coaster, with some smooth coasting but lots of highs and lows, too."

Parents who learn to cope effectively may do so, in part, because influential others, such as disability professionals and educators, expected it from them and then gave them the support they needed to understand, accept, and deal responsibly and capably with their children's impairments. Professionals tend to expect responsible parents to face the future realistically and with confidence. However, even disavowing parents may become vague or uneasy when talk turns from today to tomorrow. Once they are past the daily grind of dealing with impairment, which Featherstone calls the "tyranny of mechanics," parents of impaired children may find that their children's transition to adulthood is the greatest test.[1] Although they do not prepare parents perfectly and do not eliminate the ambiguities, worries, or uneasiness, disavowal of deviance, coping splendidly, a flexible family orientation, and dual integration seem to represent, among the four coping patterns proposed here, the most fruitful basis for parents to face the future. Further evidence to bolster these arguments is presented in future chapters about integration and preparing for the future. The next chapter focuses on the need for social support and networks.

NOTE

1   H. Featherstone, *A Difference in the Family: Living with a Disabled Child* (New York: Penguin Books, 1981).

Chapter 5
SOCIAL SUPPORT: NEEDS AND NETWORKS

The story of the mother who initially could not look at her daughter's baby pictures and eventually learned to accept her daughter's impairment and see her as normal shows the amount of resocialization that can occur during the process of coping with a child's impairment. In telling her story, this mother revealed that along with the accumulation of experience, an empathic teacher opened her mind and heart to the acceptance of her child as impaired and disabled but also normal. We can interpret *normal* here as implying a socially and morally acceptable and destigmatized identity despite not being like everyone else. The emergence of this realization occurs in breaking through and paves the way for the disavowal of deviance. In this mother's case, as well as in many others, progress in coping was significantly influenced by a strong support tie at a critical time in her socialization as a parent of an impaired child. In this chapter, I examine the social support that parents of visually impaired children said they needed for their children and themselves and the ties they sought and used to meet their need for support.

NEEDS OF THE CHILD AND NEEDS OF THE PARENT

Denying and Minimizing Parents

The parents I interviewed were asked to express their children's and their own needs in regard to visual impairment. As one might expect, the denying parents had little to say about such special needs. In responding to my direct question, they either made general comments or denied that they or their children had any special needs. It was not the sort of question they often asked themselves.

Denying parents just described did not express special needs or were not clear, precise, or expansive about concerns or needs they may have felt because, as deniers, they had difficulty coming to terms with visual impairment and they were not inclined to be emotionally expressive. What they expressed was anger, antagonism, or alienation. Minimizing parents similarly were not inclined to be expansive about their children's and, especially, their own special needs. However, they tended to be clearer or more specific in expressing needs than did the deniers, and they were less negative in the way they talked about special needs.

The minimizing couple with the mildly impaired son acknowledged his current need for eyeglasses and his possible future need for large-print materials or special equipment to help him in school. Although the boy's mother said she would like to gain a better understanding of what her son was seeing and of what the doctors were saying about visual impairment, she also said, "He'll handle it better and get stronger if we draw less attention to [the visual impairment]." The boy's father said, "I just need the reassurance he'll get and continue to get glasses, [large-print] books, whatever he needs from the special education counselor. If someone finds a problem, we go with their effort to help him." The father's words seem to imply that he hoped that responsible others (such as "the special education counselor") would identify and attend to whatever special needs his son might have. This acceptance of help without actively seeking it is characteristic of minimizers, and it can be seen in the responses of other minimizing parents I interviewed.

The father of the teenager who became impaired after a motorcycle accident described his son's and his own needs in the following terms:

> He's getting the best possible services, according to the professionals. [As for me] I don't know [what I need].... His getting independent will help us. [My wife and I, who are having problems] need to be alone for a weekend without him. But I won't impose on anyone for respite care.

Along with a restatement of the stoicism we saw earlier in this man's coping, these comments indicate a connection between the needs of parents and children that I found in many parents. That is, parents often implicitly or explicitly referred to how their own coping would be helped by support that helped their children cope better. Thus, parents often saw their needs as parents of impaired children in terms of their children's special needs and failed to distinguish between their children's and their own needs for support.

The mildly visually impaired mother of two visually impaired teenagers was not accustomed, as a minimizer, to thinking about special needs. When her daughter became mentally ill as a result of her inability to cope with low vision, this mother was faced with coming to terms with the connection between the visual impairment she had minimized and the serious mental illness that she could not minimize as easily. She said:

> I don't think [my daughter and son] have needed anything due to visual impairment. [My daughter] felt the need to be a high achiever due to visual impairment. I didn't feel that way [about myself or her]. I don't look at them as handicapped.... I don't think I need anything. I don't think I could have done anything for [my daughter]. The doctor finally had to tell her to lighten her school load. I couldn't have told her that as a mother. I don't think she would have listened.

Minimizing does not mean that parents are unconcerned about their children or unaware of the coping problems that visual impairment may cause or affect. The mother just quoted loved her daughter and did not underestimate the severity of her mental illness. However, her tendency to minimize limited her capacity to identify with her daughter, despite her own visual impairment, and to come to terms with the part that visual impairment played in her daughter's mental illness.

The other visually impaired mother who was a minimizer seemed more aware than the mother just considered of the connection between visual impairment and the social problems her teenage daughter was experiencing. This mother was more visually impaired than was the other mother, and she had dealt more directly in her own youth with the social stigma of being impaired. These factors probably made her more aware of her daughter's problems. She said:

> Most important is how she feels about herself. She needs to feel OK—not necessarily the best. She could use one close friend to share her feelings with.... There are cliques. It hurts her feelings not to be invited to a party.... Visual impairment makes a difference with peers. It's not said, but it's there.

This mother was able to recognize that her daughter was struggling with being different because she was visually impaired and that she needed support to help her feel good about herself and feel socially accepted. She also recognized that her own visual impairment contributed to problems of limited money and limited access experienced by her daughter. Nevertheless, as a minimizer, she did not worry about her daughter and remained optimistic about her future. She said, "It'll be OK.... Visual impairment won't affect her dating."

Protective Parents

Even though minimizing parents expressed their children's needs related to impairment, such as for eyeglasses, services, independence, self-esteem, and social acceptance, they tended to say little about what their children needed to cope with visual impairment or how impairment made their needs special. Furthermore, they did not elaborate on their own distinctive needs as parents that derived from having impaired children. Protective parents were much more expansive in their expression of needs and more clearly articulated the connection of their needs to visual impairment than either denying or minimizing parents.

The protective noncustodial mother of a preschooler in foster care spoke of "getting what [my child] needs for visual impairment" and about her own needs for self-esteem, information, and support groups. Another protective mother said her baby probably would need braille along with "love and care to get her going." She said that as a parent, she needed "to learn what was out there" and to get support from other parents, mainly to help her understand how other parents handled the marital stress associated with a severely impaired child.

Protective parents of school-age children identified various types of their children's expressive needs (such as moral support, praise, love, happiness, security, emotional support, acceptance, and friendship), informational needs (such as committed teachers who understood visual impairment and information for themselves), and instrumental needs (such as a good and appropriate education, "chances to do what everyone else is doing," braille, large-print materials, and a father's "wish list" of a large-screen television and special computer equipment). These parents also talked about their own needs, which included emotional support from their spouses, encouragement from the school, reassurance from someone that they were doing a good job as parents, and an occasional weekend with their spouses away from their children.

One protective mother spoke about how the special needs of a parent of an impaired child may go unrecognized when she said, "Sometimes my parents and friends forget it's still difficult [to deal with impairments despite my child reaching school age]. It would be nice to have an offer of a weekend off once in a while, but it's always hard to ask." However, she also recognized that more severe impairments made life more diffi-cult than her own: "I don't feel I have the problems of parents of severely disabled kids in getting what I need." Another protective mother talked about the informational support her husband needed "to learn the depth of [our son's] special needs and school problems and that we could ask for more [in special education]." She had pushed her husband, who was not interviewed, into a parent training workshop to help him gain the understanding she felt he needed.

Protective parents of teenagers talked about a lot of the same kinds of needs that were identified by protective parents of younger children. They also expressed the need for reassurance that the help their chil-dren required for their special needs would be available, for help to sup-port their children with their special needs, and for confirmation that they were doing a good job with parenting and impairment. The teen-agers' distinctive needs expressed by their protective parents were for support for mental health, self-understanding of their visual impair-ment and special needs, and direction in planning their transition from high school to adulthood.

Disavowing Parents

Disavowing parents expressed a variety of needs that they and their children had as a result of visual impairment. Many of these needs over-lapped with the kinds expressed by protective parents. However, par-ents who disavowed tended to place more emphasis on integration, the acceptance of difference, independence, and self-sufficiency than did parents who coped in other ways. They talked more specifically about their children's needs for self-esteem; normally sighted friends; special aids and services (such as braille materials, orientation and mobility training, and training in everyday living skills); and social acceptance in the mainstream. It is not surprising that, as disavowers, many of these parents talked about the children's need to have other people disavow their deviance. The comments of the mother of an elementary school child who was losing his sight demonstrate this point:

> People need to accept that he is different and that everybody is. I get my hackles up about his being a "special child" needing a "spe-cial parent." That's crap. He may need a cane, but beyond that, treat a person as a person. A lot of his problems stem from his feeling different.

Disavowing parents did not ignore the obstacles and challenges posed by their children's impairments and disabilities or their need for special services or other support. Instead, they realistically accepted them and saw their children as handling their lives as people who happened to be impaired. This perspective of the disavowal of deviance is succinctly captured in the words of the mother of a blind preschooler: "I don't believe my son needs to see." This mother did not mean that she was happy her son was born blind. Rather, she was suggesting that sight was not necessary for him to have a fulfilling and "normal" life. Indeed, she and her husband had high aspirations for him. However, these aspirations and their assessments of his needs were filtered through the facts of his blindness and its disabling implications. For disavowing parents, realistic acceptance and the realistic appraisal of needs tend to combine with some degree of confidence and optimism in Coping Pattern D.

Disavowing parents were able to disavow because they already had received support to help them cope with their children's impairments. Their generally confident appraisals of their children's capacity to live on their own as adults tended to reflect confidence in their own parenting skills and a feeling of being supported. In their interviews, the disavowing parents emphasized the importance of understanding for themselves, as well as their children, and they noted how understanding grew out of formal learning or parent-training experiences and informational support and the accumulation of past experiences.

Some parents also spoke about a level of understanding that went deeper than facts. For example, the mother of the blind preschooler said, "We want to understand and will put in the time to learn. We want to know why—beyond the superficial. We don't want to just be given answers." Other parents talked about the importance of experience in helping them deal with their children's needs and their needs as parents. The father of the blind girl in elementary school asserted: "[In parenting], visual impairment is not that different from having a sighted child. You learn from experience."

Coping Pattern D typically implies a disavowal of special status for the child or the parent in relation to impairment. This perspective was stated directly and unequivocally by the single mother of the boy who was losing his sight, who did not like references to her impaired child as a "special child" or to herself as a "special parent." This woman, like many other disavowers, noted that her son needed to be integrated into the mainstream, but she added, "Parents should be mainstreamed, too." By this statement, she meant that special support, such as parent groups, may be helpful but that, eventually, parents—like their children—have to wean themselves from such special support so they can find their place in "normal" society.

This argument, which will be reconsidered later in regard to a more detailed treatment of parent groups, describes the balance in relationships that is implied by dual integration. Dual integration involves a push to the mainstream without fear of contacts with those in disability networks, and it is assumed to be associated with the disavowal of deviance. The disavowal of deviance also implies an awareness of the amount and kind of support needed at a particular time. Later in this chapter, I elaborate on these ideas in terms of the notion of "appropriate support."

Associations Between Patterns and Needs

The parental coping patterns were associated with the range and types of needs that parents expressed and how they expressed them. Deniers expressed few special needs for their children or themselves, and the tone of their expression of them reflected anger, frustration, or alienation that they had difficulty suppressing. Minimizers also were restrained in the expression of special needs. However, they acknowledged the connection between impairment and the need for support more than did the deniers, even though all of them did not explicitly acknowledge or fully understand the connection. The minimizers also talked about needs with much less evidence of the latent anxiety, hostility, or sensitivity to stigma that gave deniers' comments their sharp, biting, or wary edge.

The special character of the needs of impaired children and their parents was conveyed most often by protective parents. Overall, these parents' inventory of needs was lengthy and diverse. Their comments about the needs often dramatically underscored the difficulties posed by disability, handicap, or stigma for their children or themselves, and they were the most open in expressing their worries. Parents who disavowed deviance talked about a number of the same kinds of needs as did the protective parents. However, they tended to feel they already had received or were receiving adequate support to handle most of the major impairment-related needs in their families. Indeed, this support helps explain why they were able to disavow deviance. In breaking through to the disavowal of deviance, parents were more inclined to see their own and their children's needs as ordinary or normal, rather than special, but they did not ignore, deny, or substantially minimize the facts of impairment or disability after they had "normalized" their children or parenthood.

There are times when the association between coping and needs becomes attenuated. In particular, when parents face serious crises that threaten their children's lives, survival is likely to dominate all other needs or concerns as parents focus on keeping their children alive. However, after the initial crisis fades and the child's condition stabilizes, parents are likely to display the differences in coping that are seen under more ordinary circumstances of impairment. The type of coping that parents display in response to perceived needs, concerns, and demands from their children's impairments tends to show the imprint of the support on which they rely. In the ensuing sections, I consider the various types of support that parents of visually impaired children received.

SOCIAL SUPPORT AND THE FAMILY

Parents may use existing relationships or seek new ones to get support for coping with impairment-related needs, and they may find that their existing or new relationships do not provide the support they wanted or anticipated. Most married parents who were interviewed turned first to their marital partners for support to cope with perceived problems from impairment and their impaired children. All the disavowing parents who were married named their spouses as those to whom they first turned. Among the protective wives, 10 were married and living with their husbands; 7 of the 10 named their husbands as their first "line of support." Among the 4 minimizing parents who were married, only the couple who was interviewed said they turned first to each other. Two of the 3 parents who engaged in denial were married, and 1 said he turned first to his wife. Single or separated parents turned first to their parents (with ambivalence in one case), to God, to the child's resource-room teacher, or to "anyone who will listen and I know will help or is in a position to help."

One would expect disavowing parents to turn first to their most intimate family tie and to feel supported by that person because the disavowal of deviance was associated with cohesion and good communication among the family members. In fact, married parents who disavowed were strongly tied to their marital partners by mutual affection and respect and were highly consensual in their attitudes, feelings, and actions.

Some of the married protective, minimizing, and denying parents said they turned first to their spouses to help them cope. However, the family orientation of a number of these parents was rigid or only marginally flexible, and the support many of them received from their spouses did not directly or indirectly help them cope with impairment. When marital ties were merely perfunctory and held together only by common ties to the child, parental coping tended to be complicated by marital and parental friction and disagreements and lack of support from the spouse.

Married parents who disavowed almost uniformly responded that their families were close and did a lot of things together and that communication tended to be open and honest. The single mother who was a disavower described her family life with her children in similar terms. In general, these parents also accepted change as part of life, and although they appreciated some stability, too, a number of disavowing parents welcomed change or saw it as an exciting challenge. These elements of a flexible family orientation were found in the descriptions of the family life of protective parents, but families of protective parents were less likely than were families of disavowing parents to be described as close, open and honest, and adaptable. These qualities were seldom found together in the descriptions of family life by minimizing and denying parents. The tendency for disavowing parents to rely on support from their spouses, but to turn to outside help when needed, reflected the degree of permeability of family boundaries associated with a flexible orientation. The boundaries were permeable but not *too* permeable.

Taken together, the results suggest that flexibility and acceptance of change were an important part of the foundation for Coping Pattern D. Parents who reflected back on their coping problems when their families were more rigid or static underscored the importance of flexibility and adaptability for coping effectively. For example, the mother who initially had difficulty looking at pictures of her visibly different baby daughter described changes in adaptability and marital communication in her family experience:

> At the beginning of my first marriage, I hated change. I was young and naive. But I was forced into change [by a bad marriage and divorce]. I learned to cope well with change, that was what life was about. I flow with it now.... Communication in my marriage is open now.

The breakdown in communication and cohesion of her first marriage and family deprived this woman of support that could have eased her coping sooner. A tie to a transitional kindergarten teacher provided essential expressive, instrumental, and informational support for her coping that ultimately enabled her to disavow and cope splendidly. In addition, she received general expressive and instrumental support for parenting from her new husband, which made coping with impairment easier for her.

Parents with rigid and marginally flexible family orientations spoke about having to face too many changes, trying to avoid changes, and fearing the new problems that changes could bring. In the latter regard, a protective mother said, "I probably prefer things being fairly stable—with no surprises. Surprises usually are bad. No change means no new problems. I love it when nothing happens." She also said that in her family they were able to withstand more than 10 years of changes and accompanying problems in their impaired child's life because they were closely knit and talked. In her words, "We are still a family due to communication."

What this mother did not say in this context but revealed later in the interview was that she shouldered a disproportionate amount of the burden of handling impairment problems and holding things together in the family. She was not alone. Even in flexible families of disavowing parents, the parental burden of coping with the child's impairment often was primarily a *maternal* burden. Many parents believed that this division of labor was the way it should be or had to be, but a number of mothers lamented the sacrifice of their careers or the lack of "time for themselves," and some fathers acknowledged the sacrifices and stresses and wished they had flexible jobs that would allow them to do more.

Heavily burdened mothers appreciated their husbands' love, encouragement, and faith in their parenting, but some also wished their husbands more fully understood the demands and special needs created by impairment. The protective mother who saw problems in changes and faced a series of changes and problems over her multiply impaired child's life said, "I could use more support from my husband for emotional stress. He figures that [dealing with our child's impairments and illnesses] is an extension of my job as a nurse and that I don't need support. He is beginning to understand [after attending a parent workshop]." This mother talked about communication holding her family together, but in respecting her as a professional and a mother, her husband presumed she did not need to talk about the strains of taking care of their child.

It is not clear how much expressive support this woman actually expected from her husband, because she said that sometimes it was easier to talk to another woman about feelings. It was ironic that in a number of marital relationships that were described by one or both partners as close, open, or honest, important things were not discussed. These family systems were only marginally flexible in their orientation to impairment, and thus it was difficult for the parents to break through to the disavowal of deviance without significant compensating ties outside the family.

Like the literature on parenting in general, the literature on parents of impaired children typically refers to "the maternal burden" and sometimes to "the absent (or forgotten) father." Research on parents of impaired children frequently has focused exclusively on mothers. The results of my study provide some validation for this view of parental roles. However, it also is true that in more flexible families, fathers tended to be more directly involved in supporting their wives or children to help them cope with impairment. Some fathers were heavily involved in support activities, especially in getting information and resources for their children, and a few even actively sought support for themselves (such as parent training) to help them cope more effectively with their children's impairments. Thus, a flexible orientation to family life facilitated the disavowal of deviance, and the combination of these conditions seemed to be associated with fathers assuming more responsibility for the impaired children.

There were a few noteworthy exceptions to the generalizations proposed in this section. One was the disavowing noncustodial father, who was much more active than his former wife in advocating for the educational rights of their impaired child, despite a divisive relationship with his ex-wife. However, he pointed out that they had begun coping with their child's impairment with some consensus about what the child needed and with some openness and honesty.

Another exception was a disavowing single mother, who was solely responsible for her children and benefited from experience with her own moderate visual impairment, her strong religious faith, and access to a lot of social support from the people in her religious movement, who were like an extended family. In addition, the character of her family life with her children tended to be flexible.

A third exception was the father of the teenager who had been in a motorcycle accident. His marriage was rocky, his family was rigidly oriented, and he was the primary custodian of his impaired child. A major source of the rift between him and his wife was the clash between his wife's belief that he was too tough with their son and his belief (as a minimizer) that she was too protective.

The case of the single mother illustrates the importance of establishing ties outside the nuclear family. Those who accepted the realities of impairment and its disabling effects generally recognized the need to turn to people outside their immediate families to supplement family support or to compensate for support not received within the family. For some parents, members of personal communities provided valuable support. The next section discusses more extensively the role of personal communities in parental coping.

SOCIAL SUPPORT AND PERSONAL COMMUNITIES

Support of Grandparents

Many parents cited their parents as sources of support for their coping. A few of the mothers had to rely heavily on their parents for support because they were single parents or could not rely on their husbands, and this dependence caused ambivalence or resentment. The relationship between power and dependence explains this ambivalence and resentment, which is illustrated in the case of the single mother of a visually impaired teenager who was a minimizer and was restricted by her own visual impairment:

> I wish [other people] could see what I see for a week. People complained about being housebound by the snow. That's the way it is for me all the time. I hate to be so dependent on my mom. She was nasty for a while. She does things for needs not wants. I get tired of having to decide whether something is a need or a want.
>
> I have to be totally flexible [when I depend on others to take me places]. I constantly have to adjust my schedule to others'. My neighbor involves me a lot. It lessens the pressure and my dependence on my mom.
>
> My mom has that authority over me—where I couldn't go or could go. I hate it. It's unhealthy. It gives her a superior hand over me as her child and undermines my authority as a parent. She goes over me with my children and becomes their mom at times. Mom is as defeating to me as she is positive. She is pitiful with [my visually impaired daughter]. She feels sorry a lot. She never treated me like that.... The things she hated when we were kids, she could care less about now with her grandchildren. I resent it a lot.... [But] my dad is a sweetheart.

This mother was relieved to be free of her marriage to an unsupportive husband, but with her own visual impairment limiting her perceived mobility and independence as a parent, she felt trapped. She was tied to her mother as her main source of support, but that support engendered feelings of dependence and powerlessness that caused ambivalence and resentment.

The young mother whose child was with a foster family also was dependent on her parents. She lived with them because she was unemployed. However, she did not feel the same amount of resentment as did the mother who was visually impaired. She recognized that her father did not understand her child's visual impairment and believed that her mother worried excessively about her financial status and her child's inability to see well. Nevertheless, she appreciated her parents' material support and was able to see a future in which she would be reunited with her child and be on a more independent footing. This outlook was fed by the regular support she received from professionals, friends, and parent support groups. She also was buoyed by the good relationship she had with her child's foster family. The resentment felt by the visually impaired mother may have been fueled by the absence of a similar vision of future independence and by a limited number of alternative support ties.

Parents who had alternative sources of support appreciated the help their parents offered, especially when it reflected an understanding and acceptance of the meaning and implications of impairment. However, a number of grandparents had difficulty understanding or accepting their grandchildren's visual impairment, and the parents found that the grandparents needed support themselves. The mother of the blind preschooler described how difficult it was to call her parents to inform them that their grandchild had been born without eyes, especially after they had gone through a long misdiagnosed mental illness with the mother's sister. She observed, "One out of four [of my child's] grandparents accepts, but [the others] are loving and treat him normally." Her husband added, "We don't get 'professional' help from our family. We don't ask for it or seek it. If they tell us, we tune it out, but they [provide] a loving environment."

Having a flexible family orientation and a supportive marital partner made it easier for parents to deal with grandparents who had difficulty understanding or accepting their grandchild's visual impairment. In most cases, grandparents were not a primary source of support for the grandchildren or parents, and parents were satisfied that their children knew that their grandparents loved them and that they were treated "normally" by them.

There did not appear to be a simple connection between a parent's coping and the frequency of contact between grandparents and their impaired grandchildren. However, when there was regular contact with grandparents, the nature of the grandparents' coping with impairment and their support for the grandchildren and the parents seemed to affect the parents' coping. For example, frequent contact was a source of tension and resentment for, and undermined the parental authority of, one of the visually impaired single mothers, whereas the other visually impaired single mother saw her parents less frequently but said they were a "great source of support because they handled my visual impairment [well] when I was growing up." The couple with the blind elementary-school-age daughter talked about their busy lives with their dual-career marriage and expressed their appreciation of the strong and regular involvement of the mother's parents in their children's lives. They called them "the best grandparents for our children."

Nearly all the disavowing parents mentioned the love, encouragement, or confidence in their parenting they received from at least one grandparent. Only one of these parents emphasized the problematic nature of support from parents. This mother and her family were preparing to adopt the severely impaired boy who had been with them for several years. She said, "My mother was a [registered nurse] at the state hospital. She asked me, 'Are you sure you know what you are doing in adopting?' I expected support and she has questions." The implied concern expressed in this question was voiced in various ways by other grandparents. It was not a statement of rejection of the child but an expression of their worry about the welfare of the parents and the family as a whole in the face of the stresses and demands that impairment could pose for them.

Along with the minimizing single mother who struggled with her dependence on *her* mother, a few other non-Pattern D parents had to deal with the clearly negative influence of grandparents or other members of their extended families. Most prominent was the case of the protective couple with a moderately impaired elementary-school-age daughter. The mother had lived on the street with her daughter for a while, and she and her husband (the child's stepfather) had battled drug abuse. When I interviewed them, they were establishing stability in the life of their family and expressed their strong commitment to the children. However, their visually impaired child had to deal with taunts from cousins and an aunt who called her mentally retarded. Furthermore, perhaps because of their past troubles, the parents had to deal with efforts by the mother's mother to have their visually impaired child removed from their family by a child protection agency. The grandmother argued that the girl's mother and stepfather were not competent to handle the girl's special needs. Her efforts to take away the child may have made these parents more protective.

The role of grandparents and other relatives in parental coping varied considerably. Some offered crucial expressive or instrumental support. Others were significant obstacles or antagonists. In general, though, relatives did not provide strong, frequent, or pivotal support for parental coping with impairment, per se. One visually impaired mother with two visually impaired teenagers and one visually impaired single mother whose child had retinitis pigmentosa mentioned that their parents were understanding and supportive because they had been through it before as parents. However, only one of these mothers disavowed deviance; the other minimized. Furthermore, as has been noted, having a visually impaired child does not necessarily provide the basis for an understanding and positive supportive relationship with that child when she has a visually impaired child of her own.

Support from Other 'Normal' Relationships

Most grandparents were limited in the informational support and the empathy they could offer for coping with impairment. Support from friends, neighbors, religious groups, and co-workers was similarly restricted. In addition, "normal" relationships in the personal communities of parents outside their extended family networks seldom offered as much expressive or instrumental support as did ties to extended family members. As "normal"—rather than disability—ties, these contacts might have been able to offer concern or emotional support, provide practical help with child care, or even raise money to help with medical or rehabilitation expenses or special equipment, as in the case of the couple with the baby whose church organized a benefit for them.

These kinds of support from normal relationships in personal communities typically were offered during times of substantial stress or crisis for the children or the parents, and because they were "normal," they rarely answered the parents' crucial questions about their children's impairments and how they should deal with it as parents. The mother who struggled for several years to achieve the disavowal of deviance and the capacity to cope splendidly had this to say of the role of friends in her impairment experience: "With friends, I only got emotional support, but they couldn't help me understand because they were not going through it. You need friends to pick you up when you are down but not to understand."

Several variations of this theme were expressed by parents in relation to coming to terms with the realities of impairment and disability. That is, informal ties (outside disability networks) could be helpful, especially during situations of great stress or crisis, but they did not help parents achieve the understanding and acceptance needed to disavow deviance. Parents who denied or minimized had difficulty acknowledging, or were not inclined to acknowledge, their need for ties to special disability networks to help them understand or deal with impairment. However, in crisis situations, they were likely to accept and, especially in the case of minimizers, to appreciate support for their children from their personal communities or formal disability networks.

The denying father of the baby said, "As far as blindness, I haven't concerned myself much with it." His wife contradicted him and pointed out all the questions he asked the doctors. In fact, denial often involves the suppression of anxieties and concerns and perhaps also mixed messages about the desire for support. Because deniers have not yet come to terms with the meaning or impact of visual impairment but may have seen some evidence of its effects, it is understandable that they may be confused or have questions and be ambivalent about informal or formal support. This father acknowledged that it felt good to know that people in his church cared enough to stage a benefit for his child, but he still felt self-conscious and "on the spot" about such special attention.

Minimizing parents generally were not as concerned as were other types of parents about relationships to help them understand or address special needs because they were stoics who tended to play down the significance of impairments. The father of the teenager who had been in a motorcycle accident made no special plea to help him understand or cope. Although he did not know how or when his son's behavioral problems would end, he believed that the answer was within his son. This man was waiting for his son to take control of his life once again so that his family could return to its life as it was before the accident and he could be more independent of his child.

Similarly, the minimizing mother of the teenager with serious coping problems felt compelled to try to understand her daughter's impairment situation only because of her daughter's crisis. Despite her own visual impairment, she could not fully grasp why visual impairment caused her daughter's depression. She perceived no stigma from her daughter's mental illness and appreciated the efforts of rehabilitation professionals and the outpouring of concern from relatives, friends, and classmates for her popular child during these crises. Yet, she, like the minimizing father of the accident victim, did not ask for special support for herself.

All the parents I interviewed could mention some informal relationship or member of their personal community who had provided at least a limited amount of expressive or instrumental support for their coping. Some found the support they received from relatives, friends, neighbors, or members of their religious organizations to be valuable. Others felt hurt or upset by the lack of understanding or acceptance of their children or resented their dependence on informal support ties. In general, though, the routine ties in parents' personal communities were much less important in providing direct support for coping with impairment than were their ties in the nuclear family or their weak ties to other parents or professionals in disability networks.

FROM PERSONAL COMMUNITIES TO DISABILITY NETWORKS

Many parents found the empathy or informational support that they could not get from personal communities, or perhaps even from their spouses, in contacts with other parents of impaired children or with disability professionals. However, it should be apparent by now that the nature of these ties to disability networks varied considerably in frequency, intensity, and content for parents at different times and with different patterns of coping. Furthermore, differences in the perceptions and actual demands of impairments were associated with differences in ties to disability networks for parents who generally displayed the same coping patterns. Despite these differences, connections between coping and ties to disability networks will become evident in the ensuing discussion.

Although the observations and views of the interviewed professionals varied, most noted the significant frustrations that many parents felt at one time or another, which the professionals attributed to the parents' failure to obtain appropriate educational or related services.[1] One professional noted that parental reactions to frustrations depended on their resolution of "personal adjustment issues" and added that many were reluctant to "face the facts" of visual impairment. Another said that a lack of information and education often prevented parents from seeing the need for support to cope with visual impairment. A resource-room teacher, herself visually impaired, asserted, "Parents need more support than they get; they are left out there alone."

Although the parents I interviewed had at least *some* degree of contact with special education professionals and services, most reported frustrating experiences in trying to obtain support for their children or themselves to cope with visual impairment. The nature of their coping at the time I interviewed them generally reflected the success they had in resolving those frustrations. Professionals believed that involvement in support groups could help parents resolve their frustrations and personal adjustment issues but observed parents' general lack of interest in getting involved and a number of significant obstacles to the establishment of viable groups.

Among the obstacles were a sense of uniqueness of the child's impairment; the denial of the child's impairment or disability or a desire for normalcy; the low incidence of visual impairment in children and the geographical distance among families that made meetings difficult to arrange; the changing needs of parents over time; and the related fact that relatively few parents have similar needs for support at the same time, which one professional called the "shifting reference group" phenomenon. Other barriers included the tendency for parents to fall back on previous support networks (even though the support may not be satisfactory); intellectual, socioeconomic, or cultural "gaps" among parents that inhibited their communication; and parents' insecurities about their ability to contribute to a support group.

A number of professionals thought that mothers were more likely than were fathers to be involved in support groups. One professional, who organized and ran a support group for fathers of children with impairments, had little experience with fathers of visually impaired children. He pointed out that the fathers in his group were unusual in regard to their involvement because his reading of the literature on parent support groups indicated that fathers were much less likely than were mothers to join such groups. The fathers in this group tended to be middle class and to have mentally retarded or developmentally delayed children. Although they discussed problems of parenting an impaired child, they did not consider the purpose of the group to be therapy or counseling. They were more concerned about becoming better informed and developing a better understanding of their children and their own roles. An important insight from this professional's experience is that the nature and flow of interaction change substantially when fathers and mothers interact together rather than separately. Mothers who open up easily with other mothers tend to be more restrained and deferential toward their husbands when they participate with them in a group. Because fathers generally talk less than do mothers, there usually are periods of uncomfortable silence when mothers and fathers from different families get together.

PARENTS' INVOLVEMENT IN SUPPORT GROUPS

Although I did not interview all 42 parents in the 23 families in my research, I was able to obtain information about all the parents' involvement in support groups from the comments of those I interviewed.[2] I found that 20 of the 42 parents had more than fleeting current or past involvement in a local, regional, or national group for parents. Three couples were primarily or exclusively involved in a group that was not related to visual impairment, and the remaining 14 parents were involved in a group for parents of visually impaired children. Five parents in the sample had attended local or state-sponsored conferences or had met with other parents on an ad hoc basis to discuss problems with the special education program or services for their children. These 5 parents never considered themselves members of a parent support group.

Overall, 11 of the 23 mothers and 9 of the 19 fathers had participated in a parent support group. All 4 mothers and 2 of the 3 fathers with preschool children were currently or had been involved in a group, as were 3 of the 10 mothers and 4 of the 8 fathers with children in elementary school and 4 of the 9 mothers and 3 of the 8 fathers with children in junior high school or high school. None of the 3 single mothers with custodial care had been involved in an impairment-related group for parents.

These figures describe the amount of parental involvement in groups, and they begin to identify which parents get involved. Some of these facts, such as the overall amount of parental involvement, the relative proportion of fathers versus mothers who were involved, and the non-involvement of single mothers, may seem surprising in view of the observations of the interviewed professionals. However, they do not reveal much about the nature and meaning of involvement in support groups for different parents or how involvement related to coping patterns. To discover what the statistics mean, one must take a closer look.

Three basic dimensions of involvement in a group are membership, interest in membership, and intensity of involvement. Table 6 shows the types of involvement in parent groups that were derived from a combination of dichotomous categories of membership (member or nonmember in the past year), interest (interested or conditionally/negligibly interested), and intensity (high or low). By considering combinations of these dimensions of current or recent (in the past year) involvement, it is possible to understand variations in the nature and the meaning of parental involvement and noninvolvement.

Committed Parents

True believers. Five mothers fit this category of interested and intensely involved members. Three were protective parents and two

Table 6. TYPES OF INVOLVEMENT IN PARENT SUPPORT GROUPS

Type of Involvement	Membership	Interest	Intensity
Committed			
True Believer	Member	Interested	High
Frustrated	Member	Interested	Low
Obliged			
Situational Joiner	Member	Conditionally Interested	High
Reluctant Joiner	Member	Negligibly Interested	Low
Seeker			
Active	Not a Member	Interested	High
Passive	Not a Member	Interested	Low
Uninvolved			
Former Member	Not a Member	Conditionally Interested	High
Never a Member	Not a Member	Negligibly Interested	Low

were disavowers. Four of the five were in groups focusing on visual impairment. The fifth had recently been in a group for parents of premature babies and was having difficulty meeting other parents and finding a nearby support group for parents of visually impaired children.

These mothers were "true believers" because they were enthusiastic members of support groups and believed that such groups provide a variety of forms of support, such as emotional support, information, the opportunity to help others, and the related chance to feel needed (which boosted their self-worth). One mother said it made her "feel better to know someone else is sharing the same experiences." Another said she liked the national association to which she belonged because, unlike groups sponsored by organizations of adult consumers, it focused on parents' needs and concerns.

However, the enthusiasm even of the true believers was not unqualified. As one mother put it, these groups sometimes "get going on what's wrong" with services and service providers. Despite her membership in the national association and attendance at local seminars, another mother said she did not feel involved in an actual parent support group. As the mother of a teenager, she also realized that having an older child could result in her giving more advice than she received. She believed that with her experience "fighting so many battles [for her child]," she probably would be a good leader. However, she was unable to invest the time required to organize and lead a parent group. She still wanted to be part of one, though.

The mother just mentioned saw most parents of visually impaired children as "happy to go with the flow" types, who would not be interested in group meetings. In fact, as soon will become apparent, parents' feelings about groups and their patterns of involvement and noninvolvement are more complex than this parent's comment implies.

Frustrated parents. One couple and one mother were in this category. The couple engaged in the disavowal of deviance, and the other mother was protective. All had been involved in organizing and leading parent groups and were members of a national association for parents of the visually impaired. Only the mothers in these two families were interviewed. The mother whose husband was not involved in her group seemed to accept his noninvolvement because she thought it was "sometimes easier to talk to other females [who were more open about their feelings]." This woman had a traditional view of gender differences in communication, and her experience as an organizer of a parent group did not change that view.

All three parents had begun as true believers but had become frustrated by the lack of response from other parents to their efforts. All were motivated by the problems they had in finding services for their children and were encouraged by professionals in the fields of visual impairment and special education. When the couple found appropriate help for their child and moved him into the mainstream at his school, they became "altruists" and were able to achieve dual integration. That is, in Darling and Darling's terms, they were able to achieve normalization for their child and themselves while they remained committed to helping impaired children and their parents.[3] The other mother probably is better characterized by Darling and Darling's "crusader" concept because she was still fighting for better special education and related services and had not achieved the level of normalization for her child or herself that the couple had. Her integration was more biased toward ties to the disability subculture.

Obliged Parents

Situational joiners. One couple and another father were in this category. The father in the couple was a minimizer, and his wife was protective. The second father engaged in the disavowal of deviance. Of these parents, the two fathers were interviewed. These "situational joiners" attended meetings to get practical help or, in the case of the couple, to help them figure out how to handle their child.

The disavowing father had a blind child in elementary school. As was noted earlier, both he and his wife had careers and were busy. Neither liked to waste time. His wife shared his interest in a parent group and for the same, mostly practical, reasons, such as acquiring information about services and the latest technology and learning how to help their child with daily living skills. However, after fleeting involvement, she felt too burdened by her assorted family and occupational responsibilities to be actively involved in a parent group. Thus, she was a "passive seeker."

The disavowing father, a "situational joiner," periodically reassessed the activities he was pursuing for his blind child's benefit. Although he helped organize a regional seminar for parents sponsored by an organization of adult blind consumers and attended a number of meetings for parents of visually impaired children, he believed that "unfortunately, support groups are not much use." It was difficult to get useful information from other parents when their children had different forms of visual impairment or other impairments and attended schools in other districts. One reason he attended meetings was to learn what to expect of the school.

The other father had the teenager who had suffered brain damage from a motorcycle accident. Both he and his wife had attended meetings of a parent group attached to a head-injury association, sponsored by the local hospital where their child had been treated. This father thought that the meetings did not help much because all the cases of head injury were different, which made it difficult to learn anything from other parents about how to handle his child. As a minimizer and particularly as a stoic, he was resigned to the constraints on his freedom and did not believe it fair to place his burdens on the shoulders of other parents. He had no contact with parents of visually impaired children and considered the brain damage and behavioral problems to be much more serious than the visual impairment. He had joined a support group for practical solutions but, so far, had not found any and did not really expect he would in the future.

Reluctant joiners. The two fathers in this category both attended support-group meetings because their wives—both true believers—had pressured them to do so. One father was a denier and the other was a minimizer. According to his wife's account, the minimizing father did not have much interest in the group, often was the only father at the meetings, felt self-conscious, and substantially reduced his rate of attendance when his wife eased her pressure on him.

The denying father had attended a support group for parents of premature babies, which was organized by the hospital where his child was born. He said that when he found out the extent of his child's blindness, he thought he would like to get ideas from other parents about how they cope. However, in reflecting on his involvement in "preemie groups," he said, "I don't like the idea of that. I don't see the benefit. I have no big urges to talk to anyone about emotional things." This father tended to prefer avoidance and relative isolation, especially regarding special expressive support for dealing with his child's visual impairment. He did not see parent groups as a vehicle to help him get the answers about impairment that he had unsuccessfully sought from doctors.

Seekers

Actives. No parents could be classified exclusively as "actives." Of course, a number of those who were members of groups were actives before they joined, when they were searching for social support. In addition, there were members who wanted to find a group for parents of visually impaired children or who wanted greater involvement, especially with parents of children more like their own.

Passives. Two mothers and two fathers were in this category. The couple were protective parents, and the other mother and father in separate families engaged in the disavowal of deviance. One of these parents had a blind daughter in elementary school and was already mentioned in regard to her husband, who was a situational joiner. She felt her child was doing "fairly well" and had no major problems. However, she said, "I know where to go if it is necessary [to talk to other parents]." This was the attitude of a disavower, and it was similar to the one expressed by another father in this category.

This other father was the noncustodial parent of a boy in elementary school. He believed that support groups were important for providing information and advice about dealing with schools and doctors. He also said, "It gives you encouragement to know that other parents have the same problems.... [and] it is nice to be able to help each other." He observed, in the fashion of a disavower, that "sometimes you need them and sometimes you don't. It is nice to have them when you need them." He was among "a few parents" who had been involved in a visual impairment-related parent-teacher group several years earlier. However, at the moment, he did not think that visual impairment was a big problem (in part because of his confidence in his child's resource-room teacher). He had chosen to invest his time in the parent-teacher association (PTA) in recent years, rather than an impairment-related group, but was becoming frustrated by the lack of parental involvement in the PTA of the local elementary school, which had a large proportion of impaired children among its students.

Like the other two parents in this category, the final two—a couple with a severely visually impaired child in junior high school—were more concerned about getting help for their child than about getting help with parenting or for their personal coping with visual impairment. They had attended conferences and other activities for parents of visually impaired children and were regularly seen at special school and community events for visually impaired children. They liked the idea of meeting and talking to other parents but noted the logistical problems of sustaining a parent group when parents are "so spread out."

Uninvolved Parents

Former members. This category included two couples. All four of these parents engaged in the disavowal of deviance. One couple had a blind preschooler. During their child's first three years, they were involved in a support group of parents of visually impaired children in a center-based infant-stimulation program. The parents met five or six times a year. The other couple had a visually impaired child in high school. Their child had a number of medically anomalous conditions at birth, including a pituitary deficiency that retarded growth. During the child's early years, they were involved in a parent group in an effort to obtain the growth hormone their child needed.

The first couple appreciated the support in the beginning when they were asking the "Why us?" questions, but, as the mother observed, "We can't get into that much any more from the emotional support side." This mother suggested, and her husband agreed, that he was never comfortable at the support-group meetings. He may have felt uncomfortable because he saw the purpose of these groups as "fact gathering rather than emotional support." He also said that after going to meetings for a while, "you don't have much new to say [about visual impairment]. Once you've shared and adjusted, you don't need [the group] anymore. It's useful for a limited time." His wife shared these sentiments. However, both parents agreed with the father's statement: "If we could find another set of parents like us with a child with the same problems as our child's and 5 to 10 years older, we'd latch on to them [to learn what to expect as our child gets older]."

The other couple in this category had only "a little bit of contact" with parents of visually impaired children and did not feel the need for a support group. After getting the amount of hormone their child required, they no longer felt the need to belong to the parent group they had joined for that purpose. Thus, like the first couple in this category, they had been situational joiners. They had not liked the struggle for power and control over the direction of the group that had emerged during their involvement. The mother complained of the shift from being a practical "self-help group to a grumble group." She said, "You need to express your fears and anxieties at first," but she was more concerned with "improving public awareness of the need for more hormone than with working through our feelings." She stated that "once the group lost its practical focus, we lost interest. I'm not much of a joiner. I work for things that are useful." To these comments her husband added, "It doesn't bother me to listen to other parents talk about their feelings, but I don't feel we needed that. I had no time to talk about problems or what we were feeling [to a group of parents]." These comments and those of the other "former members" indicate a disavowal of deviance and a desire for dual integration.

Never members. By far the largest category of parents consisted of 11 mothers and 10 fathers (including 7 married couples) who had never been members of any parent group or association. However, 5 parents had attended educational conferences or meetings for parents of visually impaired children and 1 couple had tried to organize parents for advocacy purposes. These parents displayed more acceptance of visual impairment than did those who were not interested in such activities. In general, the types of reasons for nonmembership and the circumstances of nonmembership in a parent group were associated with parents' coping patterns.

The 21 parents who were "never members" included 5 disavowers, 6 protective parents, 8 minimizers, and 2 deniers. Among those who disavowed deviance, 1 couple did not like parent groups organized for expressive support but had unsuccessfully tried, on an ad hoc basis, to organize parents for advocacy purposes. They also had attended educational conferences for visually impaired students and their parents. A father who was not interviewed but who was classified as a disavower on the basis of his wife's comments, seemed an unlikely candidate for a parent support group, at least partially because he left a lot of the responsibility and stress of daily care for their impaired foster child to his wife. He had a lot of confidence in his wife, who was a true believer. Her participation in groups had been restricted by a busy schedule and her husband's assignment to a late-night shift at work.

Another disavowing parent who had not been a member of a parent group had been a passive seeker for a number of years but lacked the critical ties to professionals that might have guided her to one. She was eventually able to break through to disavowal with the help of a sympathetic transitional kindergarten teacher. The contacts she had in the classroom with other parents and impaired children fulfilled her need for a parent support group and, along with the experience she had accumulated with her daughter, made her feel that a parent group was no longer necessary.

The final disavowing parent who was never a member of an organized parent group was a single mother who was moderately impaired herself. Her own impairment, her peripatetic lifestyle, and the numerous people in her religious movement who constantly surrounded her combined with her strong mainstream orientation to make her uninterested in a parent group. She said:

> I would rather see a support group for kids themselves. I suppose it's needed, but I would not get involved myself. However, I *would* get involved with the RP Foundation to raise funds. Why get together with other parents to socialize about visual impairment.
>
> People are sent to me for help. I worked through "stuff" with a girl friend with a son with muscular dystrophy. I have a good support system around me. I went to a couple of [state-sponsored] conferences [for parents of visually impaired children] for information and support. Parent panels were helpful. They talked about what would happen when [my son] couldn't see. I started to set up a parent group, but it died. I probably wouldn't get involved anyway. [It] could become a crutch. Self-pity could be used too easily.

It was in this context that this mother remarked that "parents should be mainstreamed, too." Overall, her comments suggested a common attitude among disavowing parents, whether they had or had not been members of organized parent support groups. That is, these groups could be useful for specific practical purposes or for a specified period, but they were not useful when they dwelled on parents' emotional problems with visual impairment or when parents became dependent on them as a "crutch" for coping. Disavowing parents typically recognized the value of ties to disability networks for meeting their children's impairment needs but ultimately were interested in dual integration and a relatively normal lifestyle for their children, themselves, and their families.

The protective parents who were "never members" included the mother and stepfather of a moderately impaired girl in elementary school, the former wife of the noncustodial father, the couple with two visually impaired teenage daughters, and the mother who had a rebellious teenage daughter with low vision and a husband who was a denier. The mother and stepfather thought parent groups were potentially useful, but they were not interested in joining one at the time they were interviewed. They seemed happy that they were beginning to establish some stability in their family life after difficult times. The mother also had seen a psychiatrist in the past and knew he was available to help her in the future. She and her husband depended on their daughter's visually impaired resource-room teacher for support and, like the married parents who disavowed deviance, were able to draw emotional support from their marital relationship.

The mother with two visually impaired daughters had been unable to find a support group when her children were younger and she had felt the need for one. Now that the children were older and they had the support of a trusted counselor, she no longer felt the need for a support group for herself. She was like another mother of a teenager who had more interest in a parent group when her daughter was much younger. She and her husband also were like this other mother and her husband (who were disavowers) in their participation in educational conferences.

Another protective mother of a teenager never had contact with a parent support group but said it had not mattered. She asserted that "the problems of each child are different. You can't lump them together. You need to understand what is wrong with *your* child—what *your* child is going through. Talking to other parents doesn't help unless their children are *exactly* the same as yours." This mother, like her husband, who engaged in denial, had been unable to establish the rapport with professionals that might have made her more receptive to contacts with other parents and might have set her on the path to the disavowal of deviance.

The other protective parent who was never a member of a support group was not interviewed. However, the comments by her ex-husband, who was a committed but noncustodial father, and my telephone calls to solicit her participation in my research suggested she felt too burdened by single parenthood and a full-time job to get involved in a parent support group. She seemed satisfied to trust professionals to provide her visually impaired son with the services he needed. The nature of those services and her former husband's involvement in determining them were matters of contention between these former spouses.

Whereas most disavowing or protective parents who were never members usually had an interest at one time in joining a parent support group, most parents who minimized or denied never had such an interest. In fact, only three of the minimizing and denying parents had been involved in a parent support group, and one other had been a reluctant participant in a parent-training workshop. Two were reluctant joiners, and the other was a situational joiner who hoped for some informational support but did not really expect it. The general lack of involvement of minimizing and denying parents in parent groups reflected their biased normal or isolated integration and may have reinforced it as well.

REASSESSING PARENT SUPPORT GROUPS

Arguments for the potential value of support groups for parents of visually impaired children clash with certain realities, revealed in my research as obstacles to their formation or endurance. Two major questions quickly surface. First, what kind of support is appropriate for parents who resist or feel uncomfortable in small discussion groups, especially when the groups focus on "emotional ventilation"? Second, how can parents who might benefit from a group at a given time and be willing to join be assured that a group will be there when they need it? The first question concerns matching parents to appropriate forms and processes of support. The second question concerns logistical, administrative, and resource matters. Although parents may want to feel ownership over the support groups in which they are involved and assert their own leadership and control over them, it still may be argued that professional intervention is relevant to both questions. Appropriate parent support and the role of professional intervention are discussed next.

Appropriate Support

There were few instances of sustained involvement in a support group and even fewer cases in which a support group provided a network of friends for the parents in this study. Nevertheless, support groups served useful purposes for the parents who were involved in them and could have been helpful for parents who were seekers but could not find a group. The major forms of support that the groups provided included information and advice (about visual impairment, rights, services, and special aspects of raising a visually impaired child); help to enable parents to obtain important resources for their children; and the chance to gain emotional support, to increase their self-esteem, and to talk with other parents in similar circumstances who could help them understand and cope with their children's impairments.

Parents obviously had many perceptions of "support" and support groups, and what attracted some was precisely the reason others lost interest or would not join. It is easy to agree with Gottlieb that "we will probably find that there is no such thing as a 'network (or support group) for all seasons.' "[4] Thus, instead of trying to identify the ideal parent support group or network, it seems more fruitful to consider the concept of fit between the needs for or interest in support groups and alternatives in the forms and processes of parent-to-parent contacts.

Appropriate impairment-related social support should involve parents in relationships with other parents that meet mutual or shared needs and goals, occur in places and represent a style of communication with which the interacting parents feel comfortable, and take into account potential problems that may arise because of differences in social or cultural background and perceptions of visual impairment and disability. Parents may be unable to find appropriate types of support on their own or in formal gatherings of parents and professionals at conferences. Therefore, professionals who work with impaired children and their parents can play an important role as bridges or gatekeepers in facilitating the access of parents to appropriate support groups.

Role of Professionals

Professional intervention can be useful even though parents may not always get along with professionals and some professionals think it would be intrusive or otherwise inappropriate for them to get involved in a group that is supposed to be of and for parents. In fact, different types of professionals—from ophthalmologists to social workers, to special educators, to educators of the visually impaired, to rehabilitation teachers, to mobility instructors, to vocational educators, and to school and family counselors—can help parents find and get involved in a fruitful group or network of some type. To be effective, these professionals must overcome the barriers to parent-professional cooperation that have been identified by many experts on families coping with impairment.[5]

Professionals must try to understand the personalities of parents and how parents convey their concerns and needs, as well as what they say about them. Even though parents are not always consistent in what they think, feel, say, and do, it still seems especially important to understand the general type of coping patterns of parents. Darling pointed out that professionals have a special responsibility to be sensitive to the differences between their perspectives and parents' perspectives on impairment and their impaired children.[6] The actual relationship between professionals' and parents' perspectives is discussed in Chapter 6. However, it should be mentioned here that professionals also should recognize that parents' beliefs, feelings, actions, and overall coping patterns may change over time and that parents have different types and amounts of need for support at different times. Professionals may look at parents who deny or minimize and presume that social support will not be welcome. If professionals back away in these cases, they may contribute to a self-fulfilling prophecy that reinforces denial or minimizing for the future. If they ignore parents who said in the past that they did not need help, they may be ignoring parents whose needs for support and receptiveness have changed.

Parents of visually impaired teenagers in this study revealed the need for the types of social support for their children or themselves that could have been provided through contacts with other parents. It is easy to presume that parents of older children have "adjusted" and no longer need help. The evidence from this study contradicts that premise, however. In fact, the low incidence of visual impairment among children means that the normal uncertainties of growing up are compounded for parents and their visually impaired children. Parents have fewer clear guideposts for parenting and the normal transitions are less predictable when their children are impaired. Professionals must be aware that parental coping is never "secure" and that new and unexpected stresses or crises may surface at any time during the visually impaired child's or parent's life. During any of these periods of crisis or unusual stress, parents who already have gotten through such experiences could be helpful to those who are just beginning to confront them.

Helping parents find other parents may pose challenges that call for creative approaches. For many parents, perceived cultural, social, and social-class differences may be relevant to the kinds of social support they will seek and accept. Surely, it is essential for professionals to be able, directly or indirectly, to understand the parents' language and culture and to show respect for them if they hope to help these parents develop useful parent-to-parent contacts in their communities or want to provide other kinds of support to them. Correa's analysis of interaction between teachers and Hispanic parents of visually impaired children suggests that professionals are unlikely to reach culturally different parents and help them get the social support they need in the absence of cultural sensitivity and some linguistic proficiency.[7]

My difficulty getting black and Asian parents to participate in this research indicates the need to find professionals or community members whom these parents trust to mediate or facilitate interaction until sufficient trust is built between the white professional and the minority family to permit a more direct relationship. The need to get help to give help may exist whenever prospective recipients of support perceive salient differences in status, background, or lifestyle between themselves and professionals. Such differences can spawn suspicion, intimidation, or even alienation when they are associated with differences in power. Thus, professionals have to be concerned about matching the social and cultural characteristics of parents when they try to get them together for mutual support and need to be aware of possible obstacles created by differences in status and background between themselves and the people they are trying to help.

Another major "matching" issue, beyond cultural background, race, ethnicity, and social class, is gender. Professionals sometimes assume that only mothers will be interested in a support group. However, this study found that although fathers may become involved only after they are pressured by their wives or when they have practical reasons, the fathers' rate of current or past involvement was not significantly different from the mothers'. Of course, the fathers' tendency to display different types of involvement than the mothers underscores the importance of identifying the types of support that groups can provide and of matching their support and style of interaction to parents' distinctive needs and aims. This point was made by the professional who worked with fathers and recommended separate groups for mothers and fathers.

My findings lead to the conclusion that mixed-gender groups of practically minded situational joiners would be viable but that mixing mothers and fathers in an emotional-support environment could be counterproductive in that it would stifle self-disclosure and openness for fathers and mothers. This is not to say that fathers do not need emotional support from other parents, but that option should be available in fathers-only groups. In general, it appears that married fathers—and married mothers—in families with a flexible orientation get the emotional support they need for coping with impairment from their marital partners.

Another point in this context is that some practical situational joiners are resource seekers, whereas others are politically minded advocates. The evidence here is that these two perspectives are not always compatible, which professionals should keep in mind in facilitating contacts among parents and in the organization of support groups. Professionals also should not be disappointed when parents fail to heed their advice to become involved in a parent group or public advocacy activities. As the parents' comments have indicated, parents have many reasons for their lack of involvement in such activities, and these reasons usually reflect something other than neglect, a lack of concern, or a lack of commitment to their children. The next two sections present various forms of parental contact that could meet parents' needs for support. Professionals who want to help parents find appropriate support from other parents need to keep an open mind about the form that support may take.

A PERSONAL PERSPECTIVE ON PARENT GROUPS

My experience with parent groups seems relevant to mention at this point. After coming to believe that I had "adjusted" to my son's visual impairment and that I understood his special needs as a 2 year old, I had no intention of attending an exploratory meeting of parents sponsored by the state association for the blind. My wife felt differently. With her urging ("Don't you think your son is worth an hour of your time to look into this?"), I set out for the exploratory meeting as an obliged and reluctant observer. To my surprise, I found the discussion with other mothers and fathers interesting and informative and the idea of a parent group, with the support of the state association and an organization of adult blind people, potentially helpful.

I quickly lost my initial reluctance and soon became president of a new parent group in our state. My enthusiasm as a converted "true believer" led to meetings with other parents; a newsletter for parents; the organization of a statewide conference for parents, teachers, and other professionals; membership on boards and councils concerned with children, education, and disability issues; and a commitment to political advocacy.

I eventually became a frustrated parent-group leader, because I typically found more professionals and other resource people than parents at meetings. There were times when I lamented the apathy of parents, but I eventually realized the meaning of appropriate and timely support. I learned that it was difficult to get parents together on a regular basis, even with conference calls, when they were geographically scattered, had different socioeconomic and cultural backgrounds and interests, and did not always feel a pressing need to talk to other parents or to get special help for their children or themselves.

I also learned that it was important for other parents to know that there was someone to call for advice, information, or emotional support and for professionals to know that there was a parent who was experienced with the "system" to whom they could refer other parents. Furthermore, I learned that at least in a small, largely rural state, finding new members, and especially new leaders, and sustaining the group as a viable organization often are difficult and usually will depend on the support of professionals and the resources of their school system or agency. My research and personal experience have shown that some parents see professionals, the school, or special education and disability agencies as the enemy when their children are not receiving the services the parents want them to receive. These parents are not likely to be interested in parent groups with a formal or informal connection to "the system." I found, however, that professionals who volunteered their skills, time, and other individual and organizational resources to parent groups were more committed to cooperation and being helpful to parents than to the control or co-optation that some parents feared. In saying this, though, I do not mean to gloss over real and significant differences between parents and professionals. Parent-professional cooperation in parent groups, in the schools, in doctors' offices, at home, or elsewhere can be affected by differences in perceptions, values, and goals. Furthermore, parental reluctance to be involved with professionals in a parent group may reflect parental concerns about serious deficiencies in services or major problems in the treatment of parents or their impaired children. These issues are discussed in greater depth in Chapter 6.

Even with a great deal of professional support and the help of other parents, it is easy to "burn out" as the leader of a parent group. You are especially likely to burn out when you are trying to maintain the viability of the group, pursue advocacy, tend to the needs of your impaired child and the rest of your family as a parent and spouse, and maintain a serious commitment to your career.

I was fortunate to find another "committed true believer" to take over the leadership of our group, but her acceptance of this role was an act of genuine altruism. She was the mother of a blind teenager preparing to attend college. Her involvement in the group demonstrated the ongoing need for contacts with other parents and for a parent group over the life cycle of an impaired child. I suspect, however, that she gave far more than she got as a group member, because no other parents in the group had an older visually impaired adolescent. She talked to me about continuing frustrations with her son's classroom teachers, despite his excellent academic record (he went on to Dartmouth College), her need to "educate" her son's teachers every year to ensure that he got appropriate resources and treatment, and her concerns about her son living on his own as a college student. I probably provided little helpful feedback to her, but I think she appreciated the chance to talk about her problems and concerns with a sympathetic parent.

Although we spoke together as individual parents, the reason we had a chance to talk was our involvement in the parent group. Like me, she believed that it was important to try to sustain the group, even if there were few active members and few formal group meetings, because it provided opportunities for parents to talk to other parents when they needed such support, it helped as an advocate to be a representative of a formal group, and it gave professionals names of parents to whom they could refer other parents who needed support.

ORGANIZATIONAL ISSUES
IN PARENT-TO-PARENT SUPPORT

The discussion of parent-to-parent support has subtly shifted from a focus on genuine involvement in groups toward other options, including individual contacts between parents. The shift occurred in recognition of the different types of parental coping and parental needs at different times. My experience has revealed that matching individual parents or couples may be especially appropriate for parents of visually impaired children who tend to be geographically dispersed. Professionals who arrange such matches should keep in mind that the parental support they are encouraging is likely to supplement—not substitute for—existing resources and interpersonal ties. That is, parental seekers may be looking for only temporary help, not lasting friendships.

I have found that an especially useful referral for parents who are looking only for advice and information is an established national association of parents or its regional affiliate. Such organizations may publish regular newsletters and other publications, hold regional and national conferences, and offer a network of parents who can be contacted when special visual impairment-related problems, stresses, or crises arise. This support may not be as personal as a local support group, but this research suggests that parents who are seeking advice and information from another parent will be happy to get it from a distant source if that source is appropriate.

Powell suggested that parents who already feel emotionally supported by their networks of spouses, friends, and extended family members may be more responsive than may less supported or more isolated parents to efforts to supplement these networks with new contacts.[8] Isolated parents who are poor, have limited formal education, are from a cultural or ethnic minority, and feel outside the system pose a special challenge for professional intervention. Among other reasons, they may be difficult to reach because they may be invisible to those working in the school, special education, or social service agencies. Their children's needs may never have been identified, and they are not likely to be part of the informal networks of professionals or parents who could help them. They may not understand the nature of impairments such as low vision or know what to do to obtain help for their children or themselves if they think there is a problem.

The existence of these isolated, invisible parents is a strong argument for comprehensive and early assessments to identify impairments and related family needs throughout the community. Although one is less likely today than in the past to hear from parents of preschoolers that "no one ever told me about a parent support group," it still seems that parents who are outside the social, cultural, or economic mainstream do not learn about the possibility of such forms of support.[9] Such parents lack even minimal ties to professionals or others who could be bridges to critical support for their children or themselves. Needless to say, inadequate efforts by professionals and organizations in disability networks to identify children with impairments will result in an inadequate identification of their parents as well.

As a result of their perceptions that children cannot be compared, parents may not take advantage of opportunities to join cross-impairment support groups that may be more viable and available than may groups that are related strictly to visual impairment. Experience, contacts with parents of children with other types of impairments, and education about impairments could help parents expand their perspectives and make them more receptive to cross-impairment contacts and groups if they are interested in a parent support group but cannot find other interested parents of visually impaired children nearby. Parents with multiply impaired or severely developmentally delayed children are especially likely to find cross-impairment groups or networks appealing. Active seeking is likely to be correlated, to some extent, with the severity of a child's impairment and disabilities or, perhaps what is more important, with the parents' perception of the severity and their tendency to be protective.

The success or failure of a group should be measured not in terms of its size but in terms of the amount of support that members believe they are deriving from meeting with each other. The size of the group will determine the amount of formality in its organization, and small groups have the virtues of informality, flexibility, and the opportunity for members to get to know each other better than do larger groups. Organizers and leaders of support groups, like those involved in many voluntary activities in the community, should accept that only a few parents at any given time are likely to be interested and regularly involved in their group. However, for those few who are involved, the group may be invaluable.

It may be the ultimate frustration and irony for group organizers and professionals that parents who learn to cope successfully and disavow deviance and who may be especially helpful to others often turn away from a concern with impairment and become oriented to the mainstream and normalization. The success of mainstreaming and normalization efforts by professionals and parent groups would appear to deprive these groups, and parents who could benefit from contacts with other parents, of potentially valuable social support. It appears that there are relatively few altruists, like the mother who succeeded me as the leader of the parent group, who are willing to remain deeply involved in the disability subculture after having achieved the disavowal of deviance and the integration into the mainstream they had sought for their children and for themselves. However, parents who disavow deviance have not completely forsaken ties to the disability subculture and can be sources of support for those who are trying to come to terms with impairment. For denying parents or minimizing parents who are in transition to acceptance and for protective parents, a conversation with an experienced parent who has adjusted to the mainstream may be a pivotal support that ultimately makes it possible for them to break through to the disavowal of deviance. That parents who denied and minimized visual impairment were willing to talk to me, often at great length, for this research suggests their potential receptiveness to the types of ties to parents or sympathetic professionals that could open the way to better understanding, deeper or fuller acceptance, and more effective coping.

CONCLUSION

When parents understand and accept the realities and the implications of their children's visual impairments and disabilities, they become more concerned about getting professional help and finding an appropriate niche in the mainstream or an appropriate type of integration for their children and for themselves. Although all parents can face significant obstacles and frustrations in seeking integration, protective parents tend to worry the most and place the most emphasis on the need for special support and accommodations for coping with impairment.

This chapter has considered the role of professionals as bridges or gate-keepers in networks of potential social support for parents. The next chapter discusses parent-professional contacts in more detail.

NOTES

1 The remainder of this chapter draws heavily on H. L. Nixon II, "Reassessing Support Groups for Parents of Visually Impaired Children," *Journal of Visual Impairment & Blindness,* 82 (October 1988): 271-278.

2 For 10 of the 23 families, both partners were interviewed. For 4 of the single or separated parents, the parent who was interviewed was the only one who was significantly involved in the impaired child's life. In the other 9 families, the parent who was interviewed gave enough information about his or her spouse's or ex-spouse's (in the case of the noncustodial father) involvement to complete the picture of involvement by all 42 parents in the 23 families.

3 R. B. Darling and J. Darling, *Children Who Are Different* (St. Louis: C. V. Mosby Co., 1982).

4 B. H. Gottlieb, "Preventive Interventions Involving Social Networks and Social Support," in *Social Networks and Social Support,* ed. B. H. Gottlieb (Beverly Hills, CA: Sage Publications, 1981), 227.

5 See, for example, H. Featherstone, *A Difference in the Family: Living with a Disabled Child* (New York: Penguin Books, 1981); and R. B. Darling, "Parent-Professional Interaction: The Roots of Misunderstanding," in *The Family with a Handicapped Child: Understanding and Treatment,* ed. M. Seligman (Orlando, FL: Grune & Stratton, 1983), 95-121.

6 Darling, "Parent-Professional Interaction."

7 V. I. Correa, "Working with Hispanic Parents of Visually Impaired Children: Cultural Implications," *Journal of Visual Impairment & Blindness* 81 (September 1987): 260-264.

8 D. R. Powell, "Individual Differences in Participation in a Parent-Child Support Program," in *Changing Families,* eds. I. E. Sigel and L. M. Laosa (New York: Plenum Press, 1983), 203-224.

9 See, for example, B. L. Mallory, "Interactions Between Community Agencies and Families Over the Life Cycle," in *Families of Handicapped Children: Needs and Supports Across the Life Cycle,* eds. R. R. Fewell and P. F. Vadasy (Austin, TX: Pro-ed, 1986), 317-356.

Chapter 6
PROFESSIONALS AND PARENTS

Professionals help parents in a variety of ways. They support parents directly when they boost their self-esteem with encouragement and approval; when they provide a foundation for their sense of confidence, competence, and power with information and training; and when they help them understand and accept their children's impairments in unstigmatized terms. Professionals also help parents in indirect ways. When parents think that professionals are serving their children capably, they often feel supported in their own coping with impairment.

Sometimes, these services have a concrete impact on parents' lives, as when professionals heal, rehabilitate, educate, counsel, or provide adaptive devices and equipment to lessen the children's disabilities and the parents' burden of support of their children. As is noted in Chapter 5, professionals supported parents by acting as "bridges," providing referrals to other parents who could support them. Professionals also perform an important supportive role in disability networks when they act as "gatekeepers," opening the doors of eligibility or access to services for impaired children and their families.

When parents first discover their children's impairments or when they are struggling to understand, accept, or deal with the impairments or disabilities, their coping is likely to be affected by what professionals say to them as well as by what the professionals do for their children or them. That is, professionals—doctors, teachers, counselors, or rehabilitators—may, intentionally or unintentionally, act as moral guides or judges when they interact with parents. The subtle or obvious values, norms, and attitudes they convey along with their expertise reflect their own or professional moral standards for "responsible" or "good" parental coping. The range of things professionals say to parents provides a language and perspective for parental coping that may influence how parents approach and appraise their relationship with their impaired children.[1]

PROFESSIONALS' MORAL STANDARDS FOR PARENTS

The professionals I interviewed emphasized a number of moral themes about parental coping. These themes constitute a picture of parental coping that contains many of the elements associated with the disavowal of deviance and Pattern D coping in general. Professionals tended to talk about parents in terms of "ought," "should," and "need to" and often espoused these themes as the moral responsibility of a "good parent." At times, they spoke clearly, directly, and emphatically about what parents must do. At other times, their standards and expectations were more subtle or implicit in their ostensibly descriptive comments and observations. Most professionals were not hesitant to speak, without my prompting, in moral or judgmental terms about types of parents or, in some cases, about specific parents.

An analysis of the content of the interviews with professionals produced seven general themes. In deriving these themes, I gave the greatest weight to those that were expressed most strongly and widely by the special educators, other educators, and visual impairment service providers who have the most direct and frequent contact with visually impaired children and their parents. However, the comments of other professionals helped to broaden, deepen, or qualify the meaning of the themes. As the discussion of themes proceeds, it will become increasingly evident how much the themes overlapped in the professionals' statements. For each of the themes that follow, representative statements by professionals will be cited or paraphrased to define the theme.

General Themes

Understanding and acceptance. This centerpiece of the disavowal of deviance was stated in a number of ways. For instance, a principal spoke of the unrealistic demands of parents who did not understand. A special educator said, "Parents do well once they understand why things are happening." A resource-room teacher for visually impaired students said that parents needed to overcome their fears of blindness and to be able to say "blind" (in reference to their children) to be able to "make it in society" and get the services they and their children need. She added that "ignoring visual impairment does not make it go away." An ophthalmologist said that parents needed to "account for limitations without hampering development." A researcher who was studying blind and severely visually impaired preschoolers said that parents needed to accept blindness to be able to relate to professionals, and she observed that parents "wanted people to see their child as blind but not different." A special educator who had extensive experience with visually impaired children and their families in support programs and in research efforts said that parents needed to "overcome stigma to seek services" and that "parents pick up their blindness orientations from professionals."

Understanding and acceptance also encompassed professionals' emphases on the importance of parents being "aware" and "informed" regarding the nature of visual impairment and the special needs it creates. A number of professionals pointed to their own and fellow professionals' roles in facilitating or directly providing informational support to parents.

Realism. Many professionals spoke about the importance of parents being realistic about the implications of visual impairment. They viewed the lack of realism in parental demands as being a result of the parents' lack of understanding. Indeed, professionals frequently spoke, disapprovingly, of "unrealistic" parents. One professional said that parents needed early intervention to "jar them into reality." Another, who worked with parents of infants and toddlers, asserted that being realistic did not have to mean focusing on limitations, as many professionals seemed to imply. Instead, parents could be realistic about the abilities of their children.

Contrary to the strong and unequivocal emphasis on realism by most professionals was the caution expressed by a nurse who worked with severely and multiply impaired young children and their parents. She proposed that professionals sometimes expect too much realism too soon after the discovery of serious impairment. She suggested that for a while and under certain circumstances, denial could be a legitimate form of coping. She said, "Unless parents are off base and hurting the child, an overly harsh dose of reality is not needed. Illusion is a crutch for day-to-day adjustment. It gives hope. It is first aid for coping. Reality can wait until parents are adjusted enough to handle tough decisions, such as an out-of-home placement."

In contrast to this cautionary view was the uncompromising view of a vocational educator who worked with parents of teenagers with impairments. She said, "Parents help when they are realistic, involved, and flexible. Parents are unrealistic about the future, the job world." These comments anticipate the next theme of "involvement," along with a later theme of "preparation and planning."

Involvement. Many professionals stressed the importance of parental involvement in their children's programs, including educational, rehabilitative, and recreational. They believed that parents ought to be aware of the nature of these programs, participate in planning to make sure the programs meet their children's needs, and monitor their children's progress. In the latter regard, a number of professionals outside education said that parents ought to be "vigilant" in regard to their children's education. A resource-room teacher who had frequent contacts with parents lamented parents' resistance to joining support groups and ignorance and apathy about their children's education that she often observed.

It is ironic, many experienced educators observed, that in light of the mandate incorporated into P.L. 94-142, parents of impaired children in recent years have actually become less involved in their children's education when they have had a legal right to be involved. The educational administrators and special educators who observed this change made an implicitly or explicitly invidious comparison between the highly involved parents of the past and the less involved parents of recent years. While arguing for parental involvement, one special educator qualified her argument by suggesting that parents who "tried too hard" were too involved with the details of their children's education and could be as difficult to work with as could parents who did not care. She and a number of other educators said that parents needed to back away enough to allow them to do their job and allow their children to achieve some independence. This prescription for the appropriate level of parental involvement incorporated other themes of "trust" and "challenge," which are the next ones to be described.

Trust. Professionals often perceived parents as being too protective. They said that parents needed to learn to trust them and their children so they could "let go" and ask for and accept necessary services. They recognized that for parents to be able to let go, parents needed to understand and accept visual impairment and overcome their fears of blindness and worries about its implications for the future.

A principal of a school with a large population of students with impairments, including visually impaired students, said, "Parent-school trust is built gradually by design. It allows parents to let go, and it allows the school freedom to educate.... Without trust between parent and professional, it is the parent against the world." He was especially sensitive to the need for the mutual construction of parent-professional trust and cooperation because much of his day was spent as a self-described "heatilator" or "brush-fire expert," trying to mollify parents who had not established such ties with their children's teachers. Although trust was generally seen as important, a few professionals asserted that parents should not trust too much because, in doing so, they could become too dependent on professionals and relinquish too much control over crucial issues that affect their children. A director of an infant-stimulation program, who was highly regarded by parents and colleagues, stated that "parents should *not* view professionals as saints because it encourages excessive dependence." This qualification suggests an understanding of the power-dependence relationship and implies that professionals should not abuse their position. It also anticipates the theme of parental "assertiveness," which appeared in the discussion of involvement and will be considered after the theme of challenge.

Challenge. An itinerant teacher said that parents needed to "get over the worry hurdle." That is, they needed to be able to challenge their children and encourage independence without being excessively concerned about the risks. By pushing their children into the mainstream, parents would help them overcome the social and emotional immaturity that many parents recognized and many professionals viewed as a deficiency of visually impaired children and youths.

Although the professionals generally espoused challenge, several acknowledged that it was easier for them to talk about risks than it was for parents and visually impaired children to accept the actual consequences of risk taking. Some who spoke of the need for both realism and challenge recognized the potential contradiction when parents push their children toward unrealistic goals. In this context, a special education consultant said that "parents need to be less protective, but a little overprotective is better than unrealistic." A resource-room teacher seemed acutely aware of the delicate balance that parents need to strike in challenging their visually impaired children. She realized that parental overprotectiveness and an overemphasis on impairment and disability could make a child feel like a victim, which would inhibit integration and adjustment. However, she also realized that parents could push their children too much, beyond their capabilities. Her approach was to be "gently honest" with parents, encouraging them to have realistic expectations.

A major challenge for parents of visually impaired children is to get their children successfully integrated into the mainstream of the school and the community. The principle and process of integration into the mainstream are considered at greater length in Chapter 7. However, in this context, it should be noted that professionals differed in their views of how parents should approach mainstreaming. Professionals generally agreed that mainstreaming was a good idea. One principal said, "The [impaired] child needs to get into the mainstream and stay there." Yet even as a strong advocate of mainstreaming, he spoke of "unreasonable parents who wanted their visually impaired children to be exactly like their normally sighted peers." The association of unrealistic expectations—a fictionalizing of normalcy—with the desire for mainstreaming was one of the perceived problems of a parental push to the mainstream.

Another perceived problem was the absence of a "niche" in the mainstream for visually impaired children. Special educators who taught visually impaired students in self-contained classrooms or resource rooms placed the greatest emphasis on the need for parents to be cautious and vigilant about the promises of mainstreaming. Indeed, one resource-room teacher said, "Parents have been brainwashed about mainstreaming."

Thus, although other educators and service providers asserted that parents needed to give their visually impaired children "more exposure to normal kids and normal expectations," special educators were more inclined to point out the pitfalls of mainstreaming. In the words of a resource-room teacher, "They are ignoring the visually impaired child in contact classes and the mainstream. Parents think putting their visually impaired children in a regular classroom makes them like their sighted peers. It does not!" She noted the difficulty of getting teachers to recognize the special needs of students with low vision and argued that regular classroom teachers need more support to make mainstreaming work. The "deterioration of schools, resources, and the educational climate" diminished her earlier support for mainstreaming. Diminished faith and disillusionment with the implementation of mainstreaming as "plopping visually impaired students in regular classrooms with sighted peers and ignoring them" colored the feelings and beliefs of professionals who thought that parents ought to be informed, realistic, and careful in pursuit of the "challenge" of integration.

Assertiveness. It is difficult to disentangle the theme of assertiveness voiced by professionals from the other themes. A synthesis of all these themes would take the following form: Parental involvement should be assertive (about their own and their children's rights); assertiveness should be informed and oriented toward goals that are realistically challenging and should not be compromised by excessive trust in professionals. Most of the professionals I interviewed included one or more of the elements of this synthesized theme.

The theme is called "assertiveness" rather than "advocacy" (a term used by a number of professionals and parents) because assertiveness can, but does not necessarily, imply involvement in political advocacy or lobbying. According to most professionals, parents need to be able to speak up for the rights and needs of their children and themselves. However, few implied that parents who were not involved in political lobbying were irresponsible. The director of an infant-stimulation program taught parents their legal rights during the educational planning process of the IEP, but she said:

> We don't get parents involved in advocacy in our program. If the family gets a trip laid on them by advocates, they know they can say no. They need to ask, "What will this do for me and my child?" Our parent group is more for support for each other. If there were advocacy, it would have to be a *major* issue. I would say, "A letter would help."

Part of the director's concern was that parents would burn out if they got too involved in lobbying and similar political or altruistic activities. Thus, parents could engage in advocacy, but they did not have to lobby to be good parents, and their unwillingness to do so was understandable to most professionals.

A few professionals did place a strong emphasis on parental lobbying. For example, one resource-room teacher lamented parental apathy and stressed the need to teach parents how to lobby, in the face of declining special education resources for their children. However, another resource-room teacher noted that parents need to be careful not to get carried away by a newly found sense of power from advocacy and become distracted from their children's needs. She said that sometimes

> parents who gain new power [after receiving advocacy training] push, push, and lose sight of their child.... They can go from apathy and powerlessness to getting stuck with personal power issues and personal psychological agendas [based on previous guilt and powerlessness]. Kids are hurt by parents who antagonize professionals with excessive pushing.

This teacher was talking about excessive or misguided assertiveness as well as political advocacy.

In general, professionals believed that parents need to be assertive but that assertiveness should be informed, realistic, and reasonable. A number of professionals also argued that parents have to be assertive or even aggressive in demanding special services, equipment, or accommodations or risk being ignored. Some professionals even said that parents need to be the "pushy parents" whom the resource-room teacher believed could be detrimental to the children's welfare. Some administrators and consultants in special education agreed with a colleague who said that parents have to "speak up or be ignored since schools respond to demands or requests but do not seek problems." This professional also noted that there was a tendency to "discount the needs of [low vision] kids and their parents" because of the invisibility of low vision.

Planning and preparation. Professionals who worked with visually impaired teenagers and their parents were especially inclined to emphasize the importance of planning and preparation for the future. A physician noted that "good parents think about the future—about vocational things—and plan in the teen years." She faulted educational and rehabilitation professionals, who do not coordinate their efforts and, hence, form a "nonsystem," for failing to help parents plan. She went on to say that "a perceptive parent is vigilant and pushes for answers and services. The best informed parents get started in an infant-stimulation program. Passive parents get sucked along by the nonsystem."

In this professional's mind, planning and preparation were inextricably bound up with vigilance, awareness, involvement, and assertiveness. Although she did not explicitly say it, she implied what another professional, a vocational educator, stated explicitly: "Not planning is dooming a child to failure." A special educator said that parents were "poor role models when they fail to follow through." Another special educator observed that "some parents are sophisticated planners, [but] most are not."

The implied parental irresponsibility in not planning suggested a subtle or obvious social-class bias in the professionals' appraisals of parents in regard to planning and preparation. For example, a principal implied a distinction between middle- and lower-class parents when he discussed "proactive" and "reactive" parents in the following terms:

> Better educated and more intelligent parents are better prepared
> and more positive when [they see me to] look for support. They are
> one step ahead of the child and proactive [as opposed to] reactive.

Reactive parents emotionalize issues, and they are confused, apprehensive, and unrealistic because they don't understand visual impairment and its educational implications.

A social worker proposed that an orientation to the future is a predominantly middle-class characteristic and that a "dilemma of the future" is to force "parents to anticipate or plan when it [is] against their personal style." She added that parents of impaired children generally may have difficulty dealing with the future when "now is tough" and that "not planning may be taking a break rather than being a bad parent." It was not an argument against planning but a sympathetic explanation of why many parents do not, or believe they cannot, plan. It stood in contrast to what most professionals said about a "planning imperative," which they often assumed to be more within the capabilities of "better educated" and "more intelligent" (middle-class) parents.

Themes versus Coping Style

The seven general themes espoused by professionals as standards of responsible parenthood for parents of impaired children are consistent with the disavowal of deviance, coping splendidly, and dual integration. It is noteworthy that these themes are similar to general standards of responsible parenthood for all parents in our society. In this vein, Voysey proposed that parents who cope splendidly face impairment experiences that differ only in degree from the experiences of all parents.[2] This idea is similar to the notion expressed by a number of professionals and disavowing parents that visual impairment is an intensifier of the normal problems of parenthood and family life but does not make life unique for the family. However, some professionals argued that impairment could have a disruptive effect on families and parents who are not equipped to cope. As a social worker put it:

> [Impairment] can disrupt family homeostasis and unbalance relationships. [It] doesn't directly cause divorce, but, like other crises or stressful situations, such as unemployment, it will destabilize a marital relationship for a couple with immature, unhealthy coping skills.

Thus, responsible parents of impaired children will handle the crises and stresses of impairment just as any other responsible parents would handle their crises and stresses. Similarly, "bad" parents will be no more competent in handling impairment problems than they will any other problems of parenthood and may find themselves overwhelmed by the crises and stresses of impairment. As one professional stated, "Visual impairment does not turn a bad parent into a good one."

To the extent that professionals are able, directly or indirectly, to convince parents that responsible and effective coping with impairment involves disavowal, parents will become responsible in their eyes and like responsible parents in general. To the extent that professionals have preconceptions about which parents are likely to be responsible and effective, the messages they convey to parents about their coping may become self-fulfilling prophecies.

One would expect to see a correlation between the quality of interaction between parents and professionals and the degree to which parents embody the standards of parenthood that professionals hold for them. In the next section, I consider the relationship between parental coping and contacts with professionals. Having shown how professionals view parents, I will look at parent-professional interaction from the parents' perspective.

PARENTS' VIEWS OF PARENT-PROFESSIONAL INTERACTION

Dual integration is the form of integration that is most consistent with professionals' expectations for parental contacts with "normal" and disability networks. In dual integration, parents are willing to accept necessary and appropriate support from disability professionals for their children and themselves but do not become excessively dependent on such support. They are able to achieve a balance between ties to formal disability networks and their customary range and intensity of "normal" ties. Their ties to professionals are likely to vary according to changes in their own or their children's impairment-related needs. Because they tend to be most similar to the type of parent that professionals idealize or expect, disavowing parents are likely to get along best with professionals and feel most comfortable about how professionals treat their children.

When parents in this study had perfunctory or fleeting contacts with professionals, they probably did not hear much that was explicitly said to them about parental coping in general or their own coping as parents. However, every parent I interviewed had enough contact with disability professionals to form at least diffuse opinions about those contacts. Nearly all parents distinguished between professionals who helped them or their children and those who caused difficulties and singled out at least one professional who had a significant positive, or negative, impact on their coping.

The disavowing parents, like the parents who coped in other ways, did not have uniformly congenial and helpful relationships with professionals. However, as expected, they were more likely to talk about at least one professional who turned the tide or helped them understand and cope effectively with impairment. Also as expected, they were more likely to say that they were comfortable with the support their children were currently receiving and got along with teachers and other primary sources of support for their children or themselves and to suggest a sense of confidence, competence, and power in relations with professionals.

In general, parents most appreciated professionals who cared about their children and them, took the time to listen and explain, explained in a language they could understand, seemed to help their children or them in some tangible way, and affirmed the success of their parenting. In contrast, parents were unhappy with professionals they saw as cold, impersonal, insensitive, unclear, not candid or honest, incompetent, unresponsive, or negative in their judgments about their children or their parenting.

Denying Parents

The only parents who did not cite a helpful disability professional were the ones who engaged in denial, and none talked about a professional who helped them or the child. The father of the baby dwelled on his anger toward doctors, whom he blamed for his daughter's blindness, and his frustration with them for failing to answer his questions. The denying mother talked only about "the stupid people" who tried to give her child special help, which she thought he did not need. (A special educator said this woman was "irresponsible" and had "a cavalier way of treating visual impairment" but acknowledged that the child seemed to receive love at home.) The third denying parent who was interviewed asserted that no teacher or other professional had helped his daughter or him. Although he could not come to terms with his daughter's visual impairment and believed a man should suppress his feelings, he could not completely hide his frustration with teachers "who kept forgetting about her visual impairment problems at school." He said he was "tired of hearing they have not been informed about visual impairment." His wife said she had to go to school every year to inform the teachers.

Minimizing Parents

Minimizing parents were less critical than were deniers about professional support, and all had something positive to say about professionals who had helped their children. However, as minimizers, they were not effusive about the support their children received for special needs, and they did not talk about formal support that had helped them cope more effectively with visual impairment.

The mother and father of a mildly impaired boy were happy with the regular classroom teacher their son had in kindergarten because having an impaired child of her own seemed to make her more sensitive. The mother was unhappy with doctors she could not understand, and she mentioned a doctor who had put her on "a guilt trip" when her child was an infant. The doctor said that if she and her husband had been "wise" in the first six months, they might have been able to improve their son's vision. Both parents said they had gotten over their guilt feelings long ago and felt no personal blame. They even admitted that they were not very attentive parents during the first several years of their son's life, and they had few impairment-related ties.

The moderately visually impaired mother of a teenage daughter had trouble understanding doctors; did not trust them, especially in regard to additional surgery for her daughter; and thought that a new doctor she was seeing for her daughter made her feel that she had failed as a parent. She liked the itinerant visual impairment teacher and relied on that teacher to take care of her daughter's vision-related school needs. However, she noted that her daughter's main contacts with this teacher were by telephone and usually focused more on the social adjustment problems of teenagers than on schoolwork.

The father of the teenager who was impaired by a motorcycle accident said that the hospital staff had been excellent and had "put up with a lot of stuff." However, he said that nobody yet had helped his son adjust. Although the professionals tried to be encouraging, he believed they did not know what to do. In his view, the members of his family were "all living on hope, but [the professionals] never give you a great deal of hope." As a minimizer, he wanted the professionals to be more encouraging than they were.

The mildly visually impaired mother with two visually impaired teenagers appreciated the psychiatric help her daughter received to cope with depression. She also appreciated the special education that had been offered to her children, but she and the children minimized the need for it. Both children had not relied much on the special materials available to them since being mainstreamed in fourth grade.

Protective Parents

Whereas denying parents were alienated or angered by contacts with professionals and minimizing parents appreciated professional efforts to help their children but minimized the need for help, protective parents actively sought professional support for their children or themselves. The feelings of protective parents tended to be sharply divided between strong approval of one or two professionals and deep frustration or discontent with others. A number of protective parents also expressed frustration regarding their ongoing search for services to meet unmet needs in their families, and a few indicated that they learned to settle for substantially less than they originally wanted or expected in certain areas. Some also expressed their sensitivity to explicit or implicit negative judgments of them by professionals.

The noncustodial mother of the preschooler in foster care said she received help from many sources, including counselors, a chaplain, social workers, and doctors. However, she also said she had problems with medical jargon, one social worker who did not know how to listen and was "very judgmental," and representatives of the legal system whom she had to deal with to regain custody of her son. She thought she did relatively well with professionals, despite some obstacles to communication and her feeling that she was "too defensive at times."

The mother of the baby appreciated the counselors who had helped her but was ambivalent about a doctor whom she was "mad at for delaying the news [of visual impairment]" but still "felt close to." She was upset with an ophthalmologist who was "blunt and insensitive and almost made me feel we deserved [our child's impairment]."

The mother and stepfather with a child in elementary school were highly dependent on, and had complete trust in, the child's visually impaired resource-room teacher. They emphasized her love for her students and her ability to empathize with them. Both had trouble with doctors, who were difficult to understand and made them and their child wait for long periods in their offices. The stepfather said he normally got along "real well [with teachers and other professionals] until they tell me I'm wrong and I know I'm right." He added that "college-educated professionals feel they know it all. I have a bad attitude toward professionals [when] they don't give me credit for my experience." His "bad attitude" toward professionals, which was shared by a number of other parents without a college or professional education, reflected the perception that professionals are condescending toward less educated parents or try to impress or dismiss them with obscure or confusing technical jargon. As some of the professionals' comments indicated, there was some basis for these perceptions.

The two protective mothers with multiply impaired sons in elementary school had extensive contacts with numerous professionals in different fields. One mother had moved several times and found that everywhere she had been, "someone stood out." She especially appreciated an infant-stimulation teacher who "was always there and understood." She had a great deal of trouble with a young, inexperienced teacher who had caused her son to regress after the infant-stimulation program, but she thought that most teachers had been sensitive to her needs. Her experiences with doctors were mixed. She believed that most doctors did not know how to talk to parents or children but that her pediatrician was excellent because he was "real direct and was not intimidated by my [son's impairments]." It was difficult at times to get appropriate services, and she was currently having some trouble coordinating in-school and outside occupational therapy. She said, "I [generally] do pretty well with professionals but would do worse if I said what was on my mind."

The other protective mother with a multiply impaired son in elementary school noted the support she received from her pediatrician, who treated her and her son as individuals, and from a special education administrator who listened to her, encouraged her, and was an advocate for her and her son. However, she gave much more attention to her troubles with classroom teachers, who ignored or misunderstood her son's low vision and other impairments. She said that during the previous year, the teachers made her feel that because they could not get her child to perform in school, she was "a lousy parent" who made her child "a spoiled brat." Relations with teachers and the school deteriorated so badly that she pulled her son out of public school at the end of the school year and placed him in a parochial school. She said that even when relations with teachers seemed satisfactory on the surface, she had "an ulcer inside." IEP meetings to plan her son's curriculum and special services typically had been tense.

The other protective parents—two couples and the wife of the denier—had visually impaired teenagers. One couple, with two visually impaired daughters, had had contacts with many different teachers in a variety of public and private schools, as well as with several other types of professionals. They found the greatest support in ties to mental health professionals and relied heavily on these professionals for help with their daughters, especially the older one, who had serious socio-emotional problems. These parents had become extremely frustrated with educators and had difficult relations with a number of educators and doctors. The mother said:

> There has been help from the resource-room teacher in the high school, and the itinerant [teacher] gets things.... [However] there have been gaps [in services]. The older one's dyslexia has been virtually ignored.... Ophthalmologists are interested in pathology, giving it a label, and that's it. I would not say school *ever* has been much help. Lots of dead ends. What did we think we were doing? Why did we put so much energy into [finding the right school placement]? We tried, but it did nothing.... There has been poor communication, a lack of understanding of visual impairment among the teachers at the private schools. There were frustrated teachers and a frustrated child. The teachers blamed us for being poor parents, for not raising our children properly to conform to their expectations. We've had pretty good relations with teachers [in public school] the past year. We haven't asked for much. In the past, [teachers] probably hated the sight of me, and I probably wasn't very nice. I had to explain over and over the facts of visual impairment.... We've gotten satisfied with much less.

Much of the frustration of the first couple, and many other parents, stemmed from their inability to establish supportive ties with relevant impairment professionals to deal with specific special needs. For example, they had to deal with teachers in private schools or in regular classrooms in public schools who did not understand visual impairment.

The second protective couple with a severely impaired teenager had a much less critical view of teachers and other professionals than did the first couple, but they did experience frustrations. This couple, whose daughter was in a resource room with other types of impaired students, mentioned only one instance of a problem with classroom teachers. In this instance, a team of two teachers encouraged the daughter to leave the class because they were distracted by the sound of her braillewriter, which she used to take notes. The mother said that with her daughter in special education throughout her school years, "generally people are there when you need them." She and her husband aimed their major complaints at special education administrators who were slow to provide braille materials and to replace the current temporary aide with one who knew braille. In the father's words, "You always need to put pressure on [the school and special educators] to get things." The mother thought their pediatrician was "great because he is caring and doesn't rush you."

The dissatisfaction and frustrations of the final protective mother were much more intense. This mother, who struggled with the teenage rebellion of her daughter, was sensitive about the lack of understanding of her daughter's ostensibly unique visual impairment problems and needs. She said, "Only the eye doctor was good [because] he gave us the most information on the eye condition." She was upset with doctors who had used her daughter as a teaching tool when she was a baby and failed to inform her or her husband that there was nothing that could be done for the child's impairment. What stung her most was her sense that "we didn't get information because doctors underestimated our intelligence." In discussing relations with professionals since then, she stressed her unhappiness with teachers, counselors, and others who did not listen and try to understand her perspective or her daughter's. She also thought that teachers, especially in special education, underestimated her daughter's abilities and did not expect enough. She said that she would not accept "substandard performance" from teachers and that she was hard on them and pushed them. This woman's conception of teachers, her often tense relations with them, and her desire to push them may have derived, in part, from her sensitivity to professionals' underestimation of her or her child and her idea that they were looking down at her because she was not middle class or professional. Her protectiveness seemed to include protecting her child from the demeaning judgments of professionals and others who she believed did not really understand her.

This last mother was unusual among protective parents because her integration was not substantially biased toward disability networks and her grumbling about professionals was not accompanied by praise for specific other professionals. However, she shared with other protective parents a desire to locate appropriate support for her daughter's special needs, a sense of frustration about not being able to get the services her child needed, a desire to exercise more control in relations with professionals, a sense of being disparaged by some professionals for not meeting their standards, and a desire for more respect from them for her child and herself.

More than a few parents—deniers and minimizers, as well as protective ones—felt implied or direct criticism from professionals because they presumably did not measure up to the standards of responsible or effective parenthood. In casting doubt upon the success and legitimacy of parents' coping, professionals could disrupt their relations with parents and make them feel the need to justify their parenthood to retain their self-respect and social respectability. Such criticisms could also have made it more difficult for parents to establish the ties to professionals that could have increased their chances of living up to their standards of "responsible" parenthood. In response to professionals who seemed to demean or criticize them, deniers tended to lash out, minimizers tried to ignore the criticism, and protective parents seemed to rationalize their actions, but all three types of parents tended to avoid such professionals.

Disavowing Parents

Although disavowing parents also had struggles and frustrations, they were less likely to suffer criticisms of their parenting from professionals because they tended to embody the ideals of parenthood that the professionals generally valued. Even when they disagreed with professionals, disavowing parents were more likely to say they still had a relationship of mutual respect with the professionals.

In comparison with other types of parents, disavowing parents tended to feel more confident, competent, powerful, and comfortable in relations with professionals. Undoubtedly, some professionals, who lacked confidence or competence in dealing with parents, were intimidated by parents who acted like the responsible parents most professionals respected. Furthermore, there were professionals who had qualified interpretations of some of the "moral standards" for parents, as well as ones who seemed to have disagreements with one or more standards. Nevertheless, professionals tended to subscribe, at least in principle, to the kinds of moral themes presented earlier, and parents who seemed to embody most of these themes—and, hence, conveyed an impression of being "responsible"—tended to have the best chance to develop a relationship of mutual respect and trust with professionals. Respect and trust do not necessarily imply affection, but affection is not necessary for parents to work effectively with professionals and to gain the support that they or their children need.

The mother who was going to adopt her severely impaired foster child had to deal with a special school and a variety of educators and therapists, and she said she had "no complaints." She also spent a lot of time in the doctor's office because her child was often sick. There were "so many people to deal with," but she effectively coordinated the many services they provided and kept them informed with regular updates of the progress of related services. Even though her doctor discouraged her from seeing a chiropractor, she decided to see one anyway because he seemed to ease some of her child's discomfort and pain.

The disavowing couple with the blind preschooler attributed their success in coping to the early help they received from an infant-stimulation program. The mother said, "The preschool was excellent. We ate up everything [the director] gave us." Her husband added, "We are where we are today because of the foundation received from the infant-stimulation program. For parents to get into the whole adjustment—legal, educational, [and so forth]—by themselves would be frightening. The program was at the right time." These parents had some problems with doctors because doctors generally did not spend enough time with them to answer questions beyond the superficial. The mother also pointed out that doctors did not deal with the psychological, emotional, and educational issues of impairment and did not offer referrals to other professionals who could help in these areas. In general, though, both parents believed that they got along well with professionals and agreed that "they respect us [as we have] grown to respect them."

Two of the disavowing mothers had moderately visually impaired sons in elementary school. The mother who was married had "lots of trouble" with a pediatric ophthalmologist who gave misleading and frightening tentative diagnoses, ordered experimental tests that were fruitless but subjected the parents and child to great discomfort, and did not know how to talk to parents or deal with young children. This mother also had problems with a special education consultant who made it difficult for her son to get the educational and rehabilitative services he needed in the preschool years because he was not severely visually impaired. However, it was several years after those rough experiences when I interviewed her, and she had switched ophthalmologists and ultimately managed to pressure the special educator enough to get the preschool services her son needed. At the time of the interview, she was able to say that she was "satisfied with special education and regular education once things got going." She also said, "I am comfortable and confident now. My husband does not lack confidence [in dealing with professionals], and he eased the way at first. Except for [the incidents just mentioned], I generally respect competent professionals."

The other mother of a boy in elementary school was a single parent who was moderately visually impaired. She was "not overly enthusiastic about medical people [because] they label, give a diagnosis, and then they're done." However, she generally felt that she did "very well" with professionals once they understood her perspective and expectations for her child. She recognized that professionals could provide support for her child that she could not as a mother and said that "generally, if I decide he needs something and it's available, I get it." She was not one who sat back and watched things happen or who acquiesced or accommodated without good reason. In her words, "I change things if I am not happy. I have rights and I use them, [but] I work with [professionals]. I am demanding, but not too much. I try to see others' points of view." In these comments, this mother described some typical and basic aspects of disavowers' relationships with professionals.

The couple with a blind daughter in elementary school said "they had no problems since [the father] read special education [officials] the riot act" a few years earlier. The special education department became responsive to them after this father saw the director to complain about "a lack of preparation and planning that caused an excessive delay in important orientation and mobility services." This choice of words emphasizes the important point, which may have become apparent, that parents, especially ones who disavowed, tended to expect many of the same kinds of things from professionals that professionals expected from them. The mother added, in regard to her husband's advocacy episode: "That was the last time we had to do that. You don't have to yell more than once or twice. They pretty well take care of things. We know the law and our rights and follow through." In addition to disliking dilatory administration, these parents had little patience for counselors who were too vague and abstract and failed to provide concrete solutions. The mother also thought that doctors "planted false hopes, maybe because they were overly sympathetic [with a blind child]." Their problems and criticisms did not alter their overall positive evaluation of relations with professionals, which they said were "real good."

It was already pointed out that the mother who worked her way from denial to disavowal attributed her ability to get beyond stigma and accept her daughter's impairment to a transitional kindergarten teacher. She said that the teacher "changed my whole attitude about handicaps." In her transformation, this mother went from trusting professionals, such as doctors, with all her decisions to assuming responsibility for decision making about her child. Like other disavowing parents, she had become informed and assertive about her child's rights to appropriate support and her own right to participate in planning for her child, while managing to develop mutual respect and cooperative relationships with teachers and other professionals.

Assertiveness was a quality possessed by all the disavowing parents, and some described themselves as activists or advocates. For example, the noncustodial father was the president of the PTA at his son's school and was involved in legislative advocacy. In relations with teachers and disability professionals, he asked a lot of questions of those he thought would have good answers. He said:

> I follow their advice and go through proper channels to get work done. I use a third-party mediator in IEP meetings. My former wife [who is protective] chooses not to attend IEPs. She goes along with whatever the mediator says. She is doing what she thinks is best, but we don't agree on how to go about it. The You Are the Expert [parent training] program was a big help. It gives insights into politics and being an advocate.... Every parent [of an impaired child] should have [a trusted] advocate at IEP meetings.... I'm going to get what my child needs. Squeak. Squeak.

A number of other parents talked about being a "squeaky wheel" in relations with professionals, especially administrators, to get what they or their child needed. However, unlike some other parents whose advocacy antagonized certain professionals, this father was generally able to get along with teachers and other professionals as an assertive parent because he was willing to follow their advice. He also took the time to be involved in general school activities, such as the PTA, and to visit his child's classroom one or two times a year. The only serious confrontation he had in school was with a former special education administrator who tried to exclude him from the real decision making in the IEP process and give him an "informational IEP" because he was "only the noncustodial parent." He also had difficulty with the doctors who "did not take the time" and misdiagnosed his son's visual impairment at first, but he had a lot of respect for the expertise of an ophthalmologist because "he tells you what you need to know."

Respect for professional expertise and communicative ability was commonly expressed, especially by disavowing parents. One of the disavowing couples with a multiply impaired teenager expressed a strong aversion to "Edspeak," "Medspeak," and other unnecessary or confusing jargon. They said they got along fine with professionals as long as they realized that the parents knew their daughter better than the professionals knew her. They, too, spoke about being "squeaky wheels" who "went to the top" to get things done. The father spoke for his wife as well as for himself when he said:

> I write letters and make phone calls. Principals [and] special education and sight administrators listen to parents more than [to] teachers. You need to be articulate and not hysterical. You have to focus on the whole group [of visually impaired students] and long-term needs. We accelerate pressure as needed. They are terrified more by bad press than legal action. We go as high as needed. We've dealt only with special education so far, but we'd go to the superintendent, if necessary. We are quite willing to write letters of support [for professionals] if warranted.

> Administrators know we are not in there negatively. You need to be reasonable, calm, and firm. We keep interested parties, teachers, principals, and sight people, informed about our actions. We educate teachers about what our child can and can't do. Daddy has the fastest phone and pen in the West.... We are helpful avenging messengers for students, teachers, and principals [who lack the power to be listened to and get resources]. Activism is a joint effort of both of us, but [unfortunately] they listen less to mothers than [to] fathers.

These parents truly spoke with one voice and let professionals know that they should listen to both of them, not just to the father. They appreciated professionals who kept them informed, and they liked their daughter's resource-room teacher. However, they had some concern that this teacher, like other special educators, did not expect enough. They spoke approvingly of teachers who were demanding and taught responsibility.

The other disavowing couple with a multiply impaired teenager did not have the same interest in political advocacy expressed by the couple just considered. They were informed and assertive, however, and made sure that their daughter's rights were observed and needs addressed.

These parents, especially the father, still blamed the doctors who missed a test at their daughter's birth that might have enabled them to prevent her visual impairment, and they retained bitter memories of how she was treated as a "medical specimen" when she was young. They also recalled their frustrations in establishing their child's eligibility for visual impairment services because she had low vision and was not blind. Nevertheless, they remained optimistic and said they generally got along well with professionals. The mother said, "Since she has been in special education, there has always been someone who cared and we could talk to." Both parents liked and respected their daughter's resource-room teacher, especially because she was willing to get involved with her students outside the classroom (for example, this teacher had taken the class on a camping trip). They had problems in the past with another special educator whom they saw as caring but who got too emotionally involved with her students and compromised her professional objectivity; they also were not receptive to her efforts to encourage their involvement in lobbying activities.

Although one couple suggested that professionals respected parents more if they were altruistic rather than narrowly focused on their own child, the professionals I interviewed differed in their attitudes toward altruism and political activism. Parents did not have to be altruists or lobbyists to be able to engage in the disavowal of deviance or to be seen as responsible parents by professionals.

The case of the mother of the blind teenager also suggests that a parent could become a disavower and gain the begrudging respect of professionals despite major confrontations and an uneasy working relationship with them. This mother learned the news of her son's blindness from a "cold, impersonal, insensitive eye doctor" who insinuated that the child was not worthy of normal care because the mother became pregnant with him before she married. However, her greatest battles were with special educators who tried to block her efforts to remove her son from a regional visual impairment program so he could attend his local high school and be in a regular classroom. She "got educated" for the first time about her son's right to an appropriate education in the least restrictive environment at a national conference the previous year. She said:

> When I got tough, I got nasty tough. I called all over the United States for advice. Local people did not listen. I created havoc. When people called from out of state, I started getting attention. I just wanted [my son] educated appropriately. I have a new militance, [but] I compliment as well as complain.
>
> The only way to get things is to fight. If the [teachers and special educators] don't respond, I go over their heads.... Regular teachers care more than special educators [in my school district], but their hands are tied. They want help, but there is no one [with the appropriate expertise about blindness] in special education to give it to them.
>
> We have an understanding and respect for each other now. They know I won't sit still. We have clashes but we get along. We were good friends before the conference [last year]. There is no easy conversation now. It gets shorter when you want things. I want them to explain and help me understand.

Despite the risk of sparks or friction, parents who disavow are assertive in their relations with professionals and may even be militant at times. As in the case of the mother of the blind teenager who ultimately relocated her son where she and her son wanted him to be, disavowing parents frequently succeed in getting the support they seek. This mother became a disavower after learning to be assertive, even though, in the process of doing so, she probably antagonized and alienated a number of local professionals who opposed her. Eventually, she learned to get along more peacefully and effectively with them as they developed a begrudging respect for her. Throughout her struggles, she had good relations with an orientation and mobility instructor who was "excellent" because he was qualified and cared and with a counselor for families with visually impaired children because he listened. She had little tolerance for teachers and other service providers who saw their occupations as "only a job" and did not really care about the welfare of those they were supposed to help.

It is easy to understand why professionals might be unsettled or angered by this mother and find it difficult to like or respect her, especially if they were not highly committed, competent, or secure. She, along with many other parents, had high standards for their performance. Serious professionals may have been antagonized or alienated by this woman's bursts of militancy, or "nasty toughness," but they had to grant her at least begrudging respect and try to work with her after she settled down because she was acting responsibly according to their own standards.

CONCLUSION

On reflection, it should be evident that the discussion of parent-professional interaction has been largely a discussion of parent-teacher interaction and special education. Parents recalled their early experiences with doctors, and some had continuing critical relationships with them. However, after a child enters school, relations with classroom teachers, special educators, and school administrators typically assume a major place in the lives of parents who understand and accept their children's impairments and the needs they engender. Because parents usually want, or are expected to want, their children to be able to live in the mainstream of society, educators, special educators, and school administrators become important because they are assumed by "responsible" parents to be vehicles for realizing this goal.

Yet, despite nearly universal acceptance of the principle of mainstreaming among professionals and parents, there was widespread recognition of its problems and limitations for visually impaired children in practice, both in the school and in the community. Mainstreaming seldom worked out the way it was supposed to, in principle, for the children of the parents in this research. Although I have limited direct evidence, it also may be assumed that mainstreaming problems were compounded for the black and Asian children in the population I studied because their parents typically had difficulty relating to the white-run schools and human service agencies in the area. Chapter 7 examines the degree of integration of blind and visually impaired children in school and in the community and how parents reconciled the perceived moral push toward the mainstream with the practical complexities and shortcomings of actual mainstreaming efforts.

NOTES

1 Voysey proposed that professionals conveyed an "ideology of suffering" to parents of impaired children. The ensuing discussion here of professionals' moral standards for parents is related to her discussion of the ideology of suffering. See M. Voysey, *A Constant Burden* (London: Routledge & Kegan Paul, 1975).

2 Ibid.

Chapter 7
THE SCHOOL, SOCIETY, AND PARENTAL INTEGRATION

Denying parents are "isolated." Minimizing parents display "biased normal integration." Protective parents display "biased disability subcultural integration." Disavowing parents engage in "dual integration." These generalizations tend to be supported by the evidence from my research. However, the actual experiences of parents and their visually impaired children in society reveal that integration, like parental coping in general, can be varied and complex, at times making simple generalizations misleading or incorrect. Similarly, parental attitudes about integration, in the school and in the larger society, often defy simple classification. The attitudes and experiences of parents, concerning their own and their children's integration in the mainstream, are the main themes of this chapter.

DENIERS AND MAINSTREAMING

For the denying father with a baby, school was a distant thought, and mainstreaming had little meaning. The denying mother gave the impression that her son had a totally normal school placement, with no special support. Although this impression was contradicted by special educators who served her son, it reflected a conception of a normal lifestyle that she wanted me to believe and that she may have believed herself.

The other denying parent demonstrated the internal turmoil and contradictions that may beset parents who deny. He wanted his teenage daughter to be normally integrated, but he also recalled the stigma she experienced in the mainstream when her impairment was more visible and was upset by teachers who ignored her low vision. The denying parents had not developed the understanding, acceptance, or supportive ties to professionals that could help them find an appropriate niche in the mainstream for their children.

MINIMIZERS AND MAINSTREAMING

All the minimizing parents were strongly oriented to the mainstream, and all their children were in mainstream placements with limited special services. The children usually were provided with large-print materials by an itinerant teacher, but few of the children relied on these materials. The mother of the mildly impaired boy in elementary school said, "Mainstreaming fits for him. He does fine. It's like life, dealing with disappointments and people putting you down. We'd put him in a resource room if his vision got much worse and he needed it."

The moderately visually impaired single mother of a teenager said:

> At this point, she'd be bitter and hateful if I put her in the visual impairment program. She's totally mainstreamed; her large-print books are in the closet. She'd feel defeated like I did if I put her in a resource room. There's the problem for her of labels in the resource room. Mainstreaming is the only normal thing for her. She doesn't need special services.

The father who was having a difficult time with his teenage son's behavioral outbursts was unfamiliar with the visual impairment program and special education. He said he thought his son had an aide but also said his son resisted the help and opposed any other form of special educational support. He observed that "no one talked to us about special education because [my son] didn't want it." Even if someone had talked to him, it is unlikely that he would have been receptive himself, in the face of his son's opposition. Despite his son's significant impairments, this father believed that rehabilitation would happen only when his son decided to help himself. He saw little value in special support.

This man's experience and attitude raise a question about whether parents of children who become impaired in adolescence or late childhood are denied the education and attention from special educators and school officials that parents with young impaired children generally have received since the enactment of P.L. 94-142. Although this father focused primarily on the emotional effects of his son's brain damage, I was struck by how little he knew about special education. An itinerant special educator told me about her efforts to reach this father and to provide services to his son, but I was left with the impression that if the young man had been a young boy or a preschooler, the special education "system" and the school would have made a greater effort to inform the family about special resources, special education, and the rights and opportunities available to them. Of course, such conclusions need to be qualified by the recognition that the young man had spent 90 percent of his life in the mainstream without impairments, the family had not confronted impairment or special education before their son's accident; the family still was struggling with the son's emotional outbursts, which overshadowed other concerns; and his primary caretaker, his father, was a minimizer.

Although my concern about the "system" ignoring those who become impaired in late childhood and adolescence may be misplaced in this case, I believe that the question remains important enough for school officials and special educators to examine seriously. That parents deny or minimize does not absolve educators and other service providers from their responsibility to provide appropriate resources and services. In fact, the parents I interviewed generally seemed to have to work harder to ensure appropriate services for their children and gain attention for their own rights and needs as their children got older.

The other minimizing parent, who was the mildly visually impaired mother with two visually impaired teenagers, was initially upset when her children were placed in a special visual impairment classroom at the start of school. She became more comfortable with the placement after meeting the teacher. The children moved into the mainstream in fourth grade and relied only on an itinerant teacher after that. The mother said:

> I always felt great about school. There was no special treatment. I was embarrassed as a kid to say I couldn't see the board. So I tell teachers now [about my daughters' low vision]. I didn't feel special education was for them, but it made the kids a little more compassionate. If I did it over again [and even with my daughter's depression], I would do it the same way because they wanted to be with their [normally sighted] friends. It would [have held] them back to stay in special education.

As a minimizer, this mother saw little need for special education for her visually impaired children. She did not mention the educational benefits of special education but focused instead on its social implications. To her, what was most important was to get her children into the mainstream with normally sighted peers. Special education would have "held them back." Disavowing parents and especially protective parents were more likely to see special education and the resource room as a source of important academic learning experiences and adaptive resources that would enhance their children's progress in school and later in life. Feeling this way, they may have had difficulty in deciding whether to allow their children to remain in the resource room so the children could receive important services or push the children into the mainstream so the children could experience a more "normal" social development. The existence of this dilemma may be seen as a reflection of the failure of mainstreaming to meet its early promise.

PROTECTIVE PARENTS AND MAINSTREAMING

Protective parents tended to be acutely aware of the risks and pitfalls of mainstreaming. This awareness reflected their protectiveness and probably reinforced it. Protectiveness and their worries about mainstreaming help explain why so many of their children were in segregated settings. The mother of the baby, whose denying husband had not yet thought about special education or mainstreaming, had talked to a counselor to learn more about them. She envisioned her child first in special education or a special school and then mainstreamed later on, "maybe in junior high school or high school." Mainstreaming was a similarly vague goal for the noncustodial mother. Her child was in a special preschool for developmentally delayed children.

Among the protective parents of school-age children, the couple with a daughter in an elementary school resource room were most adamantly opposed to her placement in a more integrated setting. The mother said she "hated" the school where integration had been tried and was pleased that her daughter was back in the visual impairment resource room at the original school. She declared that "mainstreaming is a good idea but let [the children] do it on their own time. [My daughter] needs contact with her resource room teacher." As was noted earlier, both parents had great faith in this teacher because she was visually impaired and cared so much about her students and they depended a great deal on her. Despite their strong resistance, at that time, to more integration, they did not favor total segregation. The stepfather said that a visually impaired child needs special attention, but he added that he did not want it to be "too special to be out of the ordinary." Both he and his wife believed that their child needed to associate with peers who were not impaired.

Although protective parents accepted or sought special education placements that segregated their children in varying degrees, none favored total segregation. This view was not surprising, because mainstreaming has become the prevalent philosophy in educational circles and the number of institutional placements and fully self-contained classrooms for visually impaired children has declined sharply. Because nearly all the protective parents with school-age children had a child in a segregated setting for at least part of the school day, it means that educational practice has not caught up with philosophy. It also means that parents can easily be confused, frustrated, or disappointed when they are protective, want special services, and have to deal with discrepancies between the philosophy and the implementation of mainstreaming.

The protective mother who said that teachers in the past year had made her feel like a "lousy" parent became so disillusioned with mainstreaming and special education in the public schools that she put her son in a parochial school and risked the loss of all special educational services. Her son's public school experience had changed in one year from having no services to being pulled out of his classroom six times a day for special help. She found the latter situation much too disruptive and was upset by the unwillingness of teachers to address his visual and learning impairments, along with the more visible ones. She concluded:

> There are problems with mainstreaming.... All the higher educators in special education thought up these wonderful things and then gave [impaired] children to [teachers] who didn't want them and never had a special education background. Along with the child, they felt they were getting a mom and six other people who would be trying to interfere in their curriculum. They dumped special ed kids on unprepared and unwilling classroom teachers. They didn't ask for that. One parent I talked to gave up on the public school system and shipped her kid to the [state school for the blind] so he could have a successful year. I refused to consider it.

Instead of considering a school for blind children, this mother turned from the public schools to a parochial school. Although special services had not yet been arranged, she thought her son was "doing fine because they were treating him like a visually impaired child and giving him his medication" [for another impairment]. She was happy because they were accommodative, but she also realized that she might have to return her child to a public school where special services were more available if his special needs became too much for the parochial school teachers to handle.

This mother's solution to the dilemma about placement was temporarily satisfying but admittedly precarious. Many other parents felt caught between having to choose between mainstream settings, where their children's special needs were misunderstood or ignored, and segregated settings, where special services were available. Although protective parents tended to accept segregated settings, they were not necessarily happy with the amount of segregation. The other protective mother of a multiply impaired boy in elementary school had just returned to the area where the research was conducted after having been away for a few years, and she found the school more segregated than expected. There was no access to students in regular education. Despite misgivings, she said:

> Mainstreaming and an itinerant teacher are a great idea for kids who are just visually impaired or who don't need a lot of extra help. But most of the kids, even the ones just visually impaired, need a lot of help [in the early elementary grades]. I hope at some point [my son] will be ready for mainstreaming. My feelings have changed about it. When he was little, I didn't even want to hear the words "special education." I still had a stigma from junior high and high school. Last year, I was thrilled he was mainstreamed [in a different school district], but I realized he couldn't have been on his own. I don't have a bias anymore. I want him in special education as long as he needs it.
>
> I think they put kids in the mainstream before they are ready because it is the thing to do these days, and probably parents like it that way.... I've heard of kids who went all the way through in the mainstream who couldn't see well enough to read. It doesn't do anyone any good. [My child] won't get lost in the system. I can guarantee that. I just wish there wasn't so much segregation. Handicapped kids are in a separate building. They rarely mix. I didn't think it would be that way. I am looking for a more mixed program. I want him where he fits, though—even if mainstreaming never works out. I don't want mainstreaming just because it sounds good.

This mother's comments illustrate how parental attitudes change over time and how being protective may mean accommodating to segregation while wanting more integration and accepting that mainstreaming may never work out.

In the case of the parents with two visually impaired daughters, one also sees attitudinal changes and accommodation. In the mother's words, they had been "beaten down" by the insensitivity of teachers to visual impairment and had come to expect much less from schools and teachers. Although she said that "mainstreaming is the only way" and was pleased that her younger daughter was mainstreamed, she also was happy, or relieved, that her older daughter was having an easier time socially since being in a resource room in a public school, where her visual impairment was appropriately addressed. She and her husband were willing to compromise their academic goals for better social adjustment in special education.

What is most interesting is that the couple saw special education as a solution to their older daughter's *social* problems. Parents more typically believed that they were making a social sacrifice in placing their child in a resource room for even part of the day. This couple, however, was academically oriented, and, for them, shifting their daughters from a prestigious private school to a public school was the major sacrifice. Their case points out, once again, the importance of trying to understand parental attitudes and choices in terms of the context in which parents perceive their children's needs and make their decisions.

The teenage daughter of the other protective couple had been in a self-contained classroom or a resource room throughout her school years. Her mother said that they had "slowly mainstreamed" her, giving her more exposure to contact classes with "normal" students as she got older. She and her husband were aware that their daughter had become more sensitive to the stigma of being in a resource room and that she needed to learn to meet and talk to all kinds of people in the mainstream. They wanted her to be less shy. However, they also believed that special education and special devices were essential for her academic success. The father also expressed concern that "visually impaired kids seem to be dumped in the regular classroom" and talked about his daughter's problem with the pair of teachers in the mainstream who could not tolerate the noise of her brailler and got her to leave their class. Such incidents contributed to their cautious attitude toward mainstreaming.

Mainstreaming was a source of great frustration for the final protective mother and her teenage daughter because "teachers did not want to be bothered with mainstreamed kids." This mother added that she had "problems of dealing with unsympathetic and [unresponsive] teachers and cruel and vicious kids in the mainstream." However, because she believed that special educators "had a mentally retarded bias [and] did not push kids to excel" and because she had difficulty gaining support from special educators, she preferred the mainstream to a resource room. She said, "[My daughter] needs to be with so-called normal kids but [also] needs an extra push from teachers." At the time of her interview, this mother was concerned because her daughter's search for social acceptance had gotten her involved with "a bad crowd," and, hence, her desire for "normal" peer contacts was more specific than was the usual and more diffuse desire by parents for their children to have contacts with peers who were not impaired. Her daughter's struggles in the mainstream led to a "reentry" high school for students who had dropped out or had serious school adjustment problems and were trying to be admitted to a regular high school. Thus, for this mother, mainstreaming probably had a somewhat different meaning than it did for other parents of impaired children.

DISAVOWERS AND MAINSTREAMING

The children of disavowers were in a variety of school settings. Although they tended to share the strong mainstream orientation of minimizing parents, disavowing parents were more willing to acknowledge the value of special services in relatively segregated settings to meet certain impairment-related needs. Although the resource-room experiences of most of their children made disavowing parents seem comparable to protective parents, parents who disavowed were more likely to try to limit their children's time in segregated settings and to view the time spent there as appropriate and beneficial. They were also more likely to feel capable of altering their children's placement to a more appropriate setting, whether more integrated or less integrated, as needs changed.

For the foster mother of the severely developmentally delayed child, mainstreaming did not seem applicable at the time because "he was functioning at such a low level." She was happy her child was receiving the assorted services he needed at a special school and was aware of the "pros and cons of the state school for the blind." Like other disavowing parents, she intended to pursue the degree of integration that was appropriate for her child.

The couple with the blind preschooler wanted their child mainstreamed "as soon as possible" because they were concerned that their child could get lodged in a highly segregated special education setting and have difficulty breaking out into the mainstream. Nevertheless, they believed that the special school for developmentally delayed children that their child attended was "superb," and they were comfortable with the prospect of a resource room in conjunction with a regular classroom, especially for early development and instruction in braille. Their only question about their son's current placement was whether the teachers knew how to assess him accurately because he was the only blind child in the class.

Nearly all the school-age children of disavowing parents were or had been in a resource room and had been in a special preschool for impaired children. However, the mother of a moderately visually impaired boy, who spent part of his school day in a resource room mainly to learn braille and typing, spoke for most disavowing parents when she said, "Mainstreaming is very appropriate. My son should be in as normal a situation as possible. I'm an advocate of mainstreaming." Her son had been in a special preschool, which had prepared him for primarily mainstreamed experience in elementary school for a number of years until the current one. She and her husband had worked closely with special educators to help their son maximize his mastery of skills so he could decrease his reliance on special assistance in as many areas as possible. The boy was, however, in a new school this year and needed to learn braille and typing, which meant that he would have to spend part of his school day in a resource room. His mother was able to accept this time outside the mainstream because it was providing her son with important skills, but she and her husband carefully monitored his time in the resource room and tried to make sure that he was in it no more than was necessary.

The parents with a blind daughter and the noncustodial father also were disavowers whose children were in a resource room for visually impaired students in an elementary school. They also respected the competence of the resource-room teachers, but they, too, tried to limit their children's time in the resource room to the minimum necessary. In addition, they realized the importance of educating regular classroom teachers about visual impairment. Because they maintained regular contact with teachers and the school, these parents generally avoided the problem of having their children's intelligence and other abilities underestimated by general or special educators.

The couple with the blind child expressed a view about mainstreaming that was stated by a number of other disavowing parents. In the mother's words, "For [our child], mainstreaming is real good. She has been [almost totally] mainstreamed since first grade, with some time out for typing, braille, and cane [instruction]. There's a limit to which children can be mainstreamed. The idea everyone can be mainstreamed is wrong."

Parents' Realism

The notion that mainstreaming was not appropriate for every child reflected the realistic perspective of parents. Disavowing parents generally seemed to have a realistic sense of their children's capabilities and limitations and would not have wanted them in contact classes with normally sighted peers if they were not able to keep up with these children. The parents of the blind girl knew their child was intelligent and that her teachers shared their assessment; for that reason, they knew that regular, or even accelerated, classes were appropriate for her. The fact that most of the visually impaired children were average or above average in intelligence was not the only justification for disavowing parents to believe their children belonged in the mainstream. The children's placements typically were cooperatively arranged with teachers, who provided the children with the special support they needed to navigate successfully in the mainstream.

Two children in elementary school who had disavowing parents were not in a resource room. One was mildly impaired and received extra help in a regular classroom and special materials from an itinerant special educator of visually impaired students. Her mother said, "The amount of mainstreaming depends on the school she is in. Her teachers know her now and give her what she needs. [Right now] I don't see more involvement with the visual impairment program."

The other elementary school student who was not in a resource room also received some special support, such as orientation and mobility instruction. His mother, who was earlier characterized as a strong believer in mainstreaming for parents as well as for impaired children, said that she wanted her son "to be as integrated as possible." However, as an informed and realistic parent who was visually impaired herself, she knew that the progressive deterioration of her son's sight from retinitis pigmentosa could require a change in her son's special education arrangements. She said, "If I am given good reasons for special programs and needs, I might try [the special programs]. He doesn't need them now."

Two of the three families with disavowing parents and visually impaired children in high school were involved with a resource room. Both had worked with their children and teachers to achieve a gradual reduction in the time spent in a segregated setting, and one couple now had their child in the mainstream for all but one class per day. Both these couples also wanted resource-room teachers to push their children a little harder, but they were generally happy with the teaching and other support their children were receiving from their current resource-room teachers. One of the fathers stated he thought some students, who were too limited in skills or too disruptive, were mainstreamed so the school district could save money. (Mainstreaming was less expensive than were the more intensive services in special classes, resource rooms, or schools for impaired students.) When other parents—and some professionals—voiced their concerns about visually impaired students being "dumped" in the mainstream without adequate support, a number were at least implicitly suggesting a similar view that mainstreaming is a matter of financial expediency more than of educational philosophy or best practices. The other disavowing father of a teenager said:

> Mainstreaming is a confidence builder. [My daughter] found out she could compete with "normal" kids. She feels normal. [But] who is normal? Special education often means to people that something is wrong with a kid. But kids don't need special education. They need special things or people or tools for their education.

His wife expressed similar ideas and added:

> A child should be ready for mainstreaming and get special help when needed.... [Mainstreaming] will help her face prejudice. Some people don't believe she is visually impaired; they think she's shirking responsibility. We don't want special treatment but want her to be listened to and get reasonable accommodations. Special education is equal education. If it takes special things to get equal education, she should have them.

Mainstreaming as a Prelude to Life

The idea that the mainstream was a place where visually impaired children could compete and compare themselves with "normal" peers, could learn to deal with the normal challenges of everyday life, and could see their success as a measure of their own normalcy was an important part of the appeal of mainstreaming for many disavowing parents. The parents knew that mainstreaming could pose some formidable challenges, and they wanted their children to be prepared before confronting these challenges. However, because they saw their children living a "normal" life in the mainstream of society as adults, they believed that it was important, or essential, to face the challenges of the mainstream with the school experiences and support they needed to succeed.

The mother of the blind teenager pulled her son from a resource-room program, where he spent most of his school day, and put him in a totally mainstreamed situation in the local high school because she was concerned that he was not being challenged enough in special education. She wondered why her son, who had an IQ of 120, was in a resource room with students who were mentally retarded. In special education, all his grades had been As, but in his local high school, he initially struggled to get Cs and Ds. He was overcoming his educational deficits from his experience in the special education classroom, and his mother expected him to be on the honor roll by the end of the next school year.

His experience probably was imagined by the many disavowing parents who wanted their children to be challenged in the mainstream and tried to limit the time the children spent away from it. This young man's mother had to fight the special educators to get him into a more integrated setting. The special educators were committed to a center-based model with a largely self-contained classroom to deliver services to students with impairments, and they argued that an impaired student in a totally mainstreamed setting at a local high school would be deprived of essential services which they could not provide in that setting. However, this mother persevered. She did not want her son "set apart as different in the 'blind room.'" She believed that mainstreaming was "right for him." She realized the risks of lost services from her action, but she did what she did because she "just wanted him educated appropriately." She was like the protective mother who took a radical step (transferring her child to a parochial school) to get her child an appropriate education. However, unlike that mother and other parents who were not disavowers, the mother of the blind teenager felt confident and in control.

I am reminded here of a comment made by a parent with whom I participated on a panel of parents of impaired children. He said: "If you take a kid and keep trying to bend him to the system, you are going to end up with a kid who is bent out of shape." I would add that the child's parents might feel similarly contorted when they had to fight to get an appropriate education for their child that is responsive to his or her individual needs. The phrase "appropriate education" appeared frequently in the comments of disavowing parents. Although a number of protective parents expressed concerns about the appropriateness of their children's education and educational placements, they were less inclined to be comfortable with the challenge of mainstreaming if it presented some difficult, but surmountable, hurdles. Some protective parents actively resisted more mainstreaming when educators pushed for it, and others were willing to accommodate to segregation when more integration may have been possible and appropriate. Disavowing parents, however, tended to want to maximize the amount of integration that was appropriate and worked to make it possible, but they did not avoid special education when it provided necessary support.

The mother of the blind teenager, like many other parents, was concerned about the social, as well as academic, limitations of segregated school situations. She said that being at his local high school "opened his world" and "made a difference socially" for her son. In truth, though, her son's social life still was more limited than his mother wanted. She said, "It bothers me that he doesn't go out more. He sticks to his room and needs more social life." However, he did go out, and he did have a number of sighted friends. Despite its limitations, his social life was much more active and "normal" than was that of many other visually impaired children. In many cases, being visually impaired meant having a restricted social world, even when the visually impaired child was in the mainstream of the school. The ensuing sections focus on how parents encourage the social integration of their visually impaired children in the community, especially on parents' encouragement of their children's involvement in sports.

MAINSTREAMING AND SOCIAL INTEGRATION IN THE COMMUNITY

A high school resource-room teacher proposed that the ultimate test of mainstreaming was "where the kids go after school." [This measure is similar to using interracial friendships as a measure of the success of the racial desegregation of schools. Perhaps even more than in the case of race, desegregation often seems to fail the social test for students who are impaired.] Mainstreaming frequently does not create a "normalized" social life and a normal range of friends for students with visual impairments. A counselor of families of visually impaired children observed that "kids may be OK and [in the mainstream] in school, but they are socially isolated after school." A special educator pointed out that social integration is a matter of great concern to a number of parents, but it is one over which they can exercise little control. Parents cannot compel other children to like or befriend their children. Another special educator contended that social and recreational activities are the most neglected needs of visually impaired students.

We have seen that low vision and the serious impairments that accompany visual impairment can interfere with the social coping of visually impaired children and have considered the teenage rebellion, depression, and general social adjustment problems displayed by the children of parents in this study. These problems may have been partially or indirectly caused by parental denial, minimizing, or protectiveness. Disavowing parents of teenagers did not report such difficulties for their children. However, reports of a limited number of "normal" social ties and recreational activities cut across all types of parental coping. It appears that even a strong parental mainstream orientation and a mainstream placement in school did not assure a child a normal social life. Efforts by my wife and me to achieve both classroom and social

mainstreaming for our son testify to the difficulty of translating mainstreaming in the school into social integration beyond it. I will briefly
describe our experience and some lessons we learned from it before
considering social integration through sports.

PERSONAL LESSONS OF SOCIAL MAINSTREAMING

With the exception of one year in a segregated school and resource
room, in a school district far from home, our son has had a totally or
nearly totally mainstreamed school placement since he started kindergarten. During that time, we have lived in two small towns where he has
been the only visually impaired child in the school. Because there is a
low incidence of visual impairment among children, the experience of
being "one of a kind" is not unusual for visually impaired students. The
combination of a small community and his uniqueness made him well
known. His intelligence, perceptiveness, and outgoing personality
made it possible for him to get along well with his classmates and
teachers. Over the years in the community where we previously lived,
our son developed close friendships with two or three peers, who
shared his intellectual curiosity and interests. Since we have moved, he
has found it difficult to establish close friendships with his young teenage classmates, even though he had no difficulty being accepted at his
new school.

My wife and I have tried hard to provide as many mainstream social
and recreational opportunities for our son as possible. Our son has been
in sports, choirs, speech contests, student government, church youth
groups, and scouting. We have especially encouraged his academic and
musical interests.

My wife and I have learned a number of important things from these
experiences. First, it takes a lot of initiative and vigilance for parents to
ensure that others will attempt to achieve appropriate accommodations
to visual impairment. Part of the problem is that people seem to recognize and understand low vision less than they do blindness. In addition,
when a number of other children are involved in a program, organizers
and leaders cannot give our son even the limited amount of special
attention he needs to enable him to adapt adequately. Furthermore,
organizers and leaders of mainstream activities often are unable to
obtain or provide the special resources my son needs. In choir, for
example, he must memorize the music, and there is not always sufficient time to record the music in advance for him to study and learn it as
well as his peers do.

The second lesson is that despite our strong mainstream orientation, my wife and I have learned that in social activities, as in school, it sometimes is necessary to compromise. We know that our son ultimately must live in the mainstream of society to be able to achieve the kinds of goals of career and family to which he seems to be aspiring. Yet we have found that even when he is accepted by his classmates and involved in a variety of social and recreational activities, he still has questions that remain unanswered and needs that are not met. In deference to these concerns, we have twice enrolled him in summer programs for visually impaired children so he would have a chance to interact with other visually impaired young people with whom he might find the empathy and understanding he needs to deal with the special impairment-related challenges in his life.

Ironically, these opportunities for interaction with visually impaired peers may be increasingly important in the teenage years, when parents and educators may be most inclined to ignore them in favor of "full mainstreaming" or "normal" social contacts. With strong mainstream attitudes deeply entrenched as a result of years of contacts with mainstream-oriented special educators, service providers, and advocates, it is easy to see the involvement of your child in segregated activities as a kind of failure. When a parent sets aside his or her principles, values, and interests and tries to see things from the perspective of a visually impaired person, such perceptions may change. As my son has gotten older, I have found that the best way to determine what is best for him is to *ask him*.

The third lesson is that in the best circumstances, time is likely to be the decisive factor in determining what is possible. We, like other parents who are serious about their visually impaired children's education, have found that it takes a great deal of time for a visually impaired child to be a good student. In fact, as reading and homework assignments increase each year, it has been increasingly difficult to find time during the week to do schoolwork and other activities. In this regard, one may recall the case of the visually impaired teenager who had an emotional breakdown when she tried to do all the things her normally sighted classmates did. She was a successful student and a leader in school activities, but her downfall came when she began dating. Her boyfriend was a fine young man, but dating requires time, and it was impossible for her to meet the high standards she expected of herself in her other activities while also maintaining a serious relationship.

Thus, we parents must be aware of the tremendous demands that may be placed on our visually impaired children when we expect them to be successful students and pursue the same kind of social life that peers or siblings pursue. Although we may enjoy the applause of others who praise our children's accomplishments, we need to recognize that it is easy for an impaired child to be overloaded, even when the impaired child is bright, talented, enthusiastic, and diligent. It is important to be aware of potential stress and try to help the child find an appropriate balance of school, social, recreational, and other activities and roles.

SOCIAL INTEGRATION THROUGH SPORTS

In considering parents' encouragement of their children's involvement in sports, I will show how parents encouraged their children's integration outside the school and how complicated and difficult it was to achieve. This discussion does not imply that sports activities were the most important recreational opportunities for these visually impaired children and youths, that these young people lacked other recreational outlets, or that parents' encouragement of sports involvement reflected their general approach to social and recreational activities for their children. Rather, I will argue that a consideration of sports and physical recreation provides many important insights about the availability of social and recreational opportunities for children with visual impairments and about the role of parents in integrating impaired children into the social mainstream.

In general, I found that schools for blind children, special education programs and the local schools, disability and community associations and agencies, civic clubs, private corporations, and religious and charitable organizations periodically sponsored special events, such as an Easter egg hunt with "beeping" eggs and a circus performance with special audio headsets for visually impaired children, and special programs for children with impairments. Finding regular activities and programs that made appropriate accommodations for children with impairments was much more difficult than was finding special events and programs. Visually impaired children and their families usually had to bend to fit the program and seldom found social or recreational programs and activities that bent for them when they tried to enter the mainstream. Their experiences with sports programs illustrate the problem of finding a "good fit" and demonstrate that some parents learned the same kinds of lessons my wife and I did in trying to integrate our son into the "social mainstream."

Sports Opportunities: Segregated and Integrated

Visually impaired persons participate in a variety of segregated and integrated sports. They may be involved with normally sighted peers in intramural or extramural school athletics; community sports leagues, programs, and events open to all, males or females, or to people of specific ages; and athletic leagues, programs, and events sponsored by local or national voluntary or private organizations. Segregated sports for visually impaired persons may include leagues, programs, or events organized by residential schools for the blind, camps for the blind and other impaired people, community recreational agencies, or private or voluntary organizations. The U.S. Association for Blind Athletes (USABA) is a major organizer of sports programs for visually impaired persons. Among the sports USABA has sponsored at the national level are track and field, wrestling, gymnastics, swimming, and cross-country skiing. Organizations such as Ski for Light and the National Beep Baseball Association have focused on specific sports.

Parental Encouragement of Sports

Involvement in competitive sports activities was a realistic option for children in 16 families in this study.[1] In 11 families, parents tended to favor their children's participation. However, whether they favored their children's involvement or had misgivings about it, the strength of their feelings varied. One can conceptualize two dimensions of encouragement—direction and intensity—in simple dichotomous terms as positive or negative direction and strong or weak intensity. The combination of these dichotomized dimensions produces four major types of parental response: strong positives, called "strong encouragers"; weak positives, called "weak encouragers"; weak negatives, called "tolerators"; and strong negatives, called "discouragers."

It is noteworthy that among the parents in this study, the type of parental encouragement seemed to have no systematic connection to such factors as the parent's or child's gender, whether the parent was the head of household, social class, or even the severity of the child's visual impairment. In the latter regard, one of the families with a blind daughter was classified in the weak encourager category, and the other with a blind child, a teenage male, was classified in the strong encourager category. It is also noteworthy that with one exception, to be discussed in the section under tolerators, marital partners in intact families (interviewed alone or together) were inclined to share their spouses' views of their children's involvement in sports.

Strong encouragers. Five families had strong encouragers. In three families, the mother was interviewed and was a disavower. In the fourth family, both parents were interviewed and were protective. In the fifth family, only the mother was interviewed, and she was a minimizer.

These parents generally were athletic; tended to be realistic about their children's sports abilities; and saw positive gains in self-worth, perseverance, fitness, social adjustment, and personal enjoyment from their children's participation in sports. They were regular spectators or even coaches. One disavowing mother, with a blind teenager, was fitness conscious and thought that "being blind and out of shape were two strikes against you" when trying to fit into the mainstream. Like the other disavowers and the minimizer in this category, she had a strong mainstream orientation.

Although all the parents were strong encouragers, they were aware of the potential pitfalls in the mainstream for their children. One mother tempered her encouragement of her elementary-school-age son to do what he wanted in sports with her anticipation of problems he was likely to face in ball and group-oriented sports as he got older and competitive pressures became more intense. She also had concerns about sports organizers and coaches who were either patronizing or discriminatory. To deal with such attitudes and behavior in a community soccer program, her husband became a coach. Thus, even these strongly encouraging parents were realistic about how disability and the handicapping behavior of others could restrict their children's involvement in sports in the mainstream.

Weak encouragers. Six families were in this category: two disavowing couples, the disavowing noncustodial father, a protective couple, a minimizing couple, and a minimizing single mother. These parents had either positive or indifferent attitudes toward sports and did not actively try to get their children involved in any type of sports program. Some of them had a mainstream orientation but little understanding of what it would be like for their children to be involved in sports with sighted peers. The passive nature of encouragement by parents in this category is illustrated by the comments of a protective stepfather: "Athletics are up to her. I'd like to see her in a lot of things, but I won't push. I was pushed and now I don't care about sports." Disavowing parents in this category thought that sports could be worthwhile or fun for their children but did not offer strong encouragement because they thought their children had more important (often academic) demands on their time.

Although the disavowing parents of the blind girl in elementary school were interested in challenging their daughter and participated with her in a number of family-oriented noncompetitive physical activities, they were weak encouragers of her involvement in competitive sports per se. They were weak encouragers not only because of the constraints on their and their daughter's time but because there were few opportunities in their area for blind children to engage in competitive sports.

Another case—of the visually impaired single mother with a teenage daughter—expands our understanding of the reasons for weak encouragement. The mother enjoyed sports and saw them as a potential ego booster for her daughter. However, she thought that her daughter's junior high school peers were too aggressively competitive. She thought that a ski program for visually impaired participants was a good idea but did not think her daughter would be interested because it was "for the blind" and her daughter did not think of herself in such terms. This mother also believed that her daughter would reject her mother's active encouragement because the girl was at an age when she "did not listen much to her mother."

Tolerators. There were two families in this category. One had a disavowing single parent, and, in the other, the mother was protective and the father was a denier.

Although these parents did not actively oppose their children's involvement in sports, they had reservations about it and made no attempt to get their children involved. They might have been inclined to discourage sports, but, when faced with their children's interest in it, they tolerated it. Parents in this category had a strong aversion to "special programs for the handicapped."

Both parents in the two-parent family said they allowed their daughter to do everything she wanted to and that they wanted her to be independent. However, there were contradictions and ambivalence beneath the surface of such statements.

In fact, the protective mother expressed worries about the physical risks of sports, which were compounded by her daughter's efforts to cover up her visual impairment. Although the denying father made vague statements of support for his daughter's participation in "normal" activities, including sports, he seemed to share his wife's negative feelings about programs sponsored by the school or special education. Both believed that their daughter's visual impairment had been ignored or misunderstood and that she had been treated unfairly at school. The mother told of a confrontation with a physical educator who was going to give her child a poor grade without any consideration of the girl's visual impairment. The general doubts and confusion these parents had about their child's behavior and visual impairment seemed to translate into mixed or confused statements regarding her involvement in sports.

Discouragers. Three families had discouragers. In one, only the mother was interviewed, and she was protective. Both parents were interviewed in the other two families, in which one couple was protective and the other was disavowing. One might expect all the discouragers to be protective, but an ideological aversion to competitive sports accounted for the discouraging attitude of the disavowing couple. An antisports attitude also contributed to the discouraging attitude of the protective couple.

The protective mother with a multiply impaired and sickly son discouraged his involvement in sports mainly because she was afraid of the risks of injury. She also was upset with physical educators who did not recognize her son's impairments and seemed to want her son to do things that could hurt him. Unlike the ambivalent protective mother who was unable to constrain her daughter and was a tolerator, this protective mother limited her child's physical activities to ones that seemed safe.

The two couples were not as concerned about physical risks and even encouraged their visually impaired children to become involved in the risky physical activity of skiing. Thus, they were proponents of physical recreation but did not like the competitive nature of sports. The protective couple skied with their two visually impaired daughters, and the disavowing couple allowed their daughter to ski without them in an organized cross-country ski program. The disavowing father said, "Sports are a bore," and his wife added, "Physical education [and sport] will not get [our daughter] a job. We are the least sports-minded people." In fact, none of the discouragers had an athletic background.

Patterns of Involvement and Parental Encouragement

There were 18 visually impaired children in the 16 families we have been considering. Two of the 8 children in grades 1-6 and 2 of the 10 youths in grades 7-12 participated in integrated competitive sports. Three with integrated experiences were children of strongly encouraging and disavowing parents, and the other was the daughter of a minimizing parent who was a weak encourager. In the first three cases, involvement in integrated sports included participation in soccer in a community program, indoor Nerf soccer, and outdoor track and field for one of the moderately visually impaired boys in elementary school; participation in soccer with her brother by a mildly impaired girl in elementary school; and the blind teenager's brief participation on his high school wrestling team, which was cut short to give him more time for his studies. In the other case, a teenage girl ran laps before school in a competitive program at her junior high school.

Five of the 10 youths in grades 7-12 participated in segregated sports, mainly a downhill ski racing program for visually impaired people in which 4 youths from 2 families were involved. In the case of the visually impaired sisters, competitive involvement in skiing was limited to "a couple of races" over a few years of participation in what their parents called the "ski school." They, like their parents, did not enjoy the competition. The parents were protective, had a discouraging orientation to sports, and tended to view the skiing as a family recreational outing in which the parents also had a chance to ski. However, eventually, the entire family became so disenchanted with the competitiveness of the program that they withdrew.

The family's experience contrasted with the experience of the other family in the program. The two teenagers in this other family were athletic and enjoyed the competition. In fact, the young man excelled as a ski racer and competed in championship races for visually impaired and otherwise impaired skiers around the United State and Europe. The mother of these enthusiastic skiers was a minimizer who thought about the skiing not as a segregated activity for impaired people but as a "racing program" in which she strongly encouraged her children to compete.

The other teenager with experience in a segregated program had protective parents who, nevertheless, were strong encouragers. She was severely visually impaired and participated in sports at a camp for blind children and in track and field during the annual field day at the state residential school for the blind. She also enjoyed roller skating and figure skating with her father but did not compete in these activities as sports. She was one of the two young people (the other was the blind girl) whose parents noted her avid interest in a local professional sports team, in this case, in a pro football team. As a protective parent, who was more protective than her husband, the mother of this teenager was comfortable with her daughter in sports programs for visually impaired young people. She and her husband had also gotten their daughter involved in a variety of other special recreational programs for visually impaired children and youths.

Like the two visually impaired sisters, the severely visually impaired teenager had never participated in an integrated sports program. The visually impaired brother and sister had been involved in various casual athletic activities, such as swimming, with their normally sighted friends. Their mother's minimizing pattern and understatement of her enthusiastic encouragement are evident in the following comments:

> I let them find out on their own what they could and couldn't do. I let them kind of choose sports. [My son] knew he couldn't play baseball because he was visually impaired, [but] he played basketball in the backyard with friends. He was never one to say, "I don't do things" with [my] friends. He tried most things. I [generally] left it up to them, but I encouraged individual [rather than team] sports [when they got older]. Both are good swimmers.

Perhaps the most striking finding is the children's limited involvement in integrated sports activities. In fact, 9 of the 18 children and youths were not significantly involved in any type of sport. Although involvement in sports increased when children moved into junior high school and high school, it was predominantly in segregated activities.

At the elementary-school level, one of the five boys was in a number of integrated sports, one of the three girls was in an integrated sports program, and the remaining six boys and girls were not involved and never had been involved in competitive sports. At the junior high school and high school levels, one of the two boys was briefly in an integrated sport, and the other was extensively and successfully involved in a segregated sport. Among the eight junior high school or high school girls, one participated in an integrated competition, four were or had been involved in segregated sports to various degrees, and three had never had a noteworthy involvement in sports.

Overall, it appears that the greater involvement in competitive sports with increased age was in predominantly segregated programs, and that participation in competitive sports was limited to a few sports, rarely occurred in regular school athletic programs, and seldom was sustained from year to year. The limited amount of sustained sports involvement did not mean these young people were physically inactive. In fact, a number of those who were never involved in competitive sports engaged in such recreational activities as bicycling, swimming, kicking a soccer ball, and roller and figure skating. One teenager who never participated in a sport took part in an organized but noncompetitive cross-country ski program.

Sports and school. Although there was no systematic effort to assess parents' perceptions of the amount of their children's participation in physical education, the parents' comments implied that virtually all the children who were fully mainstreamed and received only itinerant services in school took physical education as part of their school curriculum. Even though some of these young people had difficulties in physical education because their low vision was poorly understood by physical education teachers, they were given the opportunity to take physical education. In sharp contrast, none of the seven young people who spent part of their school day in a resource room for visually impaired students had regular physical education classes. Their limited participation in physical education was the result of their parents' aversion to it or belief that it would take valuable time from more serious academic activities or their inability to fit physical education into a curriculum already filled with special activities to help with their visual impairment. The mother of the child who had just transferred to a parochial school worried that physical education teachers would not understand the physical risks related to the combination of his low vision and arthritis and hence tried to limit what was expected of her child in physical education classes.

Even though most of the 18 visually impaired children were at least occasionally active, their patterns of participation in competitive sports or physical activities seem to be in marked contrast to the typical experiences of their "normal" peers.[2] Some had been in a private school, but none had been in a residential school for blind students, and all but one were in (or had just graduated from) public school at the time of this study. In general, for boys in public schools, sports have been a rite of passage into youthful masculinity and a source of status among peers. In general, for girls, sports have become increasingly popular in recent years. For visually impaired boys and girls in this study, participation in any form of sport was not as significant as it typically is for their sighted peers. Indeed, sustained involvement in organized competitive sports (for more than a year) was evident in only two families—one with a child in elementary school and the other with the teenage brother and sister.

A retired teacher of blind students noted that the blind students (especially boys) he had taught in high school tended to gain more respect from sighted peers for accomplishments in school sports than from academics. This observation seems to mirror Coleman's findings about the male value hierarchy in the adolescent subculture of the general student population.[3]

The cases of the two teenage boys in this study demonstrate the academic sacrifices required of visually impaired high school students who are serious about athletics. One boy was a champion skier in competition with impaired athletes. In his mother's words, he was not a serious student and "barely made it" through school. However, he was not fully compensated in terms of his status among his peers or opportunities for the future, such as an athletic scholarship to college, by his concentration on sports and other extracurricular activities. He was a star athlete outside the mainstream. The other youth had only a brief experience on his high school wrestling team before having to give it up for his studies. He was having a tough time making the academic transition from a resource room at a special education-oriented school to a fully mainstreamed situation at his local high school. His withdrawal from wrestling, a sport his parents had encouraged, came from his recognition of the conflict between athletic and academic roles for a visually impaired student.

Having less sight makes schoolwork even more time consuming for visually impaired students than for normally sighted students. So just as intense participation in sports may be pursued at the expense of academics, those who place a higher priority on academics—or whose parents do so—may have little time for sports, especially on a school or club team or in a highly competitive program.

Need for active support. Apparently, significant and sustained involvement in sports requires that parents actively seek opportunities for their visually impaired children, especially outside the environment of residential schools for blind children. In 11 of the 16 families in this study, parents did not strongly encourage their children to participate in sports either because they did not like sports themselves, felt it was risky for their children, did not want to commit the time or energy to seek opportunities, or believed that sports would interfere with more valued activities, such as schoolwork. Although children are not necessarily fated to reflect the values and interests of their parents, visually impaired children may be more likely to do so because they have fewer opportunities and face more obstacles in sports and other mainstream activities and depend more on their parents to find activities for them. When their parents take little initiative and are strongly protective, the children are likely to live in a narrow social world that barely stretches beyond their families and to have few experiences in integrated sports or social and recreational programs.

Despite the need for strong parental encouragement, it seems apparent that there is not a simple cause-and-effect relationship between parental encouragement and serious and sustained involvement in sports. Although parents who did not actively seek sports opportunities had children who did not participate in competitive sport to any noteworthy extent, and vice versa, in one case, there was strong parental encouragement but limited involvement (for the high school wrestler), and, in another case (the junior high school student who ran laps in a competition at her school), parental encouragement followed from the child's involvement in an accessible program at her school. In yet another case, two teenagers participated in sports despite their parents' aversion, but they were reluctant competitors, competed in only a couple of ski races over a few years, and quit the program when it seemed to their parents *and them* to be too competitive.

If visually impaired children of weak encouragers, tolerators, or discouragers are to have a chance to participate in sports, or perhaps any type of organized physical recreation, they must be exposed to other socializing agents, such as supportive physical educators who will nurture their involvement.[4] Few of the children of the parents in this study had this opportunity, because few were more involved in sports than their parents seemed willing to allow.

Coaches in the downhill ski program saw the successful racers as having parents who were more involved and supportive, who cared about them more than the usual parents but who were not overprotective. They saw the parents of the less competitive skiers as more protective. Parents of successful skiers let their children try, fall, and get up to try again. It was in this context that a teacher, who was a booster of the ski program, described this type of parental encouragement as "getting over the worry hurdle" to allow their child "calculated risks," which involved "accepting the bruises."

Professionals and parents recognized the potential hurdles of inaccessibility and inhospitality to be faced in mainstream sports by children with impairments, as well as the possible academic or other costs. Furthermore, my own observations of visually impaired children in mainstream sports have revealed that these children may find there are not even minor accommodations to their impairments, such as using a bright ball in a children's soccer league, and that they face the aspersions of highly competitive teammates and coaches because they are not seen as "good enough" to help the team win. It is a case of visual impairment turning into a sports-performance disability in unadapted sports. In fact, given that most parents of visually impaired young people do not actively seek sports opportunities for them, the issues of successful mainstreaming and appropriate integration lose most of their relevance.

Parents of teenagers who wanted to see their children in sport (or physical recreation programs) may have perceived that predominantly segregated activities offered the best chances. These parents also seemed to think that the most realistic types of sports opportunities for their visually impaired children as the children got older would be in individual sports, such as track and field, running, swimming, skiing, and wrestling.

Most of the parents either seemed not to care about sports or were worried about the potentially adverse physical or psychosocial effects of the competition that went along with serious sports. Even some of the encouragers were concerned about how their children would be affected by competitiveness in sports. Parents who favored mainstream sports seemed to see them as a vehicle for their children's adjustment to the larger social world, as a means of developing perseverance in the face of frustration, or as an ego booster. Of course, sports can offer these benefits only if it is structured to allow visually impaired participants a fair chance of improving and feeling like winners, at least occasionally.

THE CHALLENGE OF INTEGRATION IN SPORTS AND BEYOND

The sports arena is not necessarily a microcosm of society, and sports are different in a variety of ways from other kinds of activities in the mainstream. However, for children and youths with impairments, sports can be demanding and competitive in the same way as are many of the most valued roles and activities in the mainstream of American society.

When impaired young people are in sports activities they cannot handle, physically or socially, they may feel personally defeated or inadequate, and the stigma of their impairments may be reinforced. Athletic arenas are filled with overmatched and crushed competitors who are not impaired but, like their impaired counterparts, lack the talents needed to compete successfully or even minimally. However, failure in the athletic arena may be even worse for impaired than for unimpaired competitors when they are woefully underskilled, unprepared, or embarrassed because it may compound the sense of inadequacy or insecurity they already feel from the impairment stigma. When impaired children and youths compete with and against unimpaired peers who have comparable talent and performance disabilities in activities appropriate for both, sports may benefit the impaired competitors in the ways that professionals said they could. Other kinds of activities in the social and recreational mainstream have a similar capacity to benefit impaired young people when these young people are equipped with the necessary attitudes and skills to handle them.

Integrated sports may provide a number of the same challenges and benefits found in other integrated activities in the mainstream outside the school. Mainstreaming in school often falls short of the promise of integration, despite parental encouragement and professional support. Teachers and students may ignore or misunderstand visual impairment, and the stigma of impairment can cause cruelty and rejection from classmates. Yet, even the limited support for integration that visually impaired children and youths find in the school is likely to be more than they find in the community beyond the family's personal community networks. Thus, the role of parents in integration may be especially important outside the school, where special educators are not available to facilitate understanding and acceptance or compensate for parental discouragement, indifference, or ignorance.

The case of sports suggests that parents can have much to do with whether their children are in integrated, segregated, or any organized activities outside the school. The kind and amount of involvement in sports that parents encourage, tolerate, or discourage both reveal how parents cope with impairment and affect their children's chances to make it to the mainstream. Their children's success in the mainstream also will reflect parental encouragement, but there are other factors, such as the appropriateness of the situation and encouragement from others, that parents may be less able to influence. Nevertheless, visually impaired young people seem most likely to make it to, and in, the mainstream of their schools and communities when their parents are strong proponents of appropriate integration in the mainstream and engage in the disavowal of deviance.

In the three families in which parents were disavowers, strong encouragers, and able to get their children involved in integrated sports, the parents realistically accepted the visual impairment as a disability, had a strong mainstream orientation, and were committed to giving their children concrete opportunities to develop independence. Many parents talked about wanting their children to be independent and able to handle interaction in the mainstream, but to translate those desires into action, it was necessary for them to overcome worries about socio-emotional and physical risks. They needed to overcome the "worry hurdle." Doing so may not be easy, though, especially if a parent has fears of visual impairments and doubts the capabilities of those with impaired sight.

A number of the parents appeared unwilling to let go of their visually impaired children and allow them to be tested in the mainstream of the school or in the subcultures of normal peers in the community. However, letting go cannot be an arbitrary process. Parents need to encourage their children to participate in challenging activities that are appropriate for them—activities that match the children's aptitudes, skills, and interests. Otherwise, the consequences may fulfill and reinforce the parents'—and their children's—worst fears.

Parents who embrace and try to live up to professionals' moral standards for them seem most likely to get the professional support they need to learn to overcome worry hurdles and become disavowers. Disavowing parents are most likely to understand the complexities of appropriate integration and the need, at times, to accept some segregation to enable their impaired children to face the challenges of integration successfully. They also are most likely to fend off or deal with the warnings or pessimism about mainstreaming that some professionals may express.

A LOOK AHEAD

Parents do not instantly learn to disavow, and, for some, learning to become a "responsible" and effective parent of an impaired child is a long and stressful journey. Parents who learn to disavow may do so, in part, because influential others, such as professionals, expected it from them and gave them the support they needed to understand, accept, and responsibly and capably deal with their child's impairment. Professionals tended to expect responsible parents to face the future realistically, ready, and with confidence. However, even some disavowing parents may become vague or uneasy when talk turns from today to tomorrow. Chapter 8 focuses on issues of transition and the future.

NOTES

1   This discussion draws heavily on H. L. Nixon II, "Getting Over the Worry Hurdle: Parental Encouragement and the Sports Involvement of Visually Impaired Children and Youths," in *Adapted Physical Activity Quarterly* 5 (1988): 29-43.

2   See H. L. Nixon II, *Sport and the American Dream* (Champaign, IL: Leisure Press/Human Kinetics, 1984), chap. 2.

3   J. S. Coleman, *The Adolescent Society* (New York: Free Press, 1961).
4   See C. Buell, "Blind Athletes Successfully Compete Against Able-Bodied Opponents," and C. Sherrill, "Social and Psychological Dimensions of Sports for Disabled Athletes" in *Sport and Disabled Athletes*, ed. C. Sherrill (Champaign, IL: Human Kinetics, 1986), 217-233; 21-33, respectively.

Chapter 8
THE FUTURE, TRANSITION, AND PARENTAL COPING

Even in difficult times, Americans seem to hang on to a vision or hope of a better life for themselves or their children. Studies of American values over the past few decades have shown the great importance that Americans attribute to personal achievement, happiness, material comfort, and social and economic mobility.[1] In combination with beliefs in equality of opportunity, ambitiousness, and hard work, these values form a complex of values regarding success and the means of attaining it that represent the American Dream.[2] The idea that the United States is a land of unlimited opportunity, where dreams of success are realized by all but the unambitious and lazy, is perhaps the closest thing to a national ideology in this country.

THE AMERICAN DREAM AND
PARENTAL COPING WITH THE FUTURE

Parents who aspire to be the "normal" parents professionals encourage them to be and who are inspired by the vision of the American Dream may feel compelled to push their impaired children to pursue independence and success. Many of the parents I interviewed talked about mainstreaming as the means by which their impaired children would learn how to be independent and successful and secure their piece of the

191

American Dream. Even when parents became disillusioned with their children's mainstream placement or nervous about the prospect of it, they tended to see mainstreaming as the answer to success for their children at some unspecified time. The pervasive emphasis on mainstreaming among parents, either as a source of disillusionment or as their impaired children's ultimate hope, helps explain the title of this book: *Mainstreaming and the American Dream.*

In pushing their impaired children toward the mainstream and the American Dream, parents may be pushing them toward goals of integration, normalization, and success that are inappropriate or inaccessible for them. For insightful parents who are aware of this possible contradiction, the confidence and security they otherwise feel about their children's coping may dissolve into uncertainty and anxiety when thoughts turn to their children's transition from the relatively protected environs of the home and special education to the world of adulthood. In this context, the words of a disavowing father of a multiply impaired 17 year old that were quoted in an earlier chapter seem to bear repeating:

> The future is a big fat stress. With all the uncertainties of the future, at least [my child] has the closeness of our family as a constant. We protect—but don't overprotect—with our "shelter of love." I know there is an irony about our happy family. It will not prepare our child for the harsh realities of the world, and I worry about when we will not be there for her. We worry about our daughter and worry more as time goes by. Stress is never more than an inch below the surface. She will have to be on her own eventually. But we are concerned about what she will do, how she will handle her finances, how she will handle her life. The future is a question mark, a big blank. She needs more career direction.

Disavowal obviously does not insulate parents from concerns and worries about their children's future. It is worth recalling that this man and his wife were activists, highly involved in their daughter's education, self-described realists and pragmatists, and concerned about "transition." They knew their daughter's future had to be in the mainstream, and because they were older parents, they knew that she ultimately would have to be on her own. Yet, despite all their disavowal, they still were not ready for what lay ahead.

In Darling's words, the years of adolescence have a way of "bursting the bubble of normalization" that had been created so carefully, and then confidently, in the childhood years by professionals and parents.[3] The encroachment of the reality of the transition to adulthood during adolescence could eat away at confidence, especially for the disavowers and protectors who recognize potential disabilities or handicaps that could stand in the way of their impaired children in society. Among the parents I interviewed who understood and accepted impairments and disabilities, there tended to be a growing recognition, with the increasing age of their children, that impairment, disability, and handicaps could make a difference in their children's future. The next section relates the remarks of the disavowing father, just quoted, to denying, minimizing, and protective parents' views of the future. It also shows how hopes and doubts become mixed as children get older and parents become more concerned about the impact of visual impairment on their children's future.

HOPES, DOUBTS, AND IMPAIRMENT

Implicitly or explicitly, professionals often criticized parents for being unrealistic, for failing to plan, and for being unprepared for the future, which was tomorrow or, at most, a year away for many parents. Beyond these limited time frames, the future often seemed vague and abstract, especially for parents of younger children. What professionals often ultimately meant by "the future" and perceived as the goal of planning was the transition to competitive employment and a relatively independent lifestyle in the mainstream of adult society. Although parents seldom had charted a specific and concrete path to adulthood for their impaired children, they did think more about the future when their children became adolescents. The disavowing father's remarks reveal the concerns, worries, and stresses that can be interwoven with these thoughts, and the dismal statistics of high unemployment and underemployment rates for impaired adults indicate that these concerns, worries, and stresses may be realistic and appropriate for "responsible" parents.[4] Even though questions and concerns about the future were expressed by many parents, the ways that they expressed them and the ways that they related them to dreams, hopes, and future expectations varied.

A paramount desire for their children's happiness or personal adjustment often tempered parents' wishes to see their children achieve economic and social success. Nevertheless, belief in the American Dream, or at least recognition of its potency in American society, was widespread. In some cases, parents made defiant, resentful, or self-serving comments that reflected the envy and invidious distinctions that may be provoked by talk of the American Dream for those who have been largely deprived of its rewards.

For example, a lower working-class and protective father said, "People have spent years in college and aren't any better off than I am. You don't need college. Being rich is not one of my hopes. My money is my kids." This man also resented college-educated professionals who tried to tell him he was wrong and did not give him "credit for [his] experience." His stepdaughter's visually impaired resource-room teacher was one professional whom he respected and trusted. Because he thought this teacher had overcome her impairment and become successful, he believed that his stepdaughter had "as much chance as anyone" to do so. Although he thought that visual impairment would "definitely affect her in the teen years," the positive role model of the resource-room teacher fueled his American Dream for his child. His wife, who had an eye disease that could seriously impair her sight in the future and who had endured some rough times on the street and in a violent former marriage, did not think visual impairment would affect her daughter's future. However, her hopes for her daughter's future focused more on her daughter's ability "to survive" than to achieve loftier kinds of success.

A single mother on welfare said that "rich people are as unhappy as people who are poor. They get depressed, too. The only way they are better than me is because they think they are. Rich people try to impress you. Poor people have more time to care. I'm doing the best I can.... What do you have when you are at the top?" She believed that her teenage daughter's future was "open and hard to predict." However, despite her ostensible cynicism about the American Dream, she said, "I hope [my daughter] makes better choices than I did." This woman did not spend much time thinking about her own or her daughter's future because she had "too much to think about today." As a minimizer, she was not inclined to worry much about the future. She felt relatively powerless to do much about it, but she hoped her daughter would do better than she had.

This woman felt trapped by her own visual impairment and limited education, and she did not want to see her daughter caught in the same way. The American Dream had eluded her, and this had made her cynical and resentful. However, accompanying her cynicism and resentment were implied feelings of envy and regret, and the latter feelings reflected the continuing hold of the American Dream on her. She was trying to reconcile her sense of failure with an awareness of the importance of doing better, and doing well, in American society.

Like the protective couple and minimizing single mother, whose hard lives were reflected in their comments about the American Dream, a number of other parents made statements about success and successful people that reflected their economic and social circumstances and competitive striving. The influence of the parents' experiences with mobility and success also could be detected in how they expressed their hopes, dreams, and future expectations for their impaired children.

Denying and Minimizing Reactions

When parents shifted from talking abstractly or generally about the American Dream to their hopes, dreams, and expectations for their own children, the imprint of their parental experiences with impairment became more evident in their comments. Denying and minimizing parents tended to have a vaguer sense of their children's future than did parents who were protective or disavowing. They valued an independent and normal lifestyle; said little about the specific obstacles that impairment or disability might pose for their children; and, even the parents of teenagers, engaged in little or no formal planning or preparation to ease their children's transition to the independence and normalization of adulthood that they hoped or expected to happen. Of course, deniers and minimizers did not seek special support for the transition or vocational planning because they generally rejected, avoided, or saw no need for formal support from disability networks.

Denial is clearly revealed in the comments of the father of the rebellious teenager. This father wanted and expected his daughter to go to college and do what she wanted with her life and believed that her educational program was pointing her in the wrong direction. He knew that she was receiving poor grades in school and that teachers were ignoring her visual impairment, but he failed to acknowledge the potential value of impairment-related support for vocational or career planning and preparation. Instead, he mouthed a diffuse faith in the American Dream for her. He said he had taught her that she was "capable of doing anything" and was "as good as anyone else." He went on to say:

> I want her to have a normal life as much as possible. Getting a job and getting married will not be affected by limited sight. She's going to do what she wants. Education is not pointing her in the right direction. I don't see her as a nurse's aide.

The cases of visually impaired minimizing mothers presented earlier showed that their own visual impairment did not make these parents more interested in seeking special support from disability networks. One of these minimizing mothers saw her daughter's future as "open" and "hard to predict," and she wanted her to avoid the life of entrapment she was living as an occupationally disabled single mother on welfare. However, as with other special needs, she did not make an active effort to obtain the special support that could clarify her daughter's future and make success more attainable for her.

The other visually impaired minimizer, the mother with a visually impaired teenage son and daughter, did no special planning for her son, who had just graduated from high school. Her son had held a number of jobs in high school but still seemed restricted by his skills to entry-level service jobs. She realized that he needed more education to do better and was exploring junior college, but she did not mention a role for vocational rehabilitation counselors in training him or facilitating his attendance at college. Although she had begun to think about a vocational counselor for her more visually impaired daughter, her daughter's serious bout with depression had sidetracked such plans. Even though neither child had received career or vocational guidance or training, this mother said, "I think they'll live normal lives." The minimizing couple with a mildly impaired son had similar expectations for their child and believed that visual impairment would have little to do with his future. The minimizing father whose son had been in a motorcycle accident also wanted independence and a normal life for his son, and the rest of the family, but he was not sure when, or if, they could be attained. He spoke about vocational rehabilitation, but characteristically as a minimizer, he left the arrangements for it entirely to the hospital staff.

Protective Reactions

A number of protective parents expressed "high hopes" for their impaired children, and parents in two of the three families with teenagers had attended a special conference in the area on vocational planning and training for visually impaired students and their parents. Several disavowing parents of older children and teenagers also attended this conference. Both types of parents generally were receptive to professional efforts to help with planning and preparation for the transition to adulthood. However, even the highly committed and assertive disavowing parents were not completely reassured by the availability of such support.

The protective parents generally worried about the limiting effects of impairment, were less confident and clear about the future, and seemed less willing to face the challenges of the future and less willing to make sure that their impaired children ended up on their own. The following comments reflect the vagueness, uncertainty, lack of confidence, and, of course, protectiveness of many of them regarding impairment:

> *Mother of a visually impaired boy in an early elementary grade*: I try not to think a lot long term. I seek out adult blind people to see [that] they live happy, good lives. You have to change your thinking a little. I get some reassurance from seeing even the most disabled can be happy.
>
> *Mother of a second, and older, multiply impaired boy in elementary school*: Time is measured in school years. Everything is done because later on he'll need things. I always thought of his being a contributor to society, not a leech. Education is crucial because he can't do physical labor. Without school [success], forget employment.
>
> *Mother of two visually impaired teenage girls*: I don't know what will happen after high school. Will there be a niche for the older one?... My impression is that there's not much out there. [My husband] and I are intelligent and interested in finding out what there is. I can't imagine what less interested parents do because we are not coming up with much ourselves. We are trying to figure out about college. If not college, where is the wonderful vocational education? We haven't seen anything. [This statement was made before she and her husband attended the special education vocational planning conference, referred to earlier.]
>
> *Father of two visually impaired teenagers*: I don't know if [our older daughter] will be able to live on her own when she is older. Visual impairment will affect the rest of her life, how she relates to society, the job she can get. I don't know about vocational rehabilitation or after high school. We're dealing with that now.
>
> *Mother of a severely visually impaired teenager*: We wonder how far she would have gone without visual impairment....I want her to get the best education so she can be on her own. I expect she'll be on her own. The only problem will be her eyesight.
>
> *Mother of a moderately visually impaired teenager whose husband was a denier*: We push her to do as well as she can. She has to learn to do for herself and ask questions. I hope it will be easier for her to admit visual impairment as she gets older. She has no vocational education. They're teaching her menial work [in her current school program]. She's not pushed to excel like the nonhandicapped. I want college for her, but she's doing poorly now. They don't teach special ed kids to try for college. It'll turn around for her in the future. She's talented. Right now, she's trying for peer acceptance instead of academics.

These comments show the range of protective thinking about the future and the more specific and detailed thinking that may develop as children get closer to the critical transition point before adulthood. The normal hopes, expectation of independence, and desire for challenge expressed by some protective parents imply disavowal more than protectiveness. However, the consideration of these comments in the broader context of the parents' coping reveals associated or underlying protectiveness. For example, the mother of the two visually impaired daughters expressed normal hopes for one daughter but had serious doubts about the other's future. She and her husband tended to have a disavowing relationship with their younger daughter, but their lives seemed more affected by the struggles of their older daughter, with whom they were protective.

The mother of the severely visually impaired teenager talked about her daughter being on her own, but the daughter was in junior high school, had never been in a fully mainstreamed school, and continued to participate in a number of segregated social and recreational activities with impaired peers. She had experienced one major setback in a mainstream class, where the teachers encouraged her departure because they disliked the sound of her braillewriter. Furthermore, although her mother spoke proudly about her good grades, I discovered that she did not realize that they were "special education grades" [from her resource-room teacher], rather than "regular grades."

The last-quoted protective mother spoke about pushing her daughter and having optimistic hopes for her future. But there was not any concrete basis for her optimism, because her daughter was struggling academically and rebelling socially. It is interesting to contrast this mother's comments with those of her denying husband about their daughter's future. Even though both had optimistic things to say, the mother's comments included a recognition that there were some serious problems to overcome before their daughter realized their hopes. Unlike the father, this mother suggested that getting her child on the track they wanted depended on the child's acknowledgment of her visual impairment. Peer pressure and her father's denial seemed to be encouraging this teenager's efforts to "pass" as normally sighted and hence to avoid coming to terms with being visually impaired.

Most of the protective parents expressed doubts or concerns about the future and their children's capacity to handle life on their own. For parents with severely developmentally impaired children or whose children had serious ambulatory, communicative, cognitive, or emotional disabilities, doubts about independence may be fully justified by impairments or disabilities. The expression of these doubts by parents of partially sighted or even blind children without other severe impairments suggests, however, that the parents were influenced more by handicapist or fictively normal experiences, and the coping problems spawned by them, than by impairment or disability per se. The evidence and analysis in earlier chapters should have made it clear by now that there is not likely to be a simple correlation between the degree of a child's impairment or disability and parents' doubts, worries, or concerns about the future. Indeed, if anything, the invisibility and marginality of moderate low vision appear to be associated with more anxiety and confusion for visually impaired children and their parents than do experiences with blindness. This point seemed to be recognized implicitly by the mother of the two teenage girls, who referred to the "great deal of difference between totally blind and partially blind" children and their parents. It was articulated more explicitly elsewhere by her and a number of other parents of children with moderate low vision.

Although in many respects coping with blindness may be less ambiguous and perhaps less problematic than may be coping with moderate low vision, parents of blind children are not without significant coping problems. Indeed, the transition to adulthood may be fraught with as much doubt and concern for parents of blind children as for parents of children with low vision. Parents of moderately—or mildly—visually impaired children may have to deal with their children's impairments and disabilities being ignored. Parents of blind or severely visually impaired children may have to deal with the fears or overprotectiveness of others, including professionals, for although low vision may not generate any awareness or compassion, blindness may generate too much. Thus, unlike parents who have to worry that their visually impaired children are being overextended by challenges that are beyond or incompatible with their abilities, parents of blind children have to be sure that their children are being adequately challenged and not inhibited by handicapist barriers based on ignorance or pity, rather than on real disability.

The mother of the blind teenager described the struggles she experienced in getting an appropriate placement for her child in the mainstream of the local high school. She became aware of the deficiencies of his special education and his right, and need, for more mainstream experiences to prepare him for the future when she attended a national conference on issues of transition for parents of visually impaired children. This conference was a turning point in her coping, transforming her from a minimizer or protector into a disavower. However, she learned that the road to disavowal was not easy and that the severity of her son's visual impairment was an obstacle to achieving the educational challenge that she thought his intellectual ability warranted.

Special services and the rest of his education were delivered in the protective environment of a self-contained resource room. In that environment, her son had learned to manipulate and play on the sympathies of his teachers and make his school day undemanding. The switch to regular classes at his local high school was a rude awakening for him and his parents. However, his mother felt driven to push him into and through the mainstream because she expected him to be employed and self-sufficient as an adult.

As a disavower, this mother was informed and realistic about the unemployment and underemployment problems of blind adults. With these problems in mind, she was trying to form a clearer picture of what he could do and to formulate concrete plans for her son's transition from high school. However, because she had learned to disavow, she sought information and training opportunities, encouraged, and pushed despite her frustrations and worries. She was like the disavowing father quoted earlier, who worried but knew that his daughter had to be on her own eventually.

Whereas protective parents had doubts, disavowing parents generally assumed that their children would be relatively independent—eventually. The doubts of protective parents often reflected questions about whether their children could measure up to the standards of the American Dream, but the premise of independence expressed by many disavowing parents often reflected a different conception of the kind of life their visually impaired children should live. That is, disavowing parents often talked somewhat differently about the future than did other types of parents, and they tended to talk differently about the American Dream.

DISAVOWING PARENTS AND THE AMERICAN DREAM

Protective parents frequently had worries, regrets, or disappointments regarding the limiting effects of impairment, disability, and handicaps on their children's life chances. However, they also generally expressed faith in the American Dream or acknowledged its importance. Thus, perhaps intertwined with their sensitivity to stigma was the idea that their children might not be able to measure up to standards that they thought were, or were supposed to be, important.

Disavowing parents seemed more inclined than did protective parents to question, or even to reject, the American Dream. The small number of parents in this study makes notions of causality highly speculative. However, it seems reasonable to assume that experiences with severe impairments and disabilities or with significant handicaps can make disavowing parents more inclined to question the relevance or legitimacy of the American Dream for their children because being disavowers implies that they are informed, realistic, and assertive. It also may be that having prior questions or reservations about the American Dream makes it easier for parents to disavow and think realistically about their children's future.

Impairment and Conventional Success

According to the classic version of the American Dream, success is within the grasp of all those who try hard enough. In reality, effort may be insufficient for impaired people and for others who lack the natural talents, social backgrounds and connections, or physical attributes that are needed to "make it" in this competitive society. Even for highly capable impaired people, effort may not be adequate when there is no accommodation or special support to overcome disabilities. In such cases, the competitive contest for success—in educational, occupational, and social arenas—is inherently biased. When parents learn to understand and accept their children's impairments and the implications of these impairments, they tend to develop at least an intuitive awareness of the entrenched cultural and structural biases that their children are likely to confront in trying to achieve conventional success by conventional means.

The example of sports is instructive in revealing what may happen when impaired people try to emulate conventional values of success and outcompete others by playing by the normal rules of competition. The structure of sports is like a pyramid, with many competitors at the bottom and few able to reach the top. Although the competition is fair in the sense that opponents follow the rules, usually the strongest, toughest, and most gifted survive. Winners find that their success is short-lived, with others constantly striving to take their spot.

In the discussion of sports in Chapter 7, I propose that when impaired people with athletic disabilities try to compete against opponents without impairments, they are likely to be outclassed or embarrassed unless there are adequate accommodations for the disability or the opponent lacks athletic ability. The competition will provide relatively equal opportunity only when accommodations make the competitors similarly able in that sport. However, in many sports, accommodations cannot eliminate enough of the disparity in the abilities of impaired and unimpaired competitors to make the competition equal. Indeed, in most mainstream sports, accommodations are minimal or absent. Because highly competitive sports often present insurmountable barriers to most impaired people, Hahn questioned whether their interests in integration, equal treatment, and success are appropriately served by efforts to emulate conventional mainstream competitive values in sports.[5]

Looking realistically at the chances for conventional success of impaired people in society could lead to a similar critical questioning of conventional values of success. Although, as I mentioned earlier, the realm of sports is not exactly like all other realms of society, unaccommodating and ruthless competition for personal success can be found in most areas of American life, especially as the prizes get bigger. It has been said that the integration and success of impaired people in school, sports, the job world, or anywhere else in the mainstream require that parents "overcome the worry hurdle" and accept some risks. Disavowing parents seemed to understand best that the risks were inappropriate or excessive when the odds were substantially stacked against their impaired children under the conventional rules of the game.

There is no question that people with moderate and severe impairments have achieved a great deal of conventional success in American society, as doctors, lawyers, business people, educators, and athletes, among other roles. However, they could not have done so without considerable social support, as well as exceptional drive, determination, compensatory abilities, and either significant accommodations or the selection of roles that required little use of abilities they did not have. In general, though, for most parents of impaired children, like parents in general, less lofty hopes and dreams are more realistic. In fact, in this stigmatizing and handicapping society with deeply rooted prejudices and deeply entrenched discrimination, the attainment of modest goals of a relatively independent lifestyle, a secure job, and a moderate income in the mainstream usually is much more difficult for impaired people than for those without impairments. Impaired people with other minority characteristics face even tougher obstacles.

In this context, informed and realistic disavowing parents may raise questions about the appropriateness of their children pursuing success in conventional terms and by conventional means. The father of a bright, independent, and self-confident blind girl observed that "to her, there are no limitations." He also believed that "she can reach the sky if she wants, but how she does it will be a problem." He knew that "society may not let her do what she wants [and] she has to fight."

A number of other disavowing parents and some protective ones expressed a similar combination of optimistic hopes and realistic expectations for their impaired children's future. In most cases, however, these parents said little or nothing about the conventional American

Dream's emphases on making money, holding a prestigious job, or having an affluent lifestyle. There also were some parents who explicitly rejected the American Dream even as they spoke about wanting their children to be successful or reach their potential. Clearly, "success" and "potential" had less conventional meanings for these parents. Whereas both protective and disavowing parents questioned or criticized the American Dream and expressed both hopes and doubts regarding their impaired children's future, disavowing parents seemed more convinced than did protective parents that their hopes were realistic and appropriate and that their doubts would be overcome.

Realistic Perspectives

Some disavowing parents had conventional dreams, but the ensuing comments about the meaning and relevance of the American Dream indicate the kinds of reservations and criticisms about this issue that a number of these parents expressed:

Foster mother of a severely developmentally delayed and multiply impaired child with serious health problems: The American Dream makes me slightly sick. I want the bills paid, but money is not everything. I want my child to be successful emotionally and physically. I am hoping he'll make it through life.
Father of a blind preschooler: I don't believe in [the American Dream] for ourselves, but we have what our parents wanted. We adopted the lifestyle they taught. But happiness is beyond the material and even a career. Money is a means to short-term ends. We value education. It helps in making choices.
Mother of a moderately visually impaired boy in elementary school: The American Dream is not very important. We want all our children to be good people and care about others. Visual impairment doesn't change my dreams. I still want him to reach his potential. It is the fault of capitalist society that people are too self-centered and concerned with personal goals and not community involvement.
Father of a blind girl in elementary school: You have to be satisfied with what you have. Success is not how much you have but what's inside yourself. The family and relationships to others are more important than material success. I have nothing against someone who strives to be the boss as long as that's not above the family and relationships to people.
Mother of a mildly impaired girl in elementary school: I want to teach [my daughter] something different than traditional woman's roles—of getting married, having kids, having a home, and that's it. I want her to be confident and have choices. I don't see her handicap holding her back. She has learned to compensate.
Father of a multiply impaired teenager, who expressed the viewpoint of his wife as well: The American Dream does not relate to me. I don't think about it. It is not reality. It is manufactured by

advertisers who create myths. By and for what? We can see through the dream. We tend to be realistic.

Mother of another multiply impaired teenager: The American Dream has gotten less important over time. When we were younger, it was an important part of what we strived for. Now we've gotten that and are going in other directions. We are trying to take some stress out of life, to simplify, avoid the rat race.... We have a pretty good picture of what [our daughter] will be like as an adult. She'll go to college. She wants to be a teacher of visually impaired kids. She's making good grades and going in that direction. She'll move out at 24 or 25. Maybe she'll get married. We're not worried.

The dreams of many disavowing parents were expressed in terms of their children reaching their potential, having choices, pursuing their own goals, going as far as they can, and reaching the sky. These are dreams fed by the recent era of talk about mainstreaming, normalization, integration, and new rights and opportunities for impaired people. The dreams became less lofty when parents talked somewhat more concretely and specifically about wanting their children to go to college, to have a career or a job, to have a family, to have a home, or to live on their own. However, the fact that disavowing parents talked about normal kinds of roles and lives in the mainstream, although recognizing the barriers their children would face as impaired people, reflected an inspirational and challenging vision of accomplishment that is compatible with the imagery of the American Dream and aspirations that professionals often seemed to hold for them. Because they were disavowers, these parents wanted their children to be challenged, but they tempered their dreams and hopes with expectations that were based on a realistic sense of their children's capabilities and an awareness of the barriers of handicapism in society.

Professionals often said that parents were not concrete or specific enough about their dreams, hopes, or plans for their children's future. Nevertheless, as their children got older, disavowing parents, as well as some protective ones, were taking concrete steps to get some formal support for planning and preparing for their children's transition to adulthood that addressed impairment concerns. A number of these parents also seemed willing to sacrifice or delay their own dreams so their children's special needs could be met. A major advantage that disavowing parents had over other types of parents was their ability to find and interact effectively with professionals who could help them and their impaired children prepare for an appropriate transition to adulthood.

THE DYNAMICS OF COPING: SUMMARY OF MAJOR GENERALIZATIONS

Although I have been careful to point to distinctive aspects of coping by individual parents, I also have tried to identify a number of aspects of coping that are shared by different parents. In addition, I have tried to show that there are some significant social and cultural factors that may have an impact on how coping forms different patterns among parents. In this section, I summarize some major sociological generalizations that help explain the nature of parental coping as a process of ongoing growth or change.

Parents differed in their coping with impairment and its implications in a number of ways. Some parents demonstrated substantial growth in their understanding and acceptance of their children's impairments and in their capacity to deal with the stigma of impairment. Those who learned to disavow the deviance of their children's impairments and disabilities were the most effective in handling the dynamics of coping with changes in impairment conditions and changes from maturation and the environment. They also were most likely to have children who were disavowers themselves.

Parents do not immediately understand and accept the meaning and implications of their children's impairments or fend off the stigma of impairments or disabilities. They are socialized into responsible and effective disavowing relationships with their impaired children and others. Parents with more education, middle-class or professional status, and a supportive family and flexible family orientation seemed more predisposed than did others to become disavowers. They seemed more likely to disavow because they were in a better position than were others to form and sustain cooperative relationships of mutual respect with professionals who could help them and their children cope appropriately with impairment. It probably was in these relationships that parents were encouraged to be the type that professionals respected and expected them to be.

A college education, middle-class status, and a mutually supportive marriage were not always sufficient for the establishment of ties to disability networks that could propel parents into disavowal. However, lower socioeconomic status, an unsupportive marriage, and a marginally flexible or rigid family orientation seemed to make it difficult or undesirable for parents to form such ties which could help them be "responsible and effective" in coping with their children's impairments. Professionals may help create self-fulfilling prophecies in which their favorable or unfavorable biases toward parents may lead to more, or less, cooperative, supportive, and encouraging interaction with parents.

Some parents who are presumed to be good parents may not seem to live up to professionals' expectations, in part because they are perceived as "too pushy" or seem unable to control their children. Other parents who are presumed to be bad parents probably will have a hard time defying negative stereotypes because the stereotypes inhibit the development of the respect and trust on which cooperative and supportive parent-professional interaction rests. There was evidence that a number of parents sensed professionals' disapproval of them, and some of them reacted with negative stereotypes of professionals.

The cases of a number of protective parents show that it is possible to learn to understand and accept impairment despite ongoing stormy relationships with professionals. However, protective parents also tended to have at least one highly supportive tie to a professional that helped them understand and accept. In comparison with protective parents, disavowers were not as immersed in or dependent on ties to professionals, but the range of their professional ties was consistently more supportive. Disavowing parents understood their own limitations and appreciated the need for critical professional ties at critical times. They were not reluctant to reach out when necessary, but they also had confidence in their own coping abilities and resources. Some parents developed friendly ties to professionals, but most of these ties were weaker, more formal, and time limited. Even when they clashed with professionals, disavowing parents tended to be able to cooperate on the basis of their own power and mutual respect.

The size and composition of the disability networks of disavowing parents tended to change according to current needs and the demands of critical impairment situations. In general, the social networks of disavowing parents provided more expressive, instrumental, and informational support for coping with their impaired children than did the networks of other types of parents. This support appeared crucial in reinforcing appropriate and fruitful beliefs, feelings, and behavior and in creating new aspects of coping that made impairments and their implications seem more understandable, acceptable, and manageable and less stigmatized. The availability of appropriate support in critical impairment situations—of crisis, substantial stress, or major change—enabled these parents to continue coping responsibly and effectively and to help their impaired children and other family members disavow. It appeared that along with beneficial ties to professionals, who acted as bridges and gatekeepers as well as direct providers of support, consensual and mutually supportive marital ties were major factors in helping parents to disavow.

Marital partners helped each other to disavow. Even though a few parents learned to disavow when they were single, they seemed to have already learned to disavow with their own visual impairment or had strong support from professionals who were significant to them. Rocky marital relations or prominent marital differences in coping complicated or undermined the parents' and children's coping in a number of cases. Impairments may not have directly caused marital rifts, but they seemed to contribute to more instability in precarious marriages, and they certainly did not make bad marriages into good ones. In some cases, disagreements about how to deal with their impaired children revealed deeper marital divisions. In stable marriages, both spouses tended to display the same general coping pattern. The patterns of coping by married couples in this study suggested that once coping patterns were established, protective parents in stable marriages mutually reinforced their protectiveness, just as stable disavowing couples reinforced each other's disavowal.

Although marital partners often displayed the same general types of coping, there still were some gender differences in parental coping patterns that reflected traditional expectations. There also were coping patterns that defied traditional gender stereotypes. For example, even among disavowers, mothers generally assumed a disproportionate amount of the parental burden, but there also was the case of the classically stoic minimizing father who was the primary custodian of his multiply impaired son. More mothers than fathers were interested in groups for emotional support, but a number of mothers had no more interest than their husbands did in such groups. In addition, a couple of fathers openly acknowledged that they were at least as "emotional" about their children's impairment as were their wives. Mothers often were more protective than were their husbands, but there were protective fathers as well as mothers and single and married mothers who were relatively uncompromising in their expectations for their impaired children.

In general, for this population of parents, explanations of parental coping based on gender stereotypes alone are too simple, because all four general types of coping patterns were displayed by both men and women. Clearly, the nature of parents' social networks and the dynamics of their support relations in those networks provide much more insight into the reasons for parental coping patterns than do more simplistic and conventional explanations based on single factors, such as gender, social class, or even severity of impairment. The effects of background, status, and impairment may be important, but they need to be understood in the context of more general considerations of the size, composition, structure, content, and dynamics of social networks and the influence of networks on socialization by and of parents.

It is difficult to generalize about the effects of parents' own impairment on coping with their children's impairments. It appears, though, that the coping of the small number of visually impaired parents I interviewed was influenced by how their parents coped with them—a factor that may have been more important than their impairment, per se. Unless impaired parents interact with other people who are able to change the conception of visual impairment they learned when they were growing up, they are likely to reproduce, or try to reproduce, that same learning experience for their impaired children. In the case of minimizers, this kind of socialization could be problematic if it prevents impaired children from dealing with the full reality and disabling implications of their impairment and prevents them from preparing realistically for the future.

THE TRANSITION TO ADULTHOOD: QUESTIONS AND EXPECTATIONS

During the years that I have been a parent of a visually impaired child, I have spoken about the parenting experience to audiences of parents, legislators, policymakers, educators, and service providers, as well as students. I have spoken as a parent and as a sociologist, and usually as both. My personal insights have been broadened, sharpened, and deepened by the many exchanges I have had with these varied audiences and by the responses of parents and professionals to my questions for this research. It should not be surprising that a frequently expressed concern, raised by many different kinds of people, has been the transition from high school and special education into the world of work or college and adult independence for young people with impairments. As is clear from material presented in this chapter, this issue is on the minds of even the most effective and confident parents.

For all of us, life is a series of small and large passages, or transitions. For parents of impaired children, the discovery of impairment usually is a period of crisis that leads to relationships with their children and others that were unanticipated. The predictable transitions in a child's and family's life—birth, infancy and toddlerhood, early childhood, the preschool years, the start of school, puberty, adolescence, middle and high school, and leaving the family home to enter young adulthood—

can be complicated by the unanticipated ones of the discovery of impairment or changes in impairment and disability.

Before concluding, I will share some of the insights about transition that I have learned from my varied experiences and observations in the form of questions and expectations. These kinds of questions and expectations may be important to many parents, but for a variety of reasons, parents may never express them explicitly or directly to the professionals serving their children.

The questions are about transition, but they are, more fundamentally, about relationships between parents and professionals to achieve successful transitions for impaired young people. My list is not meant to be exhaustive, but it should address a number of important issues of transition and parent-professional relationships. My questions are as follows:

• How carefully have professionals considered the meaning and implications for parents of planning for the transition?

• How well do they know the child for whom they are doing the planning or his or her parents?

• How well have professionals conveyed their best professional judgments about the child's prospects, and to what extent have those judgments been colored by personal stereotypes, prejudices, or convenience rather than by professional competence and best practices?

• How much do professionals listen to and respect what parents and their impaired child say?

• How much do plans for the transition reflect realistic challenge along with the prevailing professional philosophy?

• How much power are professionals willing to grant parents and their disabled child in the process of planning for the transition, and how much are they committed to the role of facilitator rather than of authority figure?

• How much have professionals tried to include parents and the impaired child in the planning process?

• How much are they concerned about the success of their careers relative to the success of the impaired child or the welfare of his or her family?

• How much are professionals committed to using the full range of relevant institutional resources to make plans for the transition work for the student?

• I generally assume that professionals care about their impaired students or clients. To what extent, however, does that caring imply a willingness to take the extra time, make the extra phone call, knock on the extra door, and meet the extra person to arrange for the most appropriate program for the young person they are serving?

• Finally, how much do professionals think ahead to where their efforts may be leading the impaired student?

There may appear to be an underlying critical or judgmental tone to these questions, suggesting a rejoinder to the moral standards and expectations professionals often apply to parents. I believe that the work professionals do is a high calling and can have profound effects on the people who they are responsible for helping. For these reasons, it seems appropriate to apply high standards and expectations to them.

The expectations implied by my questions are the kinds of things I expect from professionals when we are dealing with my son. To some extent, they are a summary of themes expressed by many of the parents I interviewed. More specifically and personally, though, they are the expectations of a parent informed by sociology and a sociologist informed by parental experience. I expect professionals to try to do the following:

1. Listen to my wife, me, and my son and, to the extent possible, strive for "informed empathy";

2. Be sensitive to the complexity of parental adjustment to my child's impairment and to parenting in general;

3. Be sensitive to our anxieties as well as to our hopes;

4. Respect the competence and commitment of parents and recognize that my wife and I are similarly prepared to be respectful of professional competence and commitment;

5. Cooperate with my wife and me and with relevant professionals in their own and allied fields and agencies;

6. Avoid interorganizational and professional battles for turf and status that may interfere with serving my child;

7. Be informed about my child's rights, stand up for them, and use them to the fullest possible extent to provide him and his parents with a wide range of appropriate transitional experiences and career options;

8. Develop plans for the transition that have clear, precise, and concrete goals and objectives that reflect my son's abilities and capabilities;

9. Help me and my wife arrange for my son to have concrete and meaningful experiences—of mobility, of social interaction, and of work—outside the school and in the community that will develop and test his ability to work and live on his own;

10. Use local, regional, and state resources to the fullest possible extent to meet my son's needs during the transition; and, perhaps most important,

11. Understand my son's needs, abilities, capabilities, and desires along with his parents' hopes and expectations, and balance this knowledge with professional judgment and integrity to provide an honest assessment of appropriate paths to his future.

CONCLUSION

My son has talked recently about becoming a lawyer. I could see him as a university professor, a scientist, a musician, a writer, or a public school teacher. His adulthood seems far in the future, but I know it is not. I do not know how realistic my son is, or I am, about what he will be able to do as an adult. Because his visual prognosis is uncertain, we do not know how well he will be able to see then or how his impairment will affect what he wants to do.

I admit to the kinds of high expectations for my son that sociologists often ascribe to middle-class parents. I may be demanding and even unrealistic, but I do not think I am unreasonable or inflexible. Like most of the parents I interviewed, I know that my son needs help from professionals. Most parents of impaired children I have known, including the deniers and minimizers, who are often disparaged for their lack of realism, have wanted what was best for their impaired children. If they are willing to acknowledge the reality of impairment and disability, they are likely to seek or accept professional support for their children.

Empathic, understanding, and sensitive professionals recognize that the support parents want and need will depend on their type of coping with impairment and related forms of interactional style, family orientation, and societal integration. In applying their moral expectations to parents, they must recognize that parents cope differently and that parental coping, the needs to which it responds, and the circumstances that spawn it change over time. A crucial factor that affects whether parents learn to disavow or otherwise deal effectively with impairment is the type and amount of support that they and their impaired child receive from professionals, such as special educators, classroom teachers, and vocational counselors and rehabilitators. Helpful professionals will teach the skills and provide the resources that impaired children and their parents need and, I submit, will try to meet the kinds of standards and expectations I stated in the previous section. When they do, most parents will be reasonable and be able to learn how to be realistic.

I proposed earlier that disavowal was a good predictor of effective coping and of adherence to professionals' moral standards for responsible parenting of an impaired child. In a sense, parents are "good" and "responsible" and see themselves and are seen by others as coping effectively because they are doing what *any* good and responsible parent would do under the circumstances. Even though the crises of impairment may be more frequent and the stresses more intense than crises and stresses experienced by parents of children without impairments, disavowing parents see the challenges of coping as different in degree, not type. Thus, disavowing parents do not see themselves or their impaired children as special, heroic, or deviant. Instead, they appeal to more normal or ordinary values and motives to legitimate their own, and their children's, coping.

The disavowing parents in this study believed in challenging their children, and their expectations for their children's independence, normalization, and integration in the mainstream of adult society were significant challenges for those with more severe impairments and greater disabilities. There is a fine line between parental challenge and parental pressure, and in thinking about the idealized challenges of disavowal, one is reminded of the pressures that deaf children feel when their "oralist" parents discourage signing and try to push them into the mainstream of hearing society.[6] Parents may be respected by professionals in deafness networks, who often have had an oralist bias themselves. However, the children frequently find life in the mainstream to be an experience of stigma and social isolation, as "outsiders in a hearing world."[7]

Experiences with different impairment conditions are not the same, because the specific disabilities, stigma, and handicaps vary. It is important to recognize, however, that when disavowing parents cross the lines of realistic challenge and appropriate integration for their child, they still may be respected by some professionals but are likely to exacerbate the pressures and problems of coping for their child. They may become minimizers, lacking empathy for their child's struggles to be the "normal" child the parents seem to want and expect. Thus, even disavowing parents may have a mainstream bias that may be difficult for their children to reconcile with their awkward and uncomfortable interaction with peers who are not impaired.

In view of these possible problems in the mainstream, parents who are more protective and, thus, more readily accept segregated experiences for their children may seem more responsive to their children's needs than do disavowing parents. However, the paradox of protectiveness is that it may make life easier for impaired children but reinforce the patterns of segregation and dependence that perpetuate stigma, handicapism, and the unequal access of impaired people to the American Dream—and to more modest forms of success in the mainstream.

Disavowers cope under the constraints of a culture and society that include elements of stigma and handicapism, alongside the American Dream and expectations of normal parenthood. However, the assertiveness and challenge with which they responsibly push their impaired children into the mainstream also may ultimately help to create a mainstream in which stigma is defused, handicapist barriers drop, and people with impairments feel more welcome, comfortable, and "normal" on their own terms.

Thus, the irony of the socialization that creates disavowal and related forms of coping is that parents learn to cope according to the normal standards of responsible and effective parenting and, in doing so, ultimately create challenges to institutionalized social and cultural patterns that inappropriately restrict their impaired children. It may be that as more and more parents learn to disavow and teach their children to disavow, they will gradually produce a society in which the difference of impairment is less problematic and salient. Just as parental coping is socialized by society, so too may society bear the socializing imprint of disavowing parents and their disavowing children and become less stigmatizing and handicapist and more accommodating to people with impairments and disabilities.

NOTES

1 See, for example, R. M. Williams, Jr., *American Society* (New York: Free Press, 1970); M. Rokeach, *The Nature of Human Values* (New York: Free Press, 1973); and K. L. Schlozman and S. Verba, *Insult to Injury* (Cambridge, MA: Harvard University Press, 1979). More recently, the clash between individualistic values and a commitment to the social or public good has been analyzed by R. N. Bellah, R. Madsen, W. M. Sullivan, A. Swidler, and S. M. Tipton, *Habits of the Heart: Individualism and Commitment in American Life* (Berkeley: University of California Press, 1985).

2 This discussion of the American Dream draws heavily on H. L. Nixon II, *Sport and the American Dream* (Champaign, IL: Leisure Press/Human Kinetics, 1984).

3 R. B. Darling, "Parent-Professional Interaction: The Roots of Misunderstanding," in *The Family with a Handicapped Child: Understanding and Treatment*, ed. M. Seligman (Orlando, FL: Grune & Stratton, 1983), 112-113.

4 See F. Bowe, *Handicapping America: Barriers to Disabled People* (New York: Harper & Row, 1978). See also *Labor Force Status and Other Characteristics of Persons with a Work Disability: 1981-1988* (Washington, DC: Bureau of the Census, July 1989).

5   H. Hahn, "Sports and the Political Movement of Disabled Persons: Examining Nondisabled Social Values," *Arena Review* 8 (March 1984): 1-11.

6   See J. E. Nash and A. Nash, *Deafness in Society* (Lexington, MA: Lexington Books, 1981), chap. 5.

7   See P. C. Higgins, *Outsiders in a Hearing World: A Sociology of Deafness* (Beverly Hills, CA: Sage Publications, 1980).

Appendix 1
INTERVIEW GUIDE: PARENTS

The interview guide appearing in this appendix consists of the questions parents were asked as part of the study. Both the major topics and the specific questions covered in the parent interviews are shown. Every attempt was made during the interviews to preserve a consistent order and wording in the questions asked, but questions were modified or deleted when circumstances rendered their original wording inappropriate. In addition, questions were sometimes restated using different wording for the purposes of clarity or to encourage rapport or expansiveness. Follow-up questions were used when they were deemed appropriate or necessary to obtain an initial response to encourage parents to elaborate on initial answers. Some spontaneous follow-up questions used in individual circumstances are not included here.

Words and questions appearing in parentheses were reminders to the interviewer (i.e., the author) or were follow-up items. Notations such as "Cohesion" and "Adaptability" that appear before the questions were not part of the interviews but denoted for the interviewer the issue at hand. Questions that are listed as distinct items under a heading, such as those appearing under "Perceived Responsibility and Power" in the category of "Parental Coping Factors," reflect the interviewer's initial sense that they were conceptually distinct. Questions that appear together as part of one item, such as those relating to "The Future" in the same category, were thought to be extensions of the same basic idea.

A. Family Context Factors

1. Family Size and Composition
   a. Could you tell me:
      i. The number of children you have?
      ii. The age and sex of each one?
      iii. Whether the children have another parent living at home?
      iv. Whether any of the children was adopted?
      v. Whether anyone other than your visually impaired child has a disability or handicap?
   b. Could you tell me how old you are?

2. Family Background and Resources
   a. How long have you lived in your present home and community?
   b. *If a single parent*: How long have you been a single parent?
      If a couple: Is this your first marriage, and how long have you been living with your spouse?
   c. How would you describe your own and your spouse's occupation(s)?
   d. How many years of school have you had?
   e. How would you describe your family's financial situation? Do you have enough money to get what you and your family need?
   f. (Note ethnicity and race.)

3. Family Life and Routines
   a. Cohesion: How close do you think your family is? (Do you do things together? Get along with each other?)
   b. Adaptability: How well do you and your family handle changes? (Welcome or try to avoid them? Help each other through them?)
   c. Communication: How much do you talk and try to listen to each other in your family? (Are you honest with each other?)

4. Family Culture
   a. What are the most important things you want to teach your children as they are growing up?
   b. How important has organized religion or a belief in God been in your life?

c. Does the American Dream mean much to you or your family?

B. Impairment Context Factors

1. Severity of Visual Impairment
   a. I should explain that when I say "visually impaired," I mean "blind" or "partially sighted" or having "low vision." With that in mind, how "visually impaired" is [name of the child]? How well can she [he] see?
   b. Does [name] have any other significant impairments or disabilities?

2. Background and Onset
   a. Could you tell me when [name] first became visually impaired and how you learned about it?
   b. Has [name's] vision changed much since she [he] first became visually impaired?

3. Diagnosis: Is there a name for your child's eye condition, and how sure are you and the doctors about what it is and what caused it?

4. Prognosis: Do you expect your child's vision to change much as she [he] gets older? Is this something you think about much?

C. Parental Coping Factors

1. Impairment Awareness and Understanding: How well do you understand [name's] visual impairment and how it affects her [him]?

2. Perceived Responsibility and Power
   a. Do you ever blame yourself or anyone else for [name's] visual impairment?
   b. Do you feel there is much you can do about her [his] visual impairment?

3. Self-conception and Commitments
   a. How well do you think you are doing as a parent?
   b. Have you made any sacrifices in your life for [name]?

4. Child Care and Control

    a. How much of your time is spent taking care of the kids?

    b. How do you handle discipline with them, especially [name]?

5. Problems and Pressures

    a. Are you having or have you had any special problems dealing with [name's] visual impairment? If so, how much have your spouse and the other children helped you deal with these problems?

    b. How well are your spouse and [name's] brothers and sisters handling [name's] visual impairment?

    c. How "normal" do you think your life is?

    d. How much do you feel you are in charge of your life?

6. The Future: How much have you thought about or planned for [name's] future: As a teenager? As an adult? (Being employed? Living on her [his] own? Getting married and having children?)

7. Parental Role Differentiation

    a. Who makes the decisions in your family about [name]?

    b. Who is the most concerned with people's feelings in your family?

    c. Who is the most concerned with getting things done and solving problems in your family?

D. Societal Integration

1. School

    a. Could you tell me about [name's] school experiences and how you have been involved with them? (School? Grade? Placement? Special education arrangements?)

    b. How do you feel about her [his] school situation?

    c. How does mainstreaming apply to [name's] situation?

2. Child's Social and Recreational Activities

    a. Does [name] have friends she [he] sees after school? Are they sighted or visually impaired?

    b. Does [name] seem to have enough opportunities for recreational or social activities after school?

    c. Does [name] participate in sports? Do you like to see her [him] involved in sports? What kinds seem most appropriate for her [him]?

d. Would you like to see [name] date or date more often?

3. Parental Integration
   a. How comfortable do you feel in public places or anywhere outside the home with [name]?
   b. What do you think about parent support groups and similar kinds of groups or activities for parents of visually impaired children or parents of other types of impaired children?
   c. What is the best way to make sure that [name] gets what she [he] deserves in education and other areas of life?
   d. Do you think your own social life has been affected by [name's] visual impairment?

E. Social Support

1. Needs
   a. What are the most important things [name] needs as a visually impaired child, and is she [he] getting what is needed?
   b. What are the most important things you need as a parent of a visually impaired child, and are you getting what you need?

2. Formal Support
   a. What do you think of the people who provide services to [name] and you? Who has helped you the most? Who has caused you the most trouble? (Doctors and medical professionals? Educators—general, special, vocational? Orientation and mobility teachers? Rehabilitation teachers? Social workers, family counselors, therapists? People who do parent training? Lawyers or advocates? Anyone else?)
   b. When have you gone or would you go outside your family for professional help for you or your child regarding visual impairment or adjustment to it?
   c. Have you had any difficulties finding services to help [name] or you deal with [name's] visual impairment?
   d. How well do you get along with the teachers and others who provide services for [name]?

3. General and Informal Support
   a. Who is the first person you turn to for help when [name] has a problem? When you have a problem with [name]?

b. How much help or support regarding [name] and her [his] visual impairment do you get from grandparents? Other relatives? Neighbors? Friends? Church or community leaders?

c. Do you think you have enough contact with visually impaired children? Visually impaired adults? Other parents of visually impaired children?

Are there any questions or other things you would like to add?

Appendix 2
INTERVIEW GUIDE: PROFESSIONALS

Professionals and some volunteers were interviewed as part of the study to gain important additional perspectives on parental coping and to learn how professionals viewed parent-professional interaction. The interview guide appearing in this appendix elicited information from the individual about personal and professional attributes and job responsibilities and contacts with visually impaired children and their parents. However, it focused primarily on questions concerning the coping, societal integration, and social support received by parents. These questions were intended to relate to the items in sections C, D, and E in the interview guide used with parents.

The guide presented in this appendix was used in a more abbreviated form in a number of cases. The items were frequently modified or deleted, according to the job or program responsibilities of the persons being interviewed. Thus, the format for the interviews with professionals and volunteers tended to be more flexible than that used for the interviews with parents.

Interviewee's position and organizational affiliation:

Note Impairments_____ Gender_____ Minority status_____

A. Professional Responsibilities and Contacts

1. What are your main responsibilities in your job as they relate to visual impairment?

2. What is the nature of your contacts with visually impaired children and their parents?

B. Parental Coping: How well do the parents you know cope with having a visually impaired child?

1. What is their understanding of visual impairment and its implications for their child's development and future? How does low vision compare with blindness in affecting parental coping?

2. What are the significant differences between mothers and fathers in coping? What are the effects of the children's visual impairments on the marriages?

3. What are the effects of visual impairment on child rearing for control and discipline?

4. Are parents ready for the future and transition?

C. Societal Integration: How much do parents get involved in activities and organizations that could help their visually impaired children or themselves as parents?

1. Are they effective advocates?

2. What do you know about parent support groups, and how much do you encourage them?

3. To what extent do parents encourage their children's involvement in sports and other recreational activities after school, in the community? What have you observed about protectiveness and risk taking?

4. What do you think about mainstreaming and how parents handle it?

5. What do you think about the isolation of parents? Have you observed mother-father differences in relation to isolation or in other things regarding their visually impaired children?

D. **Social Support: What are the major needs of parents of visually impaired children in your community, and how can you and others best help them to meet their needs?**

1. Are there mother-father differences in need for support?

2. What do you think and what have you observed regarding parent-professional cooperation?

3. What are the best sources of support for mothers and fathers—formal or informal?

4. What do you think and what have you observed regarding cooperation among professionals and coordination of services?

5. What do you think and what have you observed regarding professionals' accessibility to parents?

Is there anything else you would like to say about parents, visually impaired children, or visual impairment services?

Appendix 3

PROFILES OF FAMILIES

This appendix provides brief profiles of the families interviewed and the conditions of impairment they faced. The information is intended to underscore the distinctiveness of the circumstances of coping experienced by the parents in this study. To protect parents' identities, the profiles omit certain facts, such as residential location, age of the impaired child, and age and gender of siblings, and present other information, including the age and occupations of parents, in general terms.

Families with Preschool Children

Family 1 (mother only interviewed)
- A. Parental age: 20s.
- B. Impaired child: Son in foster care (because of parental negligence and abuse), with severe visual impairment accompanied by neurological and emotional impairments.[1]
  Visual impairment appeared at age 2 from head injury caused by paternal abuse. Uncertain prognosis but signs of slight improvement in vision.
- C. Siblings: None.

D. Marital/parental situation: Separated. Mother in noncustodial relationship with child and seeking to regain custody by improving
parental skills through training, counseling, and regular supervised contact with her child. No recent direct ties of this mother
and her child to the husband/father.

E. Economic status: Mother unemployed and living with her parents.[2] Self-described as "needy" and looking for employment.

F. Education: High school graduate with vocational training.

Family 2 (full-length interview by telephone with mother only)

A. Parental age: 30s.

B. Impaired child: Foster son with irreversible congenital blindness
accompanied by severe congenital developmental and health
impairments. Very uncertain health prognosis.

C. Siblings: 3.

D. Marital/parental situation: Married. Foster parents of impaired
child for 4 years, pursuing adoption. Consensual family decision
(including other children) to adopt.

E. Economic status: Working class. Financial situation perceived as
"OK but always less than adequate." Mother supplements family
income with low-paying home work.

F. Education: Some college and vocational training.

Family 3 (both parents interviewed)

A. Parental ages: Mother, 20s; father, 30s.

B. Impaired child: Infant daughter with apparently severe visual
impairment accompanied by severe physiological impairments.
Sudden onset of visual impairment at 5 months because of excessive oxygen related to aftercare for surgery for other impairments.
Uncertain prognosis for visual impairment, but expected recovery
from health-threatening impairments within the next six months.

C. Siblings: 3 (from father's previous marriage).

D. Marital/parental situation: Very strained marriage. Husband and
wife were both formerly married. Father has 3 children from former marriage living in the family a significant amount of time.
Mother is more strongly tied to impaired child than to husband or
stepchildren.

E. Economic status: Husband is the owner of a small shop, a new business on a precarious financial footing made more precarious by

substantial medical costs for infant. Financial status of family perceived as "tight" by mother and raised serious concerns for father. Mother not currently employed.

   F. Education: Mother did not complete high school. Father is a high school graduate.

Family 4 (both parents interviewed)

   A. Parental ages: Mother and father, 30s.

   B. Impaired child: Son born without eyes and with neurological growth delay that became apparent after first two years.

   C. Siblings: None, but mother is pregnant.

   D. Marital/parental situation: Highly consensual marriage with shared commitment to the child.

   E. Economic status: Middle-class professional. "Above-average affluence for our ages" (according to both parents). Mother employed part time, with career goals deferred until after motherhood.

   F. Education: College graduates. Husband has a professional degree.

Families with Children in Elementary School

Family 5 (mother only interviewed)

   A. Parental age: 30s.

   B. Impaired child: Son with moderate congenital low vision that was first recognized at 18 months. Uncertain prognosis but probable deterioration of sight.

   C. Siblings: 2.

   D. Marital/parental situation: Highly consensual marriage with shared commitment to the impaired child.

   E. Economic status: Middle-class professional with "comfortable" financial status. Mother deferred career goals until after motherhood and is not currently employed.

   F. Education: Both parents have graduate degrees.

Family 6 (both parents interviewed)

   A. Parental ages: Mother and stepfather, 20s.

   B. Impaired child: Daughter with moderate congenital low vision discovered at birth. Uncertain prognosis.

C. Siblings: 1.

D. Marital/parental situation: Consensual marriage. Both children are from the mother's previous marriage. Mother was abused in first marriage and retained no ties with former husband. Shared commitment of mother and stepfather to children.

E. Economic status: Low-income working class. Both parents think they were doing "OK," but husband thinks "things could be better." For a while before her current marriage, the mother lived on the street with her impaired child.

F. Education: Mother briefly attended high school. Stepfather is a high school graduate.

Family 7 (mother only interviewed)

A. Parental age: 30s.

B. Impaired child: Son with moderate but worsening low vision caused by retinitis pigmentosa. "Complete blindness almost certain, but path uncertain."

C. Siblings: 1 (with specific learning impairment).

D. Marital/parental situation: Single parent. Visually impaired child's father died during child's infancy, and marriage to father of second child was annulled shortly after it occurred. Almost absent ties to second husband.

E. Economic status: Precarious middle class. Independent entrepreneur with unstable financial backing but perception that "there has been and always will be enough [money]." Current lifestyle comfortable but mobile.

F. Education: College graduate.

Family 8 (both parents interviewed)

A. Parental ages: Mother and father, 30s.

B. Impaired child: Daughter with blindness from removal of eyes by surgery related to early childhood disease. Eye surgery occurred during extended period of medical intervention in the preschool years to address the disease causing the loss of eyes. Some concern about recurrence of disease.

C. Siblings: 1.

D. Marital/parental situation: Highly consensual marriage with shared commitment to child but strains on both parents from dual-career time pressures.

E. Economic status: Middle-class professional with dual-career situation. "Plenty" of financial resources (according to both parents).
F. Education: Mother is a college graduate. Father attended college.

Family 9 (partial [45-minute telephone] interview of mother)
A. Parental age: Not given.
B. Impaired child: Son with moderate low vision having gradual onset. Mother relatively uninformed about the diagnosis and prognosis because of intentional avoidance of contacts with eye and vision specialists.
C. Siblings: Not given.
D. Marital/parental situation: Single parent living with her mother. Apparently little contact with child's father.
E. Economic status: Lower class.
F. Education: Did not complete high school.

Family 10 (both parents interviewed)
A. Parental ages: Mother and father, 30s.
B. Impaired child: Son with mild low vision discovered within past 3 years. Parents somewhat unclear about the nature of the diagnosis but believe condition will not improve. Condition was moderate without glasses but improved to mild with correction.
C. Siblings: None.
D. Marital/parental situation: Recently reunited after separation. Marriage still precarious, but couple is trying. Mother is more involved with child than father, but neither had major parental commitment during the years before the separation.
E. Economic status: Working class with dual-earner situation. "Sometimes fine, sometimes strapped" (according to mother). Father felt "better off than a lot of people."
F. Education: Mother is a high school graduate. Father took some college courses and had vocational training.

Family 11 (mother only interviewed)
A. Parental age: 20s.
B. Impaired child: Daughter with congenital low vision that gradually improved from moderate to mild with medical intervention. Further improvement uncertain.
C. Siblings: 1 (with specific learning disability).

D. Marital/parental situation: Recently remarried with 2 children from her former marriage and 1 child from husband's former marriage who did not regularly live with them. Mother and her 2 children (including her visually impaired daughter) have weak and limited contact with father/former husband. Stepfather involved with children, but parental responsibilities largely rest with mother.

E. Economic status: Working class with alternating financial comfort and tightness because of seasonal nature of husband's work. Dual-earner situation.

F. Education: Mother took some college courses.

Family 12 (mother only interviewed)

A. Parental age: 30s.

B. Impaired child: Son with severe low vision and accompanying neurological impairment. Initial diagnosis of blindness revised to limited partial sight after nearly 3 years. Uncertain prognosis.

C. Siblings: 1.

D. Marital/parental situation: Stable marriage. Father involved with children, but parental responsibilities (especially for impaired child) largely rest with mother.

E. Economic status: Middle class with husband a businessman in a new job. Mother said financial status looked "good for the near future," but she wants more money for private special services for her impaired child. Mother deferred business career until after motherhood and is not currently employed.

F. Education: College-educated mother and father.

Family 13 (father only interviewed)

A. Parental age: 30s.

B. Impaired child: Son with moderate congenital low vision discovered gradually in infancy. Relatively sure of no future change in visual condition.

C. Siblings: 2.

D. Marital/parental situation: Divorced noncustodial father with visitation rights and strong commitment to children. Strained relationship with former wife, including disagreements over custodial rights and parental roles (especially regarding child's impairment).

E. Economic status: Unstable middle-class situation strained because of investment in new business. Limited child support that father is able to provide is a continual source of tension between parents. Father recognizes his inadequacies as a financial provider but is committed to his new business venture.

F. Education: Community college.

Family 14 (mother only interviewed)

A. Parental age: 40s.

B. Impaired child: Son with moderate low vision and accompanying learning and physical impairments. Gradual discovery of visual impairment over months. History of some improvement of sight with uncertain prognosis of future improvement.

C. Siblings: None.

D. Marital/parental situation: Stable marriage with responsibility for impaired child left entirely to mother.

E. Economic status: Middle class with dual-career situation. Financial situation seen by mother as "adequate but never enough." Substantial medical expenses.

F. Education: College-educated mother and father.

Families with Youths in Middle School and High School

Family 15 (both parents interviewed)

A. Parental ages: Mother, 40s; father, 50s.

B. Impaired children: Two moderately visually impaired daughters, with one more impaired than the other. Both daughters have the same congenital impairment condition, which was discovered at birth and has a generally stable prognosis in both cases. The more visually impaired daughter also has learning and emotional impairments, and the emotional impairment has been serious at times.

C. Siblings: 1 (2 visually impaired sisters with no other siblings).

D. Marital/parental situation: Highly consensual marriage with shared commitment to children.

E. Economic status: Middle-class professional with "comfortable" lifestyle. Mother employed part time, with career goals restricted by motherhood.

F. Education: Mother, graduate study. Father, graduate degrees.

Family 16 (both parents interviewed)

A. Parental ages: Mother and father, 50s.
B. Impaired child: Daughter with severe visual impairment from early childhood illness. Uncertain prognosis but hope for possible healing of the eye damage and for improvement in sight.
C. Siblings: 3 (all older and away from home).
D. Marital/parental situation: Stable marriage with shared commitment to impaired child (and other children).
E. Economic status: Working class with "comfortable" but not extravagant lifestyle. Limited discretionary income supplemented by mother's part-time seasonal work.
F. Education: Mother is a high school graduate. Father is college educated.

Family 17 (both parents interviewed)

A. Parental ages: Mother and father, 50s.
B. Impaired child: Daughter with moderate congenital low vision tied to neurological impairment. Extent of visual impairment gradually discovered over the years. Relatively sure of no change in visual condition or sight.
C. Siblings: 1.
D. Marital/parental situation: Highly consensual marriage with shared commitment to the children.
E. Economic status: Middle class. Father self-employed professional with new business, which makes current financial situation somewhat precarious. Still "comfortable" lifestyle. Mother employed.
F. Education: Both parents are high school graduates.

Family 18 (both parents interviewed)

A. Parental ages: Mother and father, 30s.
B. Impaired child: Daughter with moderate low vision caused shortly after birth by congenital physiological impairment. Numerous chronic physiological impairments. Visual condition not degenerative.
C. Siblings: 2 (1 with a specific learning disability).

D. Marital/parental situation: Highly consensual marriage with both parents involved with children but primary parental responsibilities assumed by mother.

E. Economic status: Middle class. Upwardly mobile to industrial management. "Occasionally pinched" (according to mother) but generally "doing fine" (according to father). Comfortable lifestyle. Mother not employed.

F. Education: Both parents are high school graduates.

Family 19 (mother only interviewed)

A. Parental age: 30s.

B. Impaired child: Daughter with moderate congenital low vision discovered at birth. After several unsuccessful surgeries, a stable prognosis.

C. Siblings: 1.

D. Marital/parental situation: Single parent who saw herself as "successfully divorced" for nearly 10 years. Little or no contact with former husband/father.

E. Economic status: Low income. Self-described as "welfare recipient." Mother's job prospects hindered by her own visual impairment. Little discretionary income, but lifestyle is marginally comfortable and stable because of purchase of low-income housing many years earlier and help from mother's parents.

F. Education: Attended high school.

Family 20 (both parents interviewed)

A. Parental ages: Mother, 30s; father, 40s.

B. Impaired child: Daughter with moderate congenital low vision discovered in first year. Uncertain prognosis but hope (especially of father) for "medical miracle."

C. Siblings: 3 (including 1 gifted and 1 learning impaired).

D. Marital/parental situation: Relatively stable marriage with pressures from time demands of both parents' jobs and vocal disagreements about daughter's visual impairment and handling of her adolescent adjustment problems.

E. Economic status: Working class with dual-earner situation. "A little financially strained at times" (according to mother) but still relatively comfortable lifestyle as long as both parents continue working.

F. Education: Mother nearly completed high school. Father attended college.

Family 21 (father only interviewed)

A. Parental age: 50s.

B. Impaired child: Son with moderate low vision related to brain damage from accident within past 2 years. Also serious emotional impairment in aftermath of accident. Uncertain prognosis for all impairments.

C. Siblings: 1.

D. Marital/parental situation: Precarious marriage, destabilized by consequences of son's accident and his difficult social and emotional rehabilitation, which produced different reactions from his two parents. Father (following recent retirement) is primary custodian of impaired son while wife remains employed.

E. Economic status: Stable working class, with father recently retired and mother still employed. Financial situation "tight sometimes but enough money for basic needs."

F. Education: High school graduate.

Family 22 (mother only interviewed)

A. Parental age: 40s.

B. Impaired child: Son with blindness caused by excessive oxygen in incubator shortly after premature birth. Condition not expected to change.

C. Siblings: 1.

D. Marital/parental situation: Mother has been remarried for several years after having been a single parent for many years. Children have regular phone ties to father and annual visit to see him. Stepfather involved with children but relatively detached from most of the routine parental responsibilities, especially regarding impairment.

E. Economic status: Middle class, with "enough money for basic needs" and a comfortable lifestyle. Mother employed.

F. Education: College educated.

Family 23 (mother only interviewed)

A. Parental age: 40s.

B. Impaired children: Daughter and son with moderate congenital low vision, discovered early in lives of both. Stable prognoses. Daughter treated for serious emotional impairment.

C. Siblings: 2 others (older and not at home).

D. Marital/parental situation: Previously precarious marriage destabilized by husband's problems, which recently improved, so stability of the marriage enhanced. For many years, the mother had been, in effect, a single parent, assuming nearly all the major parental responsibilities.

E. Economic status: Middle class with dual-earner situation. Significant strains created in past year by husband's loss of job, but he recently returned to work.

F. Education: High school graduate.

NOTES

1   The distinctions in degrees of visual impairment admittedly are not precise. However, *blindness* implies virtually or absolutely no light perception. *Severe visual impairment* (or *severe low vision)* implies legal blindness as well as a reliance on adaptive devices (such as a cane, braille, tapes, or special equipment) and/or behavior associated with blindness or near-blindness in many situations. *Moderate visual impairment* (or *moderate low vision)* implies legal blindness but much more "normal" types of visual functioning than cases of severe visual impairment (for example, some use of large print; television viewing at close distance; and, especially in familiar surroundings, mobility without special assistance). Moderately visually impaired people with visual acuity problems may have little capacity to see more than highly fuzzy or blurred images in the distance beyond a few feet, but they may be able to make some discriminations in details of objects (such as print letters) within several inches. *Mild visual impairment* (or *mild low vision)* is corrected visual acuity worse than 20/70 in the better eye but not worse than legal blindness of 20/200 and/or some loss of visual field not greater than the legal blindness standard of 20 degrees. Mildly visually impaired people often *appear* to function normally in many situations and, depending on their degree of actual or perceived impairment, will rely only to a limited extent on special adaptive devices.

2   The use of *unemployed* or *not currently employed* in this section means not engaged in paid work outside the family at the time of the interview.

INDEX

ABOUT THE AUTHOR

Howard L. Nixon II is Professor of Sociology and Chair of the Department of Sociology and Social Work, Appalachian State University, Boone, North Carolina. He is the author of *The Small Group* and *Sport and the American Dream* and of numerous articles that have appeared in such journals as *American Behavioral Scientist, Administrative Science Quarterly,* and *Research Quarterly*. An organizer and presenter at numerous local and national conferences, he has been involved in national and statewide advocacy efforts in behalf of parents of visually impaired children and adults with disabilities and a member of parents' groups for more than 10 years.

*   *   *

Irving Kenneth Zola is Mortimer Gryzmish Professor of Human Relations and Chair of the Department of Sociology, Brandeis University, Waltham, Massachusetts. The author of *Missing Pieces: A Chronicle of Living with a Disability* and *Ordinary Lives: Voices of Disability and Disease* and editor of *Disability Studies Quarterly,* he is a Fellow of the American Association for the Advancement of Science and a recipient of the N. Neal Pike Prize Award for Service to the Handicapped.

3001